Priced to Influence, Sell & Satisfy

LESSONS FROM BEHAVIORAL ECONOMICS FOR PRICING SUCCESS

Utpal Dholakia

Utpal Dholakia
6100 Main Street
Houston, Texas/77407
www.utpaldholakia.com

Book cover designed by America Brink. Illustrations by Shirin Abvabi.

Special discounts are available on quantity purchases by corporations, associations, and others. For details, contact the author.

Priced to Influence, Sell & Satisfy/ Utpal Dholakia. —1st ed.

ISBN 978-0-9991867-3-2

Contents

And for a price, I will pretend absolutely nothing.

– Jacqueline Carey

What is Psychological Pricing?

All that is gold does not glitter, not all those who wander are lost.

– J.R.R. Tolkien, The Fellowship of the Ring.

Pricing activities hold the key to business success. Almost every business decision that managers make involves spending money, whether it is to invest in new assets, hire employees, develop and introduce new products and services[1], enter new markets, improve service quality, integrate vertically, or modernize the company's operations. Managers are always pulling out their checkbooks to lay out money for these and any number of other activities. The only exception is pricing decisions. Making a pricing decision is a lot like turning a spigot. A pricing decision regulates the flow of revenue and profit *into* the organization, instead of the other way. Smart and informed pricing decisions swiftly drive up the company's revenue and profit and strengthen its brand in the marketplace. On the other hand, just as quickly and decisively, ill-considered and hasty pricing decisions bankrupt a business[2].

1

The Significance of Pricing Activities

All things are difficult before they are easy. – Thomas Fuller.

Prices are the bloodstream of a business, instrumental for its sustenance and rejuvenation. And yet, a majority of managers do not pay sufficient attention to pricing activities or consider the nuances of pricing decisions. Some managers treat pricing as an afterthought, simply as tactics to be hastily sketched out and implemented after the "major" strategic decisions have been made. Others are perpetually putting pricing decisions on the backburner, either because they are intimidated by the process of making them, or because they do not know which factors to consider or which pricing methods to use systematically. Still others rely on standard but simplistic pricing approaches such as cost-plus pricing or "just-below" competitor pricing season after season, year after year, even when these methods prove to be ineffective.

Thus, it turns out that pricing strategy, the one area of business activity that brings revenue and profit into the company, is also often the one function that has the most significant opportunity for improvement. In my book, *How to Price Effectively: A Guide for Managers and Entrepreneurs*, I described a comprehensive, structured, and well-tested approach for making and implementing pricing decisions called the *Value Pricing Framework*. The *Value Pricing Framework* considers the four pillars of pricing, costs, customer value, reference prices, and the value proposition, in detail, to methodically formulate pricing strategies.

Here, a brief introduction to the four pillars of the *Value Pricing Framework* will help set the stage for understanding how you can use the principles and research findings from psychology and behavioral economics to make effective pricing decisions. Let's briefly review these four pillars of pricing, considering their foundations in customer psychology.

Figure 1.1 The four pillars of pricing decisions.

The four pillars of pricing in the Value Pricing Framework

Costs. Every manager recognizes that costs must be factored into pricing decisions. Costs set the floor or the minimum threshold on prices. If a business cannot cover all its costs, it will eventually have to shut its doors. However, effective pricing goes beyond marking up costs. It separates costs into two types, *incremental costs* that are relevant and which need to be considered carefully, and *non-incremental or irrelevant costs*, which should be ignored in pricing decisions. Understanding which costs fall in these categories, and in particular how they will change based on the pricing decision, allows the manager to design creative pricing schemes to achieve specific goals such as utilize spare resources, grow the business, and attract customers from outside the target segments, all while contributing disproportionately more to the company's bottom line.

Where customers are concerned, a seller's costs are mostly unknown quantities. If managers fail to consider and deal with customer ignorance about costs, their pricing decisions face a higher risk of failure. This is because customers' lack of knowledge of input costs and how they change and why makes prices seem high, and price increases seem unfair, exploitative, or inconsistent. Just like prices, costs have informational value for consumers, which if used judiciously, can burnish the seller's reputation and produce a sheen of high quality on the product. In this book, we will examine the symbolic meanings of price, ways to manage price and cost transparency, and how to include customers in the price determination process through participative pricing.

Customer Value. Customer value, the second pillar of pricing, brings consumer psychology into pricing decisions even more explicitly. In the *Value Pricing Framework*, customer value is defined purely and narrowly in dollars and cents. It is the total amount of money that the customer is willing to pay for the functional and hedonic (or emotional) benefits obtained from the product or service. For the pricing manager, customer value sets the ceiling or the highest possible price that can be charged.

Despite this seeming rigidity, the process by which consumers assign value to products and services is fluid. It is established by psychological factors. The resulting customer value is unstable, influenced dramatically by the context, and subject to influence by the seller. Variability is the most powerful characteristic of customer value for psychological pricing. Here are three examples of the power of shifting customer value that illustrate this.

Roses on Valentine's Day. Every year, consumers, mostly men, looking to impress their romantic partners, value products and services like chocolates, candy, and restaurant meals at two times, three times, or even more than their regular prices on Valentine's Day[3]. A bouquet of red roses that was worth $10 in late January is suddenly, but predictably, worth $49.99 on February 13. Its value subsides to $10 on February 15, only to increase again when Easter approaches in

April, and then again before Mother's Day in May, and so on. The customer value of a rose bouquet ebbs and flows.

Grocery store sale. How much faith will you have in a sign in a grocery store that says, "25% off regular price" for a tube of toothpaste you usually buy? Should it matter where the sign is placed? It turns out that when the sign is displayed on a store shelf next to the toothpaste's regular price, shoppers give it more credence than if it is pasted on the product package[4]. The size of the discount matters less to customers than how the seller communicates the promotional offer.

The list price for a house. Now imagine you want to sell your house. Should you list it at $395,000 or $395,425? Although it sounds counterintuitive, a higher precise price is likely to do better than a lower round numbered price. In one study of home sales in New York and Florida, the authors found that precise list prices increased the house's sale price by 0.6%, tacking on $3,000 in value to a $500,000 house. They concluded, "these results provide strong evidence that price precision increases buyers' WTP [willingness to pay][5]."

These are just three examples of how customer value changes dramatically for the same consumers depending on small differences. We will see numerous examples of value fluidity throughout this book and consider the psychology behind these changes. We will use our understanding to identify circumstances that enhance customer value and willingness to pay for products and services and discuss how sellers can create or capitalize on these circumstances.

Reference Prices. Customers rarely make purchase decisions or evaluate prices in isolation. When considering a price and deciding whether to buy the product or service, they compare it to other reference prices. Commonly used reference prices include prices encountered on displays, menus, or online sites, competitors' prices for similar products or services, the seller's historical prices, and even wholly unrelated prices that the customer happens to encounter during the decision process. Reference prices are unique to the individual, and they are dynamic. They change over time. Understanding reference prices provides the manager with the range of prices customers find to be reasonable. Smart marketers can also influence which reference prices customers use and how they interpret them, winning a *perception advantage* over other products in the marketplace. Often, such influence methods require relatively minor actions such as how prices are displayed or presented. These actions cost relatively little but have outsized effects on customers. We will study a variety of methods to influence customer perceptions of prices throughout this book, and particularly in Chapters 4 and 5.

The Value Proposition. The final and perhaps the most critical pillar for effective pricing strategy is the company's value proposition. For a pricing decision to be effective, it must be aligned with the company's overall marketing strategy. The company's prices must be consistent with the rest of its marketing activities, serving a common goal. The value proposition is the formal expression of the company's marketing strategy, describing the significance of the product's and the brand's unique characteristics relative to its competitors. By articulating what the company considers to be its most important points of differentiation, a value proposition provides guidelines and sets constraints on pricing activities. It determines how the manager weighs costs, customer value, and reference prices in the pricing decision. From the customer's perspective, the execution of the value proposition coincides with the creation and maintenance of a particular price image that resonates. Most of us view a Porsche as an expensive, luxury automotive brand, but we consider a Honda Civic to be an economy brand that delivers excellent value. Both vehicles are targeted to different customer groups, and each one has a clearly defined price image associated with it.

These four pillars of pricing strategy— costs, customer value, reference prices, and the value proposition, provide managers with a structured and comprehensive way to make effective pricing decisions. Using these factors successfully requires an understanding of how customers use prices in their buying activities. In this book, we will dive deep into the consumer psychology behind prices and pricing. We will study how prices are searched, evaluated, shared, determined, and used by consumers in buying decisions and what managers can do to understand and influence these processes.

What would pricing in a rational world be like?

Pricing experts will attest that the most significant challenge in a pricing decision is the human factor. If customers were not humans with their hidden motivations and biases, pricing would be a breeze! It would be a strictly quantitative endeavor, dictated by microeconomic principles of supply and demand. Let's take a few moments to imagine what pricing in a rational world would be like.

Gasoline prices in a hurricane. When a hurricane would occur, and gasoline supplies dwindle, gas stations would keep raising prices and sell their remaining gasoline to those with the deepest pockets at the highest prices. A price of $50 per gallon, or even more, would be perfectly reasonable after a hurricane. The one-percenters would drive their vehicles, while others without the money would hunker down, get around on foot, and somehow manage to survive until fresh gasoline supply was restored.

Coca-Cola vending machines. Coca-Cola would install vending machines with prices that change moment-by-moment with fluctuations of the outside air temperature. When the weather sizzled at high noon, you'd have to pay six bucks for an ice-cold Coke. Later in the day, prices would come down as the weather cooled off. And when it would snow outside, you would be in luck. Your ice-cold Coke would only cost 25 cents.

Olympic Games tickets. To attend the Olympic Games (or any other event, for that matter), you'd have to bid for tickets. The highest bidders, the billionaire hedge-fund managers and the celebrities, would enjoy the spectacle live; everyone else would stay home and watch the games on TV or go to a sports bar. No one would say a word about income inequality or privilege.

In such a rational world, every person would have a fixed and well-defined willingness to pay for every object. They would see the item, evaluate it carefully and comprehensively, compare its price against their willingness to pay, and then they would either buy it or walk away depending on whether the price was lower or higher than their willingness to pay. No muss, no fuss. And pricing researchers would ask consumers how much their willingness to pay for something was, and they would tell you the number confidently and truthfully.

When we let our imagination roam like this, we can quickly see how ludicrous this imaginary world sounds, and just how far removed it is from the way pricing decisions have to be made in our real world. Each pricing decision that was described, whether it is to raise fuel prices during a hurricane, install a vending machine with dynamic prices pegged to the outside air temperature, or use auctions to sell tickets to popular events—has been tried by companies and vehemently rejected, or even worse, outlawed in the case of fuel prices as price gouging, because of consumer outrage[6]. Where pricing decisions are concerned, there is a yawning gap between what is possible with technology, the application of microeconomic principles, and managerial ambition, and what is acceptable to consumers and can be done. And the gap only grows wider with each passing year.

As a pricing manager, when you make a pricing decision, you are dealing with consumers, flesh-and-blood human beings who are governed by complex psychological processes. These processes influence how consumers respond to prices, which in turn influences pricing success. Consumers are irrational at times, and overly analytical and calculating at others. They are regulated by fundamental motives, momentary impulses, and relatively stable traits that shape their behaviors. These are all but hidden from managers.

Consumers are outspoken critics of the company's products on some occasions and rabid enthusiasts on others, spreading positive word-of-mouth to whoever will listen. Their valuation of any product and their willingness to pay is not some number set in stone. Rather, it is dictated by a wide array of factors and is influenced dramatically by the context in which it is made. By and large, they do not obey microeconomic laws, not even approximately. So, while plotting the demand curve is normative and makes some quantitatively-inclined economics-trained managers feel good about themselves, in many cases, it provides a distorted signal for establishing profitable and attractive pricing structures and practices in an organization, and making customers happy.

Fortunately, there is over a century of research in social psychology and approximately two decades of overlapping research in behavioral economics examining the psychological factors influencing consumers' response to prices. Digging into this vast body of literature allows us to go beyond simplistic thinking and consider how consumers will respond to prices, and design pricing structures and offers that will influence, sell to and satisfy customers.

The goal of this book is to dive deeply into this research, introduce useful concepts, and explore cases of companies that have used psychological pricing to design smart and effective pricing strategies. This book provides practical ideas that every pricing strategist, manager, business owner, and startup founder can use. If you are a consumer, the contents of this book apply to you as well. By learning how companies you do business with use psychological pricing methods to influence your thinking, emotional responses, and actions, you will become a better informed and smarter consumer. But be warned; as you will see, our hardwiring and habitual inclinations make these tasks challenging.

The Definition of Psychological Pricing

At the core of behavioral pricing research is the contention that price can be considered a physical stimulus, much as light and sound. – Lillian Cheng and Kent Monroe[7].

When managers started applying pricing theory to business decisions systematically, well before the popularity of social psychology and behavioral economics-influenced thinking, they routinely used a unidimensional (and some might argue, ethically questionable) consumer model on which to base their pricing strategies[8]. Essentially, they saw consumers as powerless, ill-informed and myopic creatures, ripe for manipulation and money extraction. The goal of pricing during this era was to hoodwink customers and to earn the highest possible profit from each and every transaction, customer satisfaction and welfare be damned. Under the dominant microeconomic paradigm of the time, revenue and profit maximization for every transaction were worked out to be a shrewd and legitimate way to pursue business success.

Unfortunately, however, because it was so divorced from reality, this naïve consumer model overlooked all the adverse effects, particularly economic ones, that occur when a business poisons the well by extorting from and alienating its core customer base. Needless to say, this pricing approach led to questionable pricing decisions and adverse financial consequences for many companies.

The model of the consumer we adopt in this book could not be more different. We see our customers as empowered human beings whose decisions and behaviors are made volitionally even when they are habitual or made with little effort. They are governed by their thoughts, motivations, self-identity constructions, routines, and emotions. Their value assessments and decision processes are dynamic, context-dependent, and changeable. Our customers are susceptible to social influence, and they desire to influence others. They put the requisite amount of thinking and due diligence into their purchase decisions, but they are constrained in different ways. With everything else going on in their lives, they have limited time, cognitive resources, and money to buy and consume our products. Our model of a consumer is shown graphically in Figure 1.2.

Figure 1.2 Our model of a consumer.

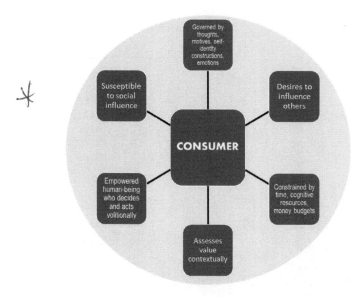

The way consumers respond to price is equally complex. On the one hand, price is a physical stimulus, subject to psychophysical laws. Consumers are hardwired to follow precisely-specified rules in how they compare prices, tell them apart, and identify that a price has changed.

On the other hand, price also produces visceral emotional responses that are unregulated. Shoppers feel pain when they have to pay money to buy something and happiness when they score a deal or buy something particularly meaningful. In one study, consumers whose brains were scanned while they saw very high prices showed increased activation in the insula region that is associated with pain[9].

In conjunction with this complex and rich consumer model, the way we view pricing strategy is that as managers, we want to sell products and services at prices that will deliver genuine value to consumers. Instead of tricking or manipulating them, we want to listen to them and accommodate their voices in our pricing decisions, and share the value generated by our offerings with them equitably. Our fundamental goal through psychological pricing is to initiate and maintain mutually beneficial, long-lasting relationships with customers where the value created by our offerings is maximized and shared. With these consumer and pricing strategy models as our guiding framework, we can now define psychological pricing as follows:

> Psychological pricing is a set of strategic and tactical managerial pricing actions designed to influence consumers' perceptions, decisions, and behaviors through processes of thinking and feeling. Its goal is to deliver a high degree of value to target consumers, while concurrently generating healthy revenue and profit for the business.

Psychological pricing requires managers to have a principled approach to creating and sharing value with customers, along with a solid understanding of social psychology and behavioral economics principles, particularly as they relate to how consumers perceive, evaluate, trade-off, infer and identify with information about prices. The purpose of this book is to share this knowledge in a practical way. Armed with an understanding of the different psychological roles and functions of price throughout the customer's journey, the manager will be able to thoughtfully and deliberately develop pricing actions to influence customers in positive ways.

The true value of psychological pricing actions lies in the fact that many (but not all) pricing actions can be performed with relatively little expense yet generate significant measurable effects on consumer behavior that, in turn, impact the company's revenue and profit. Effective psychological pricing possesses the following five properties:

1. *Psychological pricing is goal-oriented.*

A psychological pricing action is designed to achieve one or more specific business goals that the manager defines beforehand. Goals can be to support a certain image for your product or brand, to make your offer appear to be an attractive deal to your customer, to encourage the customer to complete the purchase transaction and to influence the customer's economic valuation of your product or service. For example, fine dining restaurants deliberately exploit the symbolic information conveyed by prices to create an aura of luxurious creativity by using prices ending in numbers like 3, 4, and 7, writing out prices, and using specific fonts in their menus. We will study the hidden meanings behind prices in Chapter 2.

2. *Psychological pricing is rigorous.*

All the ideas presented in this book are based on well-accepted psychological theories and empirical findings using the scientific method. There is a large and growing body of research within behavioral economics, most of it produced within the past two decades, and in social and cognitive psychology going back much further, which provides us with the foundation to design and execute psychological pricing actions. We utilize the latest and the best knowledge from these academic areas in this book. Where appropriate, the research is explained in the text and is supplemented by detailed citations of the relevant academic studies in the end notes.

3. Psychological pricing is synergistic with the Value Pricing Framework.

To use the tools and insights described in this book successfully does require that the business have a well-crafted and effective marketing strategy. It also requires the manager to have a grasp of the four pillars of pricing described earlier. If you do not know your costs and your competitors' prices, have a sense of which of your product or service features provide the most value to your customers, and if you don't have a compelling value proposition, psychological pricing will not take you very far. Rather than choosing and employing these ideas on an ad hoc basis, psychological pricing methods should be used to support and capitalize on your company's marketing strategy, in conjunction with the *Value Pricing Framework*[10].

4. Psychological pricing is measurable.

For marketing managers, one of the greatest strengths of a pricing decision is that its effects on key performance indicators can be measured reliably. When prices are changed, for instance, the impact on sales can be pinpointed. This is also the case with other psychological pricing activities beyond price changes. Psychological pricing produces outcomes that can be measured with little ambiguity using methods such as controlled experimentation. Their desired or threshold levels can also be defined in advance to make specific pricing decisions. Examples of outcomes of pricing activities include the change in sales, the shift in the customer's brand recall or brand preferences, the effects on revenue and profit margin, the change in the level of satisfaction or repurchase intent, the repurchase rate, and so on.

5. Psychological pricing is impactful.

Finally, psychological pricing produces significant outcomes. As we will see later on in the book, Subway serendipitously discovered the $5 price point for a fast food meal and exploited it for more than a decade with its "$5 footlong" sandwich promotions to become one of the largest fast food chains in the world. 99 Cents Only Stores built a multi-billion business by embracing the 99 price ending while De

Beers turned buying an expensive diamond engagement ring into a completely normal ritualistic purchase by providing consumers with an acceptable price threshold of "two months' salary." Psychological pricing actions are levered. Many of them require relatively small investments and when successful, produce disproportionately large returns to the business.

The Different Roles of Price in the Customer's Decision Journey

Wherever you go, go with all your heart. – Confucius.

In their quest to make smart purchase decisions, become knowledgeable and savvy shoppers, influence and connect with others, and maintain congenial relationships with sellers, consumers undertake a complex process involving many different psychological and behavioral states. Each state offers the seller with an opportunity to connect with the consumer, gauge their inclinations and motivations, and influence and respond to them. In this book, we will refer to this process broadly as the "customer decision journey." A major point of this book is that *prices play a number of distinct roles throughout the customer decision journey. Each role of price provides managers with unique and significant opportunities to influence, sell to, and satisfy customers.* Not only does the price level matter, but its structure (e.g., whether price remains the same or fluctuates), how it is displayed, presented, and negotiated all matter and will be considered at length in this book.

The customer journey provides a robust framework with which to understand the diverse, multifaceted ways in which price affects consumer decision making and behaviors. In this section, I will provide a brief history of the customer journey concept, then introduce the *Needs-Adaptive Customer Journey* framework that provides the theoretical backbone for this book. This framework identifies sixteen different consumer psychological states. The consumer has different motives and goals, and price performs different functions in each state.

A brief history of the Customer Decision Journey (CDJ)

The Customer Decision Journey (CDJ), shown in Figure 1.3, is a conceptual framework developed by McKinsey consultants that describes the path that consumers take in learning about, buying, and consuming products and services[11]. Typically, this path is a cyclical process. It progresses from the recognition of an unfulfilled need that motivates a process of search and the consideration of different alternatives. This leads to purchase and is followed by the product's consumption which may occur over a period of time. Afterward, the customer communicates this experience with other consumers through reviews and word-of-mouth, and bonds with the company's brands and products.

The CDJ has its roots in the Awareness-Interest-Desire-Action hierarchy of effects models used by advertisers during the heyday of advertising in the 1950s and 1960s. It captures the evolution of the customer's relationship with the company. The CDJ identifies the specific points of contact between the company and the customer, known as "touch-points," and explains how customers navigate them. Touch-points are usually controlled by the company and are used to manage the customer's experience through the journey.

Figure 1.3 The McKinsey Customer Decision Journey framework.

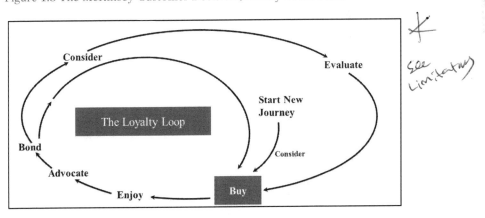

See Limitation)

Figure adapted from Edelman and Singer (2015), *Harvard Business Review.*

The CDJ framework provides powerful guidance to pricing managers. It specifies that customers progress through the decision journey in a systematic and predictable sequence of activities, implying that prices have specific roles to play at each stage. Consider a $16 one-pound bag of organic, freshly roasted, single-origin, Kenyan coffee beans. And imagine a consumer who is in the early *consider* stage of a CDJ (see Figure 1.3) to buy coffee beans. One way this consumer will use the $16 price is to decide whether to consider the Kenyan coffee brand further for purchase. If their decision heuristic says, "the highest I'm willing to pay for coffee is $15 per pound", they will simply reject the Kenyan coffee as too expensive. However, if their decision heuristic includes this price, the coffee will remain a viable choice. When the customer is considering different alternatives, price is often used for winnowing down the available options, especially when many choices are available.

When the coffee buyer moves on to the *evaluate* stage of the CDJ, they will use price quite differently. Here, the coffee's price becomes a way to judge the product's value and is traded off against its other features and quality. For instance, the consumer may ask the question, "Are the facts that this coffee is single-origin and Kenyan, and made of organically grown beans worth paying $16 a pound for?" In the same vein, price plays unique roles during the *enjoy*, *advocate* and *bond* stages of the customer decision journey.

Limitations of the CDJ framework

Although it provides useful managerial insights and guidelines, the CDJ framework suffers from two important limitations where pricing decisions are concerned. First, it is a relatively static model. For instance, the *consider* state leads to *evaluate*, which in turn leads to *buy*. However, the reality is that people may not progress in this sequence. They may go back-and-forth between *consider* and *evaluate* many times, and even visit some other states over a substantial period, before ultimately making a purchase. In many cases, they may never purchase at all, nor have any intention to do so. They may simply be in a mood to browse, to entertain themselves, or to learn more about the available choices. Alternatively, for big-ticket items, the purchase may occur months or even years after the idea first emerges. Just think about how people make buying decisions like purchasing a rental property or a boat. As we will see throughout this book, psychological pricing decisions by managers have to account for the back-and-forth, choppy aspects of consumer psychology. Treating consumer decisions as mostly linear progressions simplifies pricing far beyond what is either desirable or warranted. The manager will miss out on opportunities to influence, sell to, and satisfy customers.

The second limitation of the CDJ framework is that it does not capture the full range of psychological states that consumers experience during buying and consumption. The CDJ sacrifices nuance for parsimony. For example, instead of considering different options and evaluating them to select one option and buy it, the shopper may browse through a product assortment while waiting for a spouse or friend. They may wait to make the purchase, for a specific period or indefinitely, even after they have decided what they want to buy. Negotiation may play a considerable or even decisive role in whether the customer buys and how much they pay. And after purchase, they may refer the product to others, post a review about the product or their shopping experience on social media, and share their purchase with others. Many of these processes occur jointly with other people, adding another layer of nuance. Prices play unique and significant roles in each psychological state. More importantly, when the manager understands the underlying psychology, each state affords them psychological pricing avenues to engage with customers.

The Needs-Adaptive Customer Journey (NACJ) framework

A new and improved way to understand customer journeys is called the "Needs-Adaptive Customer Journey" (NACJ) framework. It proposes a greater number of psychological states than the CDJ. It acknowledges that in today's technology-driven and social media-infused environment, the customer's progression through the decision journey usually does not happen linearly. Instead, the customer moves back and forth between one of sixteen psychological states. These movements rely on a host of factors, such as the consumer's underlying motivations and emotions, prior knowledge, the level of interest, availability of time and money, the presence of others, and so on. Figure 1 shows the NACJ framework graphically.

Figure 1.4. The Needs-Adaptive Customer Journey framework.

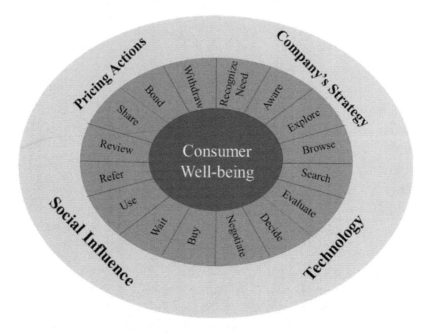

The second property of the NACJ framework is that instead of traditional measures such as sales revenue, profit, or growth, it places the consumer's welfare at its heart. The consumer's sixteen psychological states are instrumental in supporting customer journeys that contribute to well-being. Psychological pricing activities have the power to affect each psychological state, and in turn, the consumer's well-being. A third aspect of the NACJ framework is that contextual factors, such as technology, social influence, the company's broader business strategy, and its pricing actions, affect customer journeys.

Table 1.1 lists the sixteen psychological states experienced by consumers according to the NACJ framework. It describes each state briefly and explains the psychological roles that price plays when the consumer is in that state. As the table shows, the psychological functions of price are diverse and compelling.

Table 1.1 Psychological states in the NACJ framework and the cor.
functions of price.

State	Description	Psychological Fun of Price
Recognize need	To experience a state of general (e.g., "I am thirsty, I need a drink) or specific (e.g., "I want a Coke) desire.	To draw the attention the consumer by stand out; to increase percep- tions of accessibility and urgency.
Aware	To know, perceive, or be cognizant of the product.	To communicate the price and link it to other parts of the offer, such as brand image, product features, and quality.
Explore	To research alternatives, usually to discover something new, or find an alternative that is su- perior or has the desired feature.	To generate excitement or heighten interest in the offer; to minimize the consumer's resistance to buy; to increase the con- sumer's knowledge about the product.
Browse	To survey available al- ternatives casually, usu- ally without a specific purchase or consump- tion goal.	To attract attention, to create differentiation from other alternatives, and in some cases to com- municate prestige, scar- city, economy, or other desired properties.
Search	To look actively for available alternatives to achieve a specific pur- chase goal and gather in- formation about them to create a consideration set of choices.	To communicate a partic- ular level of product qual- ity and a sense of high value; to appear superior in comparison to other al- ternatives being consid- ered.
Evaluate	To appraise different brands or products in one's consideration set carefully and weigh their alignment with one's ob- jectives.	To support the use of a particular decision heuris- tic that favors the product relative to its competitors; to infuse the product with relevant meaning.

State	Description	Psychological Functions of Price
Decide	To make up one's mind about whether to make the purchase and if yes, which brand or product to purchase.	To provide a reason to choose the brand or product over others; to provide a rea-son to reject other options in the consideration set; to emphasize specific information.
Negotiate	To negotiate the final price, to make offers and counter-offers and to converge on an accepta-ble price.	To provide a mechanism (formal or norms-based) for the consumer to participate in pricing; to make the process transparent and fair; to end with an unambiguous result (deal or no deal).
Buy	To pay and make the purchase.	To influence the consumer to complete the purchase (vs. delaying it); to speed up the decision process and purchase; to reduce the pain of spending money.
Wait	To wait for a predictable or indeterminate duration until one can buy or consume the product.	To minimize the perception of waiting time until purchase or use; to convey a reasonable explanation for the delay; to provide the opportunity to reduce delay.
Use	To consume or utilize a product that one has purchased. In many cases, this is the most protracted state.	To contribute to the consumer's satisfaction; to encourage and support regular product use; to generate positive meaning for the consumed product.
Refer	To advocate on the product's behalf and rec-ommend others to consider and purchase it.	To encourage referral giving; to convey status and self-identity information to promote advocacy.

State	Description	Psychological Functions of Price
Review	To critically analyze strengths and weaknesses of the product in public venues such as social media or review sites.	To encourage customers to provide honest reviews and advocate on the product's behalf of the product; to convey desirable information about the consumer's self-identity and social roles.
Share	To participate with others in one's own or others' buying and consumption experience.	To encourage shared pre-purchase & post-purchase activities among groups; to allow easy division of costs among buyers.
Bond	To focus on the strengths of the purchased product, to strengthen the relationship with the product and brand.	To provide validation for the purchase decision; to serve as an emotional cue that triggers positive emotions; to convey desired aspects of consumer's self-identity.
Withdraw	To stop using a purchased product or to dispose of it.	To maintain consumer's engagement as long as possible; to encourage repeat purchase and use; to support returns and raise engagement after withdrawal.

As Table 1.1 shows, the psychological functions of prices go far beyond conveying information to customers about how much something costs. Prices serve a variety of psychological functions, each offering the manager with opportunities. What's more, these functions are different depending on the consumer's place in the journey. For instance, when a person is exploring or browsing, the product's price should act as a beacon, drawing them to examine the item more closely, then generating excitement and interest in purchase. Something as simple as a sale sign or a "limited quantities available" tagline displayed near the merchandise may do the trick.

When the customer is on the cusp of purchase, the job of the price is to encourage them to complete the purchase, instead of abandoning the shopping cart and walking away. It should communicate the product's quality and other properties such as scarcity. It must establish the product's value superiority over competing alternatives within the decision making context. It must provide information that will help to establish the product's value. Depending on the brand's power and price image, this could mean either a higher or a lower comparative price. The price must infuse the product with meaning that the brand manager desires, that is relevant to the target segment, and that reinforces other brand associations. It should reduce the customer's pain of spending money.

Tomatoes in Farmers Market/ Photo by Anne Preble/ Unsplash

The price should facilitate the negotiation process and define the customer's role in determining the price. It should provide reassurance and validation after the purchase is complete to minimize potential remorse or regret. It should signal validating information about the customer's self-identity, social status, and personality traits. The price should serve as a cue that triggers visceral positive emotional responses. And it should maintain the customer's engagement with the product over time, encouraging repeat purchases, advocacy, and bonding, and postponing withdrawal from the relationship. We will study these psychological functions of price throughout this book.

The organization of this book

This book investigates the different roles of price by introducing key concepts and tools of psychological pricing and using case studies to show how managers can use them. In Chapter 2, we study the hidden meanings in price. Prices have informational value and visual symbolic properties that are conveyed by the price itself and different price endings. We examine why *charm prices* (ending with 9) work so effectively and how superstitious price endings exert a powerful influence on consumers. This chapter also introduces the concept of a *price vocabulary* that a seller can use to distinguish itself, make customers feel special, and strengthen bonds with them. It concludes by considering the five components of a company's *price image*.

Chapter 3 reviews the research on *price knowledge* of consumers. We study three types of long-term memory for prices, *price recall*, *price recognition*, and *deal spotting ability*. Far more customers can spot a deal than recall the exact price of a product or service. We consider how customers form and use a *range of reasonable prices* in their decision making and what this means for managers. We introduce the *Emery model,* which explains how customers form judgments of value. We conclude this chapter by discussing the *placebo pricing effect,* showing how prices can transform the customer experience.

Chapter 4 discusses how consumers use prices in their decision making process. We consider the role of decision heuristics and examine how psychological pricing bellwethers such as *price thresholds, price points* and *temporally reframing the price offer* help consumers to answer the question, "Is this product worth the price?" We also examine ways by which the *ease of evaluation of the price* influences consumer decisions and how managers can regulate this variable to dictate how much weight customers give to price.

Chapter 5 considers the role of price in influencing the customer's context-specific value perceptions. We examine *budget-based decisions* and explain how to build and manage product lines offering *good, better, and best choices* to customers. We also review the research on how to influence customer choice within the product line and look at famous psychological pricing nudges such as the *attraction*, *similarity*, and *compromise* effects, and the influence of *incidental prices*. This chapter concludes by investigating the question of whether *all-inclusive prices* or itemized prices, also known as *partitioned prices*, are more attractive to consumers and why.

Chapter 6 examines the trend in every industry towards bargaining and fluid prices that is facilitated by the adoption of dynamic pricing methods and big data. We consider two participative pricing methods, *Pay What You Want* pricing and *Name Your Own Price* pricing. This chapter also investigates the *psychology of frequent price changes* and how they affect customer decisions adversely. The case of Uber's *surge pricing* offers useful insights into customer response and potential solutions to the problems that arise from fluctuating prices.

Chapter 7, the last chapter, covers the role of price in the customer's final step of purchase. We consider how managers can use pricing actions effectively to close the sale and influence the customer's purchase and repurchase behavior. We study how different point-of-purchase pricing tactics work, including *sale signs and other related visual cues, limited-time promotions, price-matching guarantees*, and *scarcity pricing*. We conclude the chapter and this book by considering how managers can use the *goal gradient motivation* of their customers to design *loyalty reward programs* that not only encourage customers to buy but accelerate their purchases."

All the ideas in this book are chosen to be *immediately practical*. You can pick and choose the psychological pricing concepts and tools that either intrigue you or ones that seem particularly relevant to your situation. Regardless of which industry you work in, you can apply these ideas right away in your business and see for yourself whether they help you to influence, sell to, and satisfy your customers.

Hidden Meanings in Price

Markets are... cultural constellations. Like any other type of social interaction, market exchange is highly ritualized; it involves a wide variety of symbols that transfer rich meanings between people who exchange goods with each other. – Olav Velthuis.

August 8, 2008, was a big wedding day. Although it was a Friday, wedding venues all over China, from elite resorts to small-city banquet halls, were sold out months in advance. It seemed like every engaged Chinese couple wanted to marry on that day. In the end, official Chinese statistics showed a record number of 314,224 couples tied the knot on August 8, 2008[12]. The date, 080808, is considered extremely auspicious in the Chinese culture because of its triple lucky number eights. The Chinese believed that marrying on that day would bring the couple good fortune. This surge in marriages carried over to the United States. On online wedding site TheKnot.com, four times as many members registered their weddings on that Friday compared to other Fridays in August 2008. Wedding venues in New York City were booked solid. Las Vegas hotels offered wedding packages for promotional prices of $888 and $1,888, and exclusive deals to the first 88 couples who got married there. It made sense to charge an auspicious price to a couple marrying on an auspicious date.

Price is far more than a narrow and literal expression of how much something costs to purchase. Its constituent numbers imbue every price with symbolic information that affects consumers in all kinds of ways. In this chapter, we will examine the different symbolic meanings that prices create for products and brands. We will call these meanings the representational, informational, and visual symbolic values of price.

Let's start with the representational meaning of price. If a bag of oranges has a price of $5, you must pay $5 to buy it. This is the representational symbolic value of the price. Price simply represents the amount of money the seller is asking for in exchange for the product. Nothing more, nothing less. It is an essential but straightforward function of price. The representational meaning makes the price a price, not a basketball score.

The Informational Value of Price

So help me dress for my fairytale, can't wear something I bought on sale. Love is, like, forever. This is no time to economize. – Legally Blonde, Elle, Omigod you guys.

A product's price embeds and conveys useful information about its quality. If all I tell you about one particular automobile is that its price is $85,000, images of a posh luxury car are likely to dance before your eyes when no other information about the vehicle is given. It is unlikely you will imagine a hatchback or a minivan costing $85,000. On the other hand, if I say that my lunch today cost one dollar, you will confidently guess I had a taco or a hot dog from a food truck, not a gourmet multi-course meal in a French restaurant. Even when the food, whether it is a hot dog or a carefully composed plate of risotto with seasonal vegetables, is shown to you, its price will still influence how you evaluate it, and what you expect from it. Price and quality go hand in hand. One conveys information about the other, whether it is explicitly stated or not. This is the *informational value* of the price.

The price level, in and of itself, delivers useful, and often diagnostic information about the product's quality. The price functions much like a brand does, standing for and conveying a variety of associations. The

26

informational value of the price is particularly potent when the product's price is extreme or atypical, either on the high end or the low end of the range expected by consumers. It often works in counterintuitive ways that make little economic sense, as the following examples illustrate.

The case of the bargain basement author

Consultant Dorie Clark recounts the case of a highly-regarded *New York Times* bestselling author who was invited to be a keynote speaker for a trade association's annual convention[13]. When asked his speaking fees to participate, the superstar author quoted a modest price of $3,000, a fraction of what the association was expecting to pay. Instead of being thrilled at having locked up a top-notch speaker at a price far below the budgeted amount, the event's organizers started having second thoughts. They wondered whether they had chosen the right speaker and grew concerned about the quality of speech he would deliver.

Notice that despite the author's reputation and track record, this adverse reaction still occurred among his prospective clients. It was driven by a price that was too low. Drawing lessons from this case, Clark insightfully advises, "Price is often a proxy for quality, and when you put yourself at the low end, it signals that you're unsure of your value — or the value just isn't there. Either can be alarming for prospective clients." The main lesson is that the information communicated by the price needs to be consistent with the product's quality. Asking too low a price undermines perceptions of the product's quality instead of increasing the buyer's evaluations of the product.

The highest price point is the most comforting one

In the late 1990s, when the consumer-packaged goods company P&G wanted to introduce its new *Olay Total Effects* product, the company tested three different prices, $12.99, $15.99, and $18.99, to determine which price would be the most appealing to target customers. It would presumably have made a profit at any of these prices. Now you would expect that shoppers would find the $12.99 price to be the best one. However, this was not the case.

At the low price, a fair number of mainstream consumers who shopped in grocery or drug stores expressed interest in Olay. However, the so-called prestige shoppers who purchased such products in department stores were not as enthusiastic. They thought the product was too cheap to be in department stores at the $12.99 price. When it was offered at $15.99, the amount of purchase interest from both mainstream and prestige shoppers *declined appreciably* compared to the $12.99 price.

Surprisingly, when Olay's price was increased to $18.99, both groups, and particularly, the prestige shoppers' intentions to purchase rose to levels even higher than the $12.99 price. The result of the price test showed that more shoppers wanted to buy the Olay Total Effects at the highest of the three prices. As Joe Listro, Olay's R&D manager explained[14]:

> "So, $12.99 was really good, $15.99 not so good, $18.99 great. We found that at $18.99, we were starting to get consumers who would shop in both channels. At $18.99, it was a great value to a prestige shopper who was used to spending $30 or more for a similar product. But $15.99 was no-man's-land – way too expensive for a mass shopper and really not credible enough for a prestige shopper."

Who knows what would have happened if they had tried to test an even higher price such as $21.99? The case shows that the same product, with an identical formulation and packaging, is perceived and preferred differently based solely on its price. For the Olay brand, the $18.99 price radiated assurance for the department store shoppers by signaling the product's effectiveness. The price informed the shopper that the item deserved to be sold in a department store where they would feel comfortable purchasing it. For drugstore and grocery store shoppers, the $18.99 price point made the product appear to be aspirational, representing an affordable luxury item they could splurge on every so often. A price lower than $18.99 was detrimental to the new product's success.

As the keynote speaker and the Olay Total Effects cases show, the informational value of price is particularly powerful when the buyer has difficulty in determining the item's quality. The keynote speaker's service was what marketers call an *experiential service*, the quality of which can only be evaluated after it is consumed, and perhaps fully not even then. The organizers used his asking price as a way of predicting his competence in public speaking. The low price failed because it undermined their confidence. Similarly, the Olay Total Effects product was brand new, and being introduced to the marketplace. Consumers did not know what to expect. They used their knowledge of the product category and drew inferences about the new product's potency from its price.

The main lesson for managers is this. The informational value of price is influential when selling experiential products or when introducing any kind of new product. That is when consumers are looking at the product's price for hints about what to expect. If the product is underpriced, it will convey an image of mediocrity that could cling to the product far beyond its introductory phase. Even more dangerous, a low price could create doubt and suspicion among potential adopters to such a degree that sales may never take off. Startup founders should take particular note of these cautionary cases. They often tend to be reticent to ask for prices that their innovations deserve.

As pricing consultants Walter Baker, Michael Marn, and Craig Zawada point out, "[Setting a high price] is not about gouging customers or employing tricks to gain undeserved revenues. Quite to the contrary, the real price advantage is a source of organizational pride. The highest compliment a customer can pay a supplier is to knowingly pay more for that company's goods and services. In doing so, the customer is saying, "You are higher priced, but you are worth it; you are superior to my other supplier alternatives [15]"."

The Visual Symbolic Properties of Price

Numbers feel mysterious and significant. – Mark Forsyth.

Price has symbolic value in a third broader sense that is more subtle and nuanced than either its representational or informational value. Relatively superficial and pliable properties of the price such as whether it ends with a 9, 5, 0, or some other number, whether the price is a nice round number or has jagged edges (such as $3.23), whether it includes numbers that widely signify death or prosperity in a culture, whether the price is displayed with or without a dollar sign before it, and even whether it is written out fully in words, like "twenty-four dollars" all imbue the price with unique meanings. The meaning creation involves very little effort or expense on the seller's part and generates significant influence on customers. This is the *visual symbolic value* of price because its power lies in the visual impact the price has on the consumer's assessment, and the association of price with the object and the seller.

The visual symbolic properties of a price are important to marketers for two reasons. First, a great deal of behavioral economics and cognitive psychology research is discovering how superficial and inexpensive-to-implement visual changes to prices enhance their symbolism in powerful ways, and influence consumer responses. Many of these price changes can be implemented quickly and tested conveniently, making them useful in virtually any industry. In this section, this knowledge is distilled to provide useful guidelines for pricing managers.

Second, the means by which a price's visual symbolic properties affect consumers are subtle and work below the radar. In many cases, these effects are far more influential and durable than the effects of the literal economic information or the overt quality cues conveyed by the price. What's more, the science of visual symbolic properties is rich and evolving, suggesting that there are many different avenues to influence customers depending on the manager's objectives.

The symbolic meaning of price endings

The conventional wisdom is that price endings that are just below a round number convey a lower price because of how the consumer processes information. This leads to an underestimation of the magnitude of price. To give a concrete example, a shopper will convert prices of $9.99, $9.98 or $9.95 to "nine dollars and something" instead of "almost ten dollars" resulting in a more favorable assessment of the product's value when compared to a price that is exactly $10 or slightly higher. Using this logic, marketers have embraced just-below price endings, with studies indicating that anywhere between 30% and 65% of all prices presented to consumers in the United States end with 9[16].

With just-below prices, there is a second psychological process at work beyond underestimation. Prices ending with 9 convey a low price image about the product, the seller, or both. When the seller uses prices ending with the number 9 liberally to sell its products, it creates an image of economy, coupled with high value. The CEO of the 400-store, $2.4 billion, 99 Cents Only Stores chain Jack Sinclair explains this economy association created by the 99 price ending: "We're not a dollar store, we are an extreme value retailer. Our aspiration is to give a lot more people access to the type of value we provide." The company does not adhere strictly to the 99 cents price point for every single product. About 90 percent of the SKUs (or Stock Keeping Units) in the store are priced precisely at 99 cents, while the remaining prices vary, although all prices are below $10[17]. Still, this is enough to produce a compelling low price image. 99 Cents Only Stores has built its value proposition around the brand name and 99 cent prices that draws millions of shoppers to its stores.

For those interested in academic terminology, these two effects of just-below price endings are called the *level effect* and the *image effect*[18]. The level effect is the underestimation, and the image effect is the perception of a low price image. Together, the two forces make prices ending in 9 so ubiquitous and effective.

Consumer psychologist Robert Schindler further expanded the scope of the visual symbolic properties of price, by suggesting that every price ending has specific symbolic value that conveys unique and meaningful information to consumers[19]. Table 2.1 lists the meanings discovered by Schindler, along with additional meanings discovered by other behavioral economists.

Table 2.1 Symbolic meanings conveyed by different price endings.

Symbolic Meaning	Price Ending
This item has a low price.	5, 8, 9, 95, 99
This item is of questionable quality.	9, 99
This seller offers good value.	9, 99
This seller sells cheap, poor-quality items.	9, 99
This price has been reduced from its original higher level.	3, 7, 99
This seller is trying to manipulate customers.	9, 99
This item's price hasn't been raised recently.	5, 8, 9
This price is a discounted or sale price.	3, 7
This price isn't fixed, it is negotiable.	0
This item's price is high.	0, all-text
This item is of high quality.	0, all-text
This seller is upscale (i.e., sophisticated, classy, prestigious).	0, all-text
The buyers of this product are high-status.	0, all-text
This seller sells unique products.	2, 3, 4, 6, 7, 8
This seller sells creatively designed or hand-crafted products.	2, 3, 4, 6, 7, 8
This seller has set prices thoughtfully.	2, 3, 4, 6, 7, 8
This seller offers upscale products.	2, 3, 4, 6, 7, 8
This seller has a playful approach to business.	2, 3, 4, 6, 7, 8
This seller runs its business competently.	2, 3, 4, 6, 7, 8

As the list of symbolic meanings in Table 2.1 illustrates, the same price ending conveys different, and even contradictory, inferences about prices to customers. For instance, 9-endings emphasize either the product's or the seller's superior value or highlight its poor quality and cheapness. Its association with a low price image can, in turn, lead to a variety of subsequent inferences. Some shoppers may conclude that because the product has a low price, its quality must be low. As we saw in the 99 Cents Only store example, others may conclude that the seller has taken the trouble to squeeze out costs from its operations and provide compelling value to its customers. Their conclusion will be that "Prices ending in 9 = low prices = good deals."

You must be kidding/ Tom Driggers/ Flickr

Still others may make these inferences in relative terms, by believing that the price is low relative to other sellers, or that the price is lower than it used to be. Prices ending with 9 have so many favorable symbolic meanings conveying good value that sellers have a strong preference for 9-ending and 99-ending prices. The use of 9-ending prices has a long history because of this. Marketers even have a particular name for them. They are called "charm prices" because they charm money out of shoppers' wallets.

The inferences created by other price endings in consumers' minds are just as significant. The 0-ending and 00-ending convey high quality. Using non-standard endings such as 2, 3, 4, 6, 7, and 8 is a way to stand apart from the crowd. Sit-down restaurants often use non-standard price endings to bolster their image of quirkiness or creativity[20]. Let's examine what the research says about the symbolic meanings of each price ending in more detail, starting with charm prices.

How charm prices influence consumer behavior

Academic researchers have studied the question of whether charm prices that end in 9 or 99 affect consumer behavior for over eighty years. The first known study on the impact of charm prices appeared in 1936 and was inconclusive. Since then, dozens of studies have been done. While the results are not always consistent, there is sufficient evidence that the use of charm prices by sellers leads to greater purchases. Many charm-price studies are controlled field experiments using different versions of print catalogs or different store locations of a retail chain, with some pricing merchandise using charm prices and others using slightly different prices ending with other numbers.

Across the studies that find positive effects, the increase in purchasing behavior is substantial—the lowest increase is around 5%, and the highest increase is over 75%. One study conducted with a large dataset from a grocery store involving over 1,700 products and 51 million purchase transactions found a powerful effect of charm prices on purchase behavior. The author concluded that "consumers respond to a 1-cent increase from a 99-cent ending price [to the 00-cent ending price] as if it were a 15-25 percent increase[21]." The question of what psychological decision making process lies behind the increased purchases observed at the aggregate level remains open. Are the same shoppers buying more quantity or are some non-buyers being tricked into purchasing because of the charm price? And to what extent is the *level effect* and the *image effect* responsible? The truth is we simply don't know all the answers.

What we do know is the effect of charm prices on consumers' perceptions. Let's discuss the *level effect* and *image effect* of charm prices, both of which affect consumer perceptions, in greater detail. First, charm prices create a sense in the consumer's mind that the product's price is lower than it is. Many shoppers underestimate these prices because when looking at a price, they use what psychologists call a *truncation strategy*. They only pay attention to the leftmost digits of a price instead of all its numbers. For instance, something priced at $7.99, interpreted as 7-something due to truncation appears to be a lot cheaper (and a lot more appealing) than if the same product is priced at $8.00 (interpreted as 8-something). For the level effect to work, therefore, the seller's pricing action must produce a change in the left-most digit of the price. As a concrete example, the level effect is triggered when the item's original price is changed from $3.00 to $2.99, but not when the change is from $3.50 to $3.49[22].

Research also suggests that charm prices are more effective for new products than they are for previously sold products. In one controlled experiment conducted with catalogs selling moderately-priced women's apparel, the researchers found that while sales of all items increased when a $9 ending price was used, new items showed greater increases than products that the company had previously sold in the catalog. For new products, using $9 ending prices resulted in a sales increase of 22%. For existing products, the increase was only 10%.

The second reason for a charm price's effectiveness is that when a retailer uses prices ending with 9 or 99 throughout a store, catalog or website, it creates a holistic *low price image* for the brand and store. The seller can strategically magnify the image effect of charm prices. When retailers and hotel chains price their products with a preponderance of 9-endings and then frequently offer promotions using signs such as "sale price," "25 percent off," "price reduced," and "holiday sale," their low price image is reinforced[23]. The brand becomes associated with offering a high degree of value to customers.

Sellers also use creative variations to benefit from the image effect. For example, one department store priced its regular merchandise using zero price endings and clearance items with 98 endings[24]. Once the price image is solidified in shoppers' minds, they pay less attention to actual displayed prices in the store and stop comparing them carefully to competitors' prices. They are persuaded that the retailer sells items that will be cheaper than elsewhere, and they buy accordingly. These shoppers may spend little time evaluating or deciding. Instead, they move directly to the *buy* state in the NACJ framework when they need something. This image effect of charm prices is also the reason why retailers who want an exclusive or prestige image among customers go out of their way to avoid using just-below or charm prices.

Not all effects of just-below and charm prices are favorable. Because of their use by unethical sellers, these price endings create the impression that the seller is trying to be manipulative or influence the buying decision in an underhanded way. In today's environment of widespread cynicism, distrust, and knowledge of marketing influence techniques, the negative inferences hurt the seller's marketing activities.

Even when shoppers don't react cynically when charm prices are used throughout the store, there is some danger that many otherwise receptive shoppers may think that the retailer is naïve, tacky, or lacking in sophistication. Sellers need to be cautious when using blanket charm prices to sell products. There is a fine line between being "extreme value" and being "dingy." Charm prices should be used judiciously and sparingly by most sellers, covering no more than 25-30% of all products and services. Charm prices make the most sense when the seller emphatically wants to convey a budget price image to its target audience and also uses other means to project this image in addition to charm prices.

Using charm prices at the point of purchase to influence the buyer's choice

For a retailer, one creative application of charm prices is to influence which of two alternatives a customer purchases. Customers often make comparisons between two brands in the store before choosing one (in the *evaluate* state of the NACJ framework). Prices have a significant influence in such comparisons which are made by shoppers at the point of purchase. An astute seller can use charm prices to increase sales of higher margin items.

Let's imagine your store sells two brands of pasta sauce, Brand A and Brand B. Both are national brands. Brand A is regularly priced at around $3 a bottle, and Brand B is priced at around $4 for a bottle when they are not on sale. Your store earns a higher margin when you sell a bottle of Brand B pasta sauce and a lower margin on Brand A. How will you price these two brands on the store shelf?

The correct answer: Brand A = $3.00, Brand B = $3.99

In this configuration of prices, research has shown that the share of the higher priced (and higher margin) option is the highest when compared to either Brand A = $2.99, Brand B = $3.99, or Brand A = $3.00, Brand B = $4.00[25]. This is because the perceived difference between the two prices is the *smallest* at these prices.

The reverse is also true. If you wanted to increase sales of Brand A relative to Brand B, you would price Brand A at $2.99 and Brand B at $4.00. Such an approach will *maximize* the consumer's perception of the price difference between the two brands and increase sales of Brand A.

The managerial lesson from this example is that in a direct head-to-head comparison of two competing products, pricing the higher margin product with a 9-ending and the lower margin product with a zero-ending will favor sales of the higher margin product.

The symbolic meanings of other price endings

Conveying status and high quality. When retailers want to convey that the item they are selling is of high quality or that their store is prestigious and upscale, they prefer to use prices ending with round numbers. In these cases, prices throughout the store end in 0, or 00. This is the diametrically opposite approach to the one used by 99 Cents Only Stores. Another variation is to use whole numbers such as $25 without any trailing zeros. In one classic study in which the researcher collected over 2,400 different prices from twelve different stores, they found that 79.8% of prices at Macy's and 84.5% of prices at Nieman Marcus ended in round numbers. In contrast, only 6.3% of Target's prices and 1.1% of K-Mart's prices were round numbers. None of the retailers in the study used rounded prices to sell all their products. The study's author concluded that retailers deliberately overuse prices ending with 0 when they want to signal high quality to their customer base[26].

Conveying a temporary sale. Price endings, in and of themselves, can be used to convey that the item's current price is a sale price and it is temporary. While some researchers argue that any just-below ending such as 5, 8, or 9 will be the most likely to create the association of a sale for a temporary period, others argue that endings that are not commonly used such as 3 or 7 are more effective for this purpose. For instance, if a retailer wants to place a coat that usually costs $49.99 on sale for a limited period, it should use prices such as $39.97 or $39.93 to convey both the "on sale" and "for a limited time" aspects of this reduced price. At least part of these associations come from the fact that many retailers use prices ending with 7, and to a lesser extent 3, as internal codes to indicate that the item is being offered at a deep discount or is on clearance. For instance, Costco, Gap, Old Navy, Dick's Sporting Goods, Office Depot, and Petsmart all use either one or both of these price endings to sell deeply discounted merchandise[27]. We will see more of this idea when we consider *price vocabularies* later in this chapter.

The meanings of non-standard price endings. Non-standard price endings such as 2, 3, 4, 6, 7, and to a lesser extent 8, produce a complex set of meanings for shoppers that are different from the 0, 5, and 9 price endings. Some shoppers may view sellers who use these endings liberally to be playful, adventurous, and innovative sellers that buck convention and like to do their own thing. Such meanings of innovativeness and creativity help to garner positive feelings for the seller. Contrarily, experts have argued that such endings have the potential to signify a haphazard and amateurish pricing approach, leading customers to question the seller's professionalism and competence. The third set of meanings concerns the idea that by using non-standard endings, instead of simply going with the pricing approach that everyone else does, the seller has put a lot of thought into calculating the prices it should charge customers.

Whether positive or negative symbolic meanings from using non-standard price endings take the front seat in the consumer's mind depends a lot on the seller's reputation, product assortment, and marketing performance. A popular upscale restaurant in Houston called Hugo's uses prices ending with non-standard numbers. Because of its delicious and well-reviewed food, beloved eponymous chef-owner, longstanding reputation for creative cuisine, and the comforting and plush ambiance, the non-standard price endings in its menu align with, and augment, the other positive meanings created by branding and the customer's experience. If another mediocre or poorly-run restaurant used non-standard price endings, it would backfire by producing dissonant impressions or reinforcing negative impressions.

The mythic status of the 7-ending. In technology and online marketing circles, prices ending with 7 have tended to be unusually popular, based on anecdotes of their success. Some marketing consultants in these industries have advocated for only using prices ending with 7. They claim that such offers will increase sales and profits[28]. On discussion boards and blogs, various reasons are advanced for why 7-ending prices are effective online including the idea that the number 7 is the least threatening of all numbers, that it is a lucky or happy number, that it is the most frequently occurring number in the Bible, or that it sounds the most familiar to people's ears. The fact that a fair number of Americans consider the number 7 to be lucky also contributes to its popularity in pricing. However, I could not find any credible research supporting any of these assertions. As it stands, the use of prices ending with 7 is an example of *norm-driven pricing*, in which new adopters simply use the established industry conventions, with or without accepting the mythic rationale behind them.

Lucky and unlucky price endings. Dutch sociologist Olav Velthuis insightfully observes that "Prices, which have long been considered to be devoid of meaning at all, can be thought of as cultural entities[29]." Nowhere is this more apparent than when considering symbolic meanings of numbers beyond the functional inferences they provide to customers. Superstitious beliefs about numbers and prices are sometimes far more powerful than the functional signals. These beliefs are often based on how a culture thinks of the significance of particular numbers as either auspicious or inauspicious. Superstitious beliefs play an important role in pricing, especially in which price endings are used and how they are interpreted in a culture. Unlike the United States, where prices ending with 9 are the most common, in many Asian countries, including China, Japan, and Malaysia, the most popular price ending is 8.

In Chinese culture, the number 8 has special importance. It is spoken as bā and sounds similar to fā, which has connotations of wealth, fortune, and prosperity in Cantonese and Mandarin. Because of this resemblance, there is a centuries-old belief that 8 is an auspicious number. This widespread cultural belief manifests in many ways that are relevant to pricing. We saw one of these in the opening paragraph of this chapter. Chinese couples flocked to get married on 08/08/2008, and service providers offered them wedding packages having prices awash in 8s. Telephone numbers in China usually cost nothing, but the Beijing telephone number 18888888888 sold for approximately $17 million because of its auspicious properties[30].

Illustration by Shirin Abvabi

On the flip side, the number 4, vocalized as sì, sounds very similar to sǐ, the word for death. It is considered to be an inauspicious number to be avoided. In China, and in other countries such as Malaysia, Taiwan, Singapore, and Hong Kong where Cantonese and Mandarin are spoken by a significant proportion of the population, sellers tend to favor prices ending in 8 and shun those ending in 4.

In one study of Chinese and Taiwanese print advertisements, researchers found almost 40 percent of prices ended with 8, and just 1.4 percent of prices ended with 4[31]. Another study conducted in Singapore found a similar result. 31.1 percent of prices advertised in two Singaporean newspapers ended in 8. The authors concluded that "the lucky price ending 8 can be interpreted as an element of traditional Eastern culture, which communicates a superstitious belief rooted in the Chinese language." A third study found an over-representation of prices ending in 8 in the room rates of casino hotels in Macau.

Eight is also imbued with positive symbolic value in Japan. The Japanese script for the number 8 has the shape of a mountain ("Sue Hirogari" in Japanese), symbolizing the concepts of fanning out, growth, and "to become more prosperous as time passes." Because of these positive connotations, prices in Japan also tend to lean towards 8-endings. Moreover, culturally symbolic prices ending in 8 tend to be particularly favored for high-priced items in Japan and Chinese-speaking regions, presumably because shoppers pay more attention to the auspiciousness of numbers when making consequential buying decisions[32]. In large parts of Asia, prices ending in 8 are more favored than prices ending in 9.

The symbolic meanings of numbers and the roles played by the seller in offering a price and by the buyer in accepting or declining it in market transactions have cultural significance. People's cultural beliefs about numbers play an influential role in how sellers offer prices to customers.

In the United States and other countries, when sellers use the number 9 as the last digit of their prices, they are mainly thinking about how their customers will react psychologically to the price. As we saw earlier in this chapter, charm prices lead a significant number of customers to underestimate the price and also create the perception that the seller is offering a good value. American sellers specifically, and Western sellers in general, use prices to capitalize on these psychological phenomena.

Asian sellers have an altogether different worldview when setting prices. Even though the psychological processes associated with 9-ending prices apply to Asian consumers because they are based on general cognitive and perceptual processes, many sellers choose not to focus on customer reactions to price endings or to benefit from them. Instead, they rely on the superstitious and cultural significance of numbers in their pricing decisions. Using the logic that "I want to harness good fortune for my business and my customers with my pricing decisions," they gravitate towards prices ending with the number 8.

Any price-ending (except 9) can be imbued with desired symbolic meaning when used consistently. Most of the discussion so far in this chapter has focused on the well-established symbolic meanings associated with specific price endings based on inferences customers draw from them. The truth is that when used consistently and in conjunction with other marketing tools, any number can be associated with any specific idea to generate the symbolic meaning that the seller wishes. It's a matter of patience, persistence, and broad exposure.

Consider this fascinating natural experiment that occurred in Israel a few years ago[33]. In January 2014, the Israeli government outlawed the use of all non-zero price endings to align with the obsolescence of smaller denomination coins. They also wanted to comply with public demands to ban "manipulative" 9-ending prices. In response to this ban, sellers throughout Israel widely adopted prices ending with 90 in concert. Such prices constituted only 6% of all prices before January 2014 but increased to 55% after the law came into effect. Even though they ended with zero, they became the de facto charm prices of Israel.

Without any prior symbolic meaning, the widespread replacement of previous 9-ending prices with 90-ending prices had a powerful effect. A year later, Israeli consumers, by and large, treated 90-ending prices just like they used to treat prices ending with 9. Consistent with the underestimation process that occurs with charm prices, they made larger mistakes when recalling 90-ending prices than other prices. They were also less likely to notice that 90-ending prices had changed.

The authors who conducted this study concluded that 90-ending prices had taken the identical psychological place in Israeli consumer thinking that used to be occupied by charm prices before.

The Power of a Price Vocabulary

To have another language is to possess a second soul. – Charlemagne.

For many sellers, the symbolic value of prices extends far beyond the use of individual price endings. Take the case of warehouse chain Costco. The next time you visit your local Costco warehouse store, observe the price tags carefully. In addition to showing the price, Costco's price tags encode additional information about the offer[34]. The price-endings, such as $8.99 vs. $8.97, in particular, convey special meanings to the subset of shoppers who are literate in Costco's price vocabulary. Here are a few examples of the special meanings contained in Costco's price tags:

- When a product's price ends with a 99 at Costco, e.g., $6.99, it is the regular price that shoppers would typically pay. While this is likely to be a good value compared to other sellers, it is not a limited-time promotion.
- When the price ends with 97, it is for clearance items that have been marked down from a previous higher price. Prices ending with 97 represent special, limited-time promotions run by the store's managers to sell out slow-moving or seasonal items.
- Price tags that have an asterisk in the upper right corner represent products that are discontinued and will not be available once they are sold out.
- Prices that end with either 88 or 00 are for irregular merchandise such as floor models, working returned models, etc. These items are usually one-offs and are priced much lower than their usual prices.

These and other symbols together form a price vocabulary that provides Costco's customers with potentially useful information for their purchase decisions. Costco is not the only retailer that uses a price vocabulary. Walmart has its unique price vocabulary, as do other retailers like TJ Maxx, BJ's Wholesale, and Home Depot[35].

What is a price vocabulary?

A price vocabulary *is a unique and consistent set of prices, particularly price endings, plus the use of other symbols such as glyphs, numerical codes, sale tags of specific colors, and so on, used by a seller that convey useful informational cues to consumers.* Examples of informational cues include, "this is the product's regular price, there's no need to rush to purchase right now," "this item is discontinued and drastically marked-down, it won't be available once it's sold out," "this is a sale that is paid for by the manufacturer, we are simply passing the incentive on to you," and so on. Consumers who become literate in a particular seller's price vocabulary make more informed and advantageous buying decisions. Some may even be able to form behavioral scripts and habitual buying patterns that incorporate the seller's price vocabulary consistently into their decision calculus.

How price vocabularies benefit retailers

At present, retailers use price vocabularies mainly for operational reasons and in ways that are not necessarily customer-friendly. For example, in the words of a Costco employee, "It's not really a code, more just a set of rules that we follow to track pricing and be consistent throughout the region[36]." The reality is that when designed in a way that supports common customer journeys, and publicized to customers creatively, a price vocabulary delivers powerful marketing benefits. Here are three noteworthy potential benefits of a price vocabulary for sellers.

1) *Price vocabularies create sustainable differentiation.* Every seller's price vocabulary is unique. When a seller uses a price vocabulary consistently and it becomes known to customers, it differentiates them from competitors. What's more, the differentiation created by a price vocabulary is durable. As it develops a history with shoppers, the vocabulary becomes a brand association and affects the experience of the seller's core customers positively. For example, Costco's price vocabulary was first discussed on consumer blogs in 2013 and continues to be loved by Costco loyalists six years later[37]. It has added significantly to the mystique of Costco's brand.

2) *Price vocabularies increase customer engagement.* Price vocabularies today are a lot like many secret restaurant menus used to be a few years ago. They remain mostly unacknowledged by the company and stir up controversy about whether they even exist at all[38]. Most customers are unaware, but those in the know feel special. Because of their subversive, under-the-radar qualities, they generate excitement and let customers play a more active role in their engagement with the business. When I describe the price vocabulary concept during talks and give the example of Costco's price vocabulary, I invariably get an audience member or two who will say, "I've been a Costco member for many years, but I never knew about this until just now." This reaction is usually followed by a sense of excitement and pleasure at being able to engage with a trusted and well-liked brand in a new way.

3) *Price vocabularies reward loyal customers.* Price vocabularies differ from secret menus in one crucial way. Customers who are literate in the price vocabulary derive economic benefits. For example, if they see a price indicating that a further price cut is imminent, they will hold off on making the purchase and save money. On the flip side, a final clearance signal may prompt them to purchase impulsively to avail of the best-available and limited-time deal. Because of the direct linkage between the information communicated by the price vocabulary and the customer's buying behavior, a well-designed price vocabulary effectively functions as a loyalty rewards program. It selectively rewards customers who are well-versed with the language of the retailer's prices, and who are also likely to be its loyal customers.

How sellers can use price vocabularies

Like many psychological pricing actions, using a price vocabulary is relatively inexpensive because many retailers already have specific codes for different pricing actions. It may even save the seller money by introducing new structure and consistency into the price setting and price changing process. Despite these advantages, most sellers have not yet systematically embraced the price vocabulary as a marketing program.

In-N-Out Burger's secret menu evolved over the decades and is attributed by industry experts as an essential reason for the chain's sustained financial success[39]. After letting the secret menu remain a customer-driven, under-the-radar phenomenon since the 1970s, the fast food chain embraced it officially with its not-so-secret menu. Other chains like Starbucks and McDonalds have been similarly proactive. Like secret menus, retailing managers should take a page out of the restaurant chain playbook and embrace price vocabularies as a way to enhance their customers' experience.

How the Company's Price Image Influences its Brand's Value

I've learned that people will forget what you said, people will forget what you did, but people will never forget how you made them feel. – Maya Angelou.

The most potent marketing symbol of all is the seller's brand. Today, the biggest global brands like Microsoft, Apple and Google are worth more than one hundred billion dollars apiece[40]. What creates this brand value? There are many contributors, but a company's pricing strategy is an important one. Its pricing methods and tactics, not to mention the actual prices themselves, have a significant influence in generating brand meaning for consumers and contributing to the brand's financial value. For an individual consumer, when a brand has a coherent and appealing price image, it increases the brand's attractiveness and simplifies the purchase decision. Instead of looking at each item's price and carrying out mental calculations effortfully, they can simply rely on the brand's price image as a short-cut in their deliberations.

A brand's price image is the consumer's overall impression of the company's prices, pricing strategy, and price actions that contribute to the perceptions of its brand. The price image influences the degree to which consumers see the brand in a positive or negative light, and whether they turn to it when the need arises. The price image also affects the consumers' interpretation of individual pricing actions made by the company and how they respond to them. The price image is facilitated by the company's use of a comprehensive pricing strategy, and the consistent and reinforcing use of pricing cues in its branding and pricing communications.

Consider the discount retailer Walmart. The company has used taglines to communicate its emphasis on low prices for decades. Its "Always Low Prices. Always." tagline lasted for nineteen years, from 1994 to 2007. This was followed by the tagline, "Save Money. Live Better" from 2007 onwards. Advertising expert Will Burns suggests that with the latter tagline, Walmart promised its customers, "in effect, 'We may be big and bad, but we're big and bad on your behalf, consumers, and in the form of lower prices.' Lower prices means you can afford more, which means you will live better[41]." The other core elements of Walmart's pricing strategy such as its widely-publicized decades-long use of every day low prices and its aggressive price-matching guarantees further reinforce the brand promise made by its tagline that the prices it offers will be the lowest ones[42]. Because of this consistency, Walmart's "has the lowest prices" price image has served to differentiate the company and contributed significantly to its brand value, which was estimated to be $24.9 billion in 2018.

Its competitor, Target, adopted a very different branding strategy and price image. It also makes price an important part of its value proposition, capturing the brand's promise in the tagline "Expect More. Pay Less." With this approach, Target positions itself as a retailer that provides superior value to its customers in their overall shopping experience but may not necessarily have the lowest prices for every product. The chief marketing officer of Target explained the underlying logic for this strategy by pointing out that, "we strive for a balance between making our guests aware of value while emphasizing superior merchandise and a pleasant shopping experience." To achieve this balance, Target combines its "high value but not the lowest price" price image with other consistent themes such as "enjoyable and exciting shopping experience," "friendly service," "speedy checkout" and "beautifully designed and innovative products" to create a more upscale price image for its brand[43]. To its customers, Target's price image is more compelling than Walmart's price image. They don't mind spending a few dollars more to buy trendier merchandise in a more welcoming ambiance of the Target store.

The five components of the company's price image

As the Walmart and Target examples illustrate, developing a price image is a challenging and multi-pronged undertaking. How do you develop a powerful price image for your company that contributes to your brand's value? Academic research shows that a company's price image is made up of five types of customer perceptions about its prices: (1) price level, (2) value for money, (3) price accessibility, (4) price stability, and (5) price evaluability[44], shown in Figure 2.1. The manager can use these five factors together or employ some combination of them to develop a price image that will appeal to customers. Let's consider each component in greater detail.

1) Price level. The price level is *the degree to which the company's offerings are consistently perceived as being either higher or lower than its competitors' comparable offerings.* A brand that regularly prices its products below its competitors creates a low-price image, and one that is usually higher gets pegged as the premium seller by customers, regardless of its actual prices or profit margins.

Investment company Vanguard was the first to introduce low-cost mutual funds and index funds to individual investors and charged substantially lower management fees than the similar products sold by its competitors such as Fidelity, e*Trade, and Charles Schwab. Even years after its competitors caught up and lowered their fees, to levels below Vanguard's fees in some cases, Vanguard still retains the low-cost price image among its customer base[45]. Like Walmart, the low-cost price image is an integral part of Vanguard's differentiation and fuels its appeal to millions of individual investors. Combined with high-quality service and a famous founder with a mythic origin story (the late John Bogle), the low-cost price image delivers a compelling value proposition.

Figure 2.1: The five components of the company's price image.

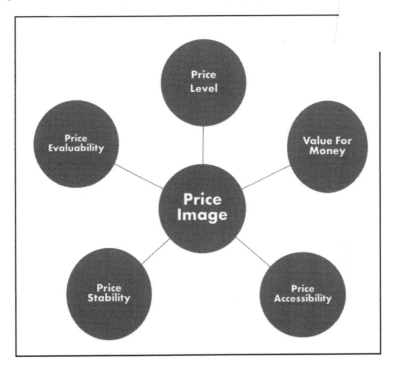

On the other end of the spectrum, consider the fashion brand Supreme (which we will look at in more detail in Chapter 7). Its products retail at two to three times its competitors' prices, which creates a premium, limited-supply image for its merchandise. The same is true of many national brands in fast-moving consumer packaged goods categories. By carefully cultivating a premium image, Proctor & Gamble's Tide detergent is able to charge price premiums of 25% or more for its Tide Plus line when compared to store brands[46].

For the price level to affect the company's price image, it needs to be consistent in its price differentials relative to its prominent competitors over a lengthy period. If price levels frequently fluctuate and are sometimes higher and sometimes lower than competitors, as is the case for the US-based full-service airlines such as United, Delta, and American Airlines, it is difficult for consumers to distinguish between the sellers, or to attribute a premium or low price image to a particular company. This is one reason why, even after decades of market dominance, it is hard for American flyers to form coherent price images for the major full-service airlines.

2) Value for money. Value for money (VFM) is *the degree to which consumers consistently perceive the company's products as providing excellent value at its chosen price level*. Both Costco, with its $1.50 hotdog and soda combo, and $4.99 rotisserie chickens, and electric car manufacturer Tesla with its top-of-the-line $80,000 Model S sedan qualify as high VFM brands, because customers perceive each of them as providing excellent value[47]. When a company earns this badge directly from customers as opposed to claiming it through advertising messages or public relations, VFM is a potent differentiator because it appeals to a wide swathe of customers. Combine the VFM image with a differentiated offering like Aldi's or Tesla's, and the result is rapid growth and strong financial performance.

There is one downside. When VFM becomes the brand's centerpiece and is based on an economy or budget positioning, it is difficult for the seller to sustain healthy profit margins or raise prices. The Indian confectionary manufacturer Parle Products built its brand around a VFM positioning by selling a pack of its flagship glucose biscuits for four Indian Rupees for decades. Because of its customers' strong affinity for the 4 INR price point, the company found it very difficult to raise prices even when its input costs went up considerably during the 2000s. The result was significant margin erosion without any obvious solution[48].

3) Price accessibility. Price accessibility has to do with literal availability of the seller's prices to a potential customer. It is *the degree to which customers and prospective customers perceive that the company provides its prices readily.* Many sellers make it difficult for potential customers to find prices during the explore, browse, and search states of their decision journeys. They have to contact a salesperson or otherwise put a lot of effort if they want to learn what the seller's products cost.

This issue is widespread in many B2B industries where companies regard prices as proprietary information or trade secrets[49]. B2B consulting firms, for example, describe their services, credentials, and client testimonials in great detail on their websites, at tradeshows, and in brochures and other marketing collateral, then ask interested customers to call them for obtaining even cursory pricing information. Similarly, in the legal services industry, it is common to charge clients by the hour. Without a clear explanation of how much time a particular task will take, prices seem inaccessible to many clients.

In B2C settings, a retailer may use small price tags that are hard to read, whereas another may place prominent price tags with large fonts throughout the store or website. Research shows that making prices inaccessible hurts low-cost sellers but is beneficial for higher-priced premium sellers because it provides customers with exposure to other product attributes first[50]. Inaccessible and opaque prices in B2B markets shield the company's pricing policies from competitors and dampen the incidence of price wars. On the negative side, they dissuade potential buyers from initiating a relationship and encourage some buyers to seek out either a known supplier or one with accessible prices when they are in the mode of gathering information or forming a consideration set.

4) Price stability. Price stability reflects *the degree to which the company's prices are perceived as frequently changing by customers.* Technologies such as price optimization software and cloud computing services allow companies to change prices quickly and at low cost, even minute-by-minute in real time if they wish to do so. It is not unusual for prices to change on sites like Amazon and Orbitz several times a day. On the one hand, frequent changes match prices instantaneously to the inputs that drive customer demand. For instance, if a tollway is exceptionally crowded, it makes sense to increase toll charges immediately to reduce congestion[51]. Or when far too many rideshare users want service in a particular area, surge pricing may be useful to manage demand and increase driver supply. Changing prices of sweaters or laptop computers eight times a day does not make as much sense. Frequently fluctuating prices without an underlying rationale make the shopping decision difficult, and shift customer's attention away from non-price attributes, hurting their brand perceptions[52]. We will consider the consumer psychology behind frequently changing prices and consider the merits of Uber's surge pricing in Chapter 6.

5) Price evaluability. Price evaluability is *the degree to which the company makes it easy for the customer to process and use prices in their buying decisions.* Prices are inherently difficult to evaluate for many customers. Online retailer Zappos displays its prices clearly, including shipping and offering a liberal return policy. With a single all-inclusive price, the company makes it easy for consumers to evaluate the price. The cell phone service company Verizon, on the other hand, breaks down and presents prices of each service separately, making it hard to assess and compare prices. When prices are shown as an itemized list (known as partitioned pricing, which we will study in Chapter 5), or on a per-serving or per-ounce basis, consumers have to expend extra effort to figure out the "real" price. On the other hand, when prices are quoted as all-inclusive, they are easier to process but hide meaningful information. The more evaluable a seller's prices are, the greater is the consumer's belief that the seller is transparent about its prices. This perception, in turn, leads to an affinity for the brand. Prices that are difficult to evaluate are appropriate accompaniments for brands that sell sophisticated or cutting-edge products.

None of the five components of price image are absolutes in the sense that a higher value of any one of them is not necessarily a good thing, nor is a lower value of the component always harmful. Take the examples of Walmart and Target that we began this section with. Having the most economical prices makes sense for one because its business is built on the idea of "Always low prices." But it is not as critical for the other because its value proposition is to offer fashionable differentiated merchandise at reasonable prices. For the manager, the core insight is that the degree of each price image component conveys a particular type of image to the consumer. The manager's task is to ensure that the five components of the price image are aligned with the brand's other associations and promises, and together, they provide a compelling and differentiated value proposition to the customer.

Knowing the Price

A good decision is based on knowledge and not on numbers. – Plato.

E very time they raise prices, managers are beset with worry. Underlying this anxiety is an entrenched assumption that customers know prices of the company's and competitors' products and services with pinpoint accuracy and will use this precise price knowledge to switch to a competitor with a lower price the next time they buy the product. A cornerstone of microeconomic theory is the principle that buyers have complete information about prices in the marketplace all the time[53]. No matter what industry they work in, managers believe that precise price knowledge drives the buying decisions of customers. This belief makes managers reluctant to increase prices even when conditions warrant such a move. They worry about all sorts of negative consequences from raising prices because of this belief, concerned that customers will be unhappy, they will buy less, they will postpone their purchases, or worst of all, they will make a permanent switch to a competitor.

Nothing could be further from the truth. Most customers have imprecise information about prices, and price knowledge itself is a nuanced and context-dependent concept. In this chapter, we will examine how much knowledge customers have about prices, even for products they buy frequently. (To give away the punchline, it's far less than you might imagine). We will study three types of long-term memory for prices, distinguishing between price recall, price recognition, and the ability to spot deals. We will consider how consumers form and use a range of reasonable prices in their decision making and introduce the classic Emery model of value formation. This chapter concludes by discussing the placebo pricing effect, a compelling demonstration of the power of knowing high prices to transform the customer's experience.

How Knowledgeable Are Customers About Prices?

We never really check the price tag, when the cost comes in, it's gonna be high. — Sleater-Kinney, Price Tag.

Every consumer wants to make smart purchase decisions. Having at least some knowledge about prices is essential to do this. Just consider how difficult it would be for an individual to answer the following questions without knowing prices:

- Is this price lower or higher than the product's normal price?
- Is this sale a real deal or is the seller trying to trick me?
- Should I buy today, or should I wait to get a better price?
- Which of these different product alternatives is the best value?
- How much did I pay for this product the last time?
- Can I afford to buy this product?

But what exactly is price knowledge, and what does it mean for the customer to be knowledgeable about prices? The answers to these questions are not straightforward. They show the nuance behind the concept of price knowledge.

Recalling prices after purchase

Imagine the following scenario. One afternoon, you are at your neighborhood supermarket, stocking up on groceries for the upcoming week. You have just wandered through the breakfast cereal aisle and picked up a 24 oz. box of Kellogg's Corn Flakes from the shelf. Just as you put the cereal box in your shopping cart and turn away, a neatly dressed, friendly man, carrying a clipboard comes up to you and says, "Excuse me, I am a university researcher. May I ask you a couple of questions about the item you just chose? In return, as a token of appreciation, I want to give you this one-dollar bill." You agree, and he asks, "Off the top of your head, without checking, can you tell me the price of the Kellogg's Corn Flakes box you just put in your shopping cart?" Will you be able to answer this man's question correctly?

In one of the most highly cited and influential of all psychological pricing research papers, marketing professors Peter Dickson and Alan Sawyer conducted this study three decades ago. They intercepted a total of 802 shoppers in four different stores of a major supermarket chain and asked them the "Can you tell me the price?" question. The study was set up in such a way that the shopper was intercepted within thirty seconds after they had placed an item in their cart. Here's what the researchers found, in their own words[54]:

> "One in five of the shoppers (21.1%) did not even offer a price estimate; they seemed to have no idea of the price of the item they had chosen. Less than half (47.1%) were able to state the correct exact price (55.6% gave a price within 5% of the objective price), and 31.8% gave a price estimate that was inaccurate... there was a systematic bias in the incorrect estimates; the recalled price was on average 10 cents lower (4.2%) than the actual price."

For items that were on sale, the price knowledge of shoppers was even worse. Just 42% of shoppers even hazarded a guess about the discount, and they were off by 47% on average. What's more, the shoppers were very quick in making their buying decisions. 75% of shoppers spent less than fifteen seconds in inspecting the display and picking out the item they wanted, 85% only handled a single brand (the one they selected), and 90% physically checked just one package size before placing it in the cart. From these numbers, it is clear that most study participants were on auto-pilot and had little knowledge or concern about prices.

Over the years, many other researchers have repeated this study and have found similar results. The percentages vary slightly from one study to the next, but the conclusion is robust: *Most customers are not good at recalling prices of items they have just purchased, and a signifi-cant number have no clue about the price.*

Despite this insight, this finding has also been widely criticized by pricing experts. They argue that when shoppers are intercepted in the store in this way, marketing researchers are mainly testing shoppers' short-term memory for price information *after the fact*. However, when shopping decisions are being made, short-term recall of prices does not matter; it's the individual's long-term knowledge of prices that drives choice. To assess the seriousness of this criticism, we need a rigorous framework to understand how memory for prices works. We will turn to cognitive psychology research for this framework.

The Three Types of Long-Term Memory for Prices

Everyone blames his memory, but never his judgment. — French Prov-erb.

Memory researchers who study how humans store numbers and arith-metic information in memory and process it have proposed a "triple-code model[55]" of memory. It says that people mentally represent and manipulate numbers in three different forms or numerical codes. These three numerical codes correspond to three different types of consumers' long-term knowledge for prices. Let's consider each one.

Price recall

At this level of price knowledge, the consumer knows the actual product price "by heart." They have stored the numerical value in memory and can retrieve it when it is needed. Prices known in this way are based on the *auditory verbal memory code* which is involved in counting verbally and in retrieving arithmetic facts from memory. In this code, an analogue of a word sequence (e.g., /ninety//nine/) is manipulated mentally by the individual. For example, a shopper may store the information, "My new Samsung microwave oven cost $199" in their long-term memory and will be able to retrieve the "one hun-dred and ninety-nine dollars" value precisely even weeks or months after the purchase. This is the deepest level of knowledge that a person can have about a product's price. But obviously, as price knowledge studies show, recallable price knowledge is relatively rare. This is because it requires mental effort and engagement with the price value to encode and store the price in long-term memory. This degree of price knowledge is not something that managers should expect a majority of their customers to have.

Price recognition

At this intermediate level of price knowledge, the consumer does not know, and cannot recall the product's price on their own, without assistance. However, when they encounter the price on a sign, a webpage, or a shelf-tag, they can discern if it is the price they are used to and consider to be the product's normal price, or whether it is an unusually high or low price. Price recognition is derived from accessing the *visual Arabic memory code*, which represents numbers in Arabic format on a spatial visual medium. For example, while I may not know the exact price of a sandwich at Panera bread off the top of my head, when I visit the store and see a Ham & Swiss sandwich on the menu for $7.19, the price seems familiar, and I feel comfortable with it. I might have enough knowledge from my past visits to Panera to judge this is the sandwich's regular price. If I see a different value instead of $7.19, I will be able to tell it is not the usual price I am used to. When the customer recognizes the price when it appears in front of them, but they cannot recall it, they require some help from external sources, typically provided by the seller, to evaluate and use the price in buying decisions.

Deal spotting

Of the three types, deal spotting is the most superficial level of price knowledge. It is possessed by far more consumers than either price recall or price recognition. When deal spotting, not only do consumers not know the product's exact price, but they cannot even tell whether the encountered price is its usual price. All they can do is judge whether the price is within the normal range of what they deem to be the product's reasonable prices, or if it lies outside this range.

Put differently, the consumer can spot a deal (either good or bad) but is immune to minute price changes within the reasonable price range. Deal spotting is the crudest level of price knowledge in the triple-code memory model because it is derived from the third processing code, known as the *analog magnitude memory code*. In this code, numbers are represented as approximate quantities on a number line in the person's head. Cognitive psychologists call it the "Approximate Number System" to capture the uncertainty that accompanies representations of numbers in the analog magnitude mode[56]. With deal spotting knowledge, all I will know is that the Panera Bread's Ham & Swiss sandwich costs around $7 and consider a price range between $6 and $8 to be reasonable. Any price below $6 will seem like a good deal and anything over $8 will appear as expensive. In the psychological state of deal spotting, cognitive psychologist Stanislas Dehaene points out:

> "To enter this putative approximation mode, arabic and verbal numerals are first translated from their digital or verbal code into a quantity code. The input modality is then neglected, and numerical quantities are represented and processed in the same way as other physical magnitudes like size or weight."

Price ignorance

Of course, there is a fourth state of price knowledge, and that is complete cluelessness about prices. In this state, the consumer is oblivious about prices and will have little sense of what constitutes a reasonable or an unreasonable price for the product or service. Price knowledge studies have found that a fair number of shoppers of any product, as many as 25-30%, fall in this category. To see a concrete example of price ignorance, google "Bill Gates guesses grocery prices" and watch the YouTube video of Bill Gates trying to estimate how much a package of Rice-A-Roni costs on the Ellen Show[57].

Researchers have tried to discover and generalize the prevalence of the different types of price knowledge in consumer groups. In an influential study of 400 French shoppers, researchers Marc Vanhuele and Xavier Drèze found that only 2.1% of respondents could correctly recall prices and 13.3% could recognize prices. Deal spotting ability was greater in their study. Just under a third of shoppers (or around 30%) were good at spotting deals. As should be clear, these are low numbers, and they match earlier research findings.

Although managers assume that the majority of customers have re-callable knowledge and know precise prices, the reality is that the price knowledge of most customers for most products and services is poor. They are more likely to know approximate prices and use price ranges when evaluating prices in purchase decisions, and a majority of customers cannot even do this. Distinguishing between the differ-ent types of price knowledge based on the triple-code memory model has significant implications for managers about how to understand, manage, and influence customers with psychological pricing. We will explore three of the consequences in greater detail in this chapter.

1) Measuring price knowledge. For any company, the proportions of customers with the three levels of knowledge—price recall, price recognition, and deal spotting, will vary. Many factors, such as the sig-nificance of the purchase, level of price competition in the industry, and the influence of price points will dictate the price knowledge among customers. It is essential to know the proportions of the three types of price knowledge in your target consumers to be able to pre-dict consumer response to price changes. In the next section, we will see a procedure developed by Marc Vanhuele and Xavier Drèze to measure price knowledge[58].

2) The influence of the range of reasonable prices. What pricing re-search on the triple-code memory model shows is that the conven-tional wisdom about consumer reactions to price changes is false. Unless you are selling a product with an iconic price that hasn't changed in decades like Costco's $1.50 hotdog and soda combo, most customers will not be able to recall your product's exact price or no-tice small price changes. Instead, they are likely to use their under-standing of the range of reasonable prices for your product to make buying decisions. As we saw earlier, far more shoppers can tell whether the item's price is a deal or not than those who know the ex-act price. Later in this chapter, we will consider how managers can use the concept of a range of reasonable prices for developing an effective marketing strategy. But the implication is clear and bears repeating: *Most consumers are unlikely to notice a small price increase, and even fewer customers are likely to react adversely to it.*

3) Subjective judgments of price and quality. The third important implication of our understanding of price knowledge and price processing is that customers are more likely to use price in the same way that they use other physical magnitudes such as size or weight in making buying decisions. The translation of objective levels to subjective levels is critical. We need a manager-friendly model which explains the process through which consumers combine subjective judgments about a product's price and its quality to form an assessment of its worth. We will do so with Fred Emery's ingenious and highly practical model that describes the process by which customers assess a product's value and consider its applications for psychological pricing.

Illustration by Shirin Abvabi

The Vanhuele-Drèze Method to Measure Customers' Price Knowledge

Marketing scientists Marc Vanhuele and Xavier Drèze developed a survey-based method to measure the price knowledge of shoppers that is easy to use and provides excellent visibility into the price knowledge of a defined group of consumers. The method is useful for measuring customers' price knowledge in any product category where customers make frequent purchases or use their long-term knowledge of prices in making purchase decisions. It will be less useful for durable or high-priced products where extensive price data is collected, and customers make price comparisons during decision making. Here's how the method works.

1) *Start with a set of specific products of interest.* In the consumer packaged goods and retailing industries, a specific product is known as a Stock Keeping Unit or SKU. For example, the 18 oz. box of Kellogg's Corn Flakes cereal is one SKU and a 20 fl. oz. bottle of Dasani sparkling lime water beverage is another SKU. To avoid confusion, show a picture or video of each SKU that you are interested in studying to the respondent.

2) *Conduct the survey at the beginning of the consumer's shopping visit.* Intercept a shopper just as they are about to enter a store or land on an online retailer's website. This avoids contaminating the individual's responses from recent exposure to prices. Ask questions only about SKUs they usually purchase and have some familiarity with, one SKU at a time.

3) *Start by asking the open-ended question, "What is this item's normal price when it is not on sale?"* Respondents provide their recalled price in the units they prefer, whether it is by item, by the pack, by weight, or by volume. This question measures the consumer's *price recall knowledge*. Compare the individual's responses to the product's current non-promotional price in the store or website to judge the accuracy of the respondent's recall.

4) *Show the respondent three prices one after the other, in random order.* These prices include the product's actual price, along with a 10% higher price and a 10% lower price. For each price that is shown,

ask the respondent, "Is this the price you recognize as the normal price at the store?" Obtain answers using "Yes" or "No" responses. This set of questions measures the consumer's *price recognition knowledge.* Note that some respondents will get the answer right just by guessing. To manage this concern, Vanhuele and Drèze recommended calculating a "corrected" measure of price recognition by subtracting 33.3 from the observed percentage of correct responses to adjust for guesswork. For example, in their study, 42.2% of consumers recognized the correct price. Their corrected percentage of non-guessers was therefore 13.3%. The actual value of customers recognizing prices will lie between 13.3% and 42.2%.

5) Show the respondent a series of hypothetical prices, one at a time. Ask them to indicate whether each price appears to be a good deal, a normal price, or a bad deal to measure deal-spotting knowledge. Randomly assign the respondent to one of two price series. The first price series starts with a price that is 20% below the actual price, followed by prices that are 5% below, 5% above, and 20% above the actual price. The second series uses the opposite order, going from high price to low price. Use the responses to identify consumers with good deal spotting ability if their responses follow the correct pattern (they are able to recognize high prices as bad deals and low prices as good deals), those who are oblivious to deals if they call 20% higher prices good deals, or 20% lower prices bad deals, and those with some deal spotting ability, if they get some but not all of the pattern right.

6) Repeat the same procedure with each SKU in your set. After all the SKUs are covered, conclude the survey by asking demographic characteristics including gender, age, annual household income, zip code, plus any other desired measures.

With this procedure, the manager understands the degrees of the three types of price knowledge that a particular group of consumers has about the company's products. This, in turn, informs the manager's concerns about changing prices.

How Customers Use the Range of Reasonable Prices in Buying Decisions

There is neither happiness nor misery in the world; there is only the comparison of one state with another, nothing more. – Alexandre Dumas.

The triple-code memory model showed that it is unrealistic to expect most customers to know the prices of the company's products or to use precise price knowledge and calculations in their buying decisions. It is far more likely that customers will be able to spot deals or tell that the price has increased significantly. If it is a product category they deal with frequently, they will have first-hand knowledge and a collection of past experiences to call upon to make this determination. They may be able to recall some price information from the seller's messaging, snippets from social media, and perhaps (less often) even have conversations with other customers about prices. Based on this imprecise information harvested from different sources[59], they will form an idea about the range of prices that the product sells for. *Few customers make buying decisions using precise prices; many more do so using a range of reasonable prices.* And as we shall learn in this section, this is good news for managers.

When I go to buy a sandwich for lunch, I expect it to cost around $5. I am using the *analog magnitude memory code* of the triple-code memory model. I have acquired my reference price knowledge over years of buying sandwiches and staying within a lunch budget. The "around $5" phrase is important here because it captures the imprecision of my price knowledge. It means that I consider a range of prices centered on $5, say between $4 and $6, to be reasonable for a sandwich. As an aside, five dollars is an accessible price point for fast food meals. We will discuss price points at length in Chapter 4.

Figure 3.1 The customer's range of reasonable prices vary with the product's quality level.

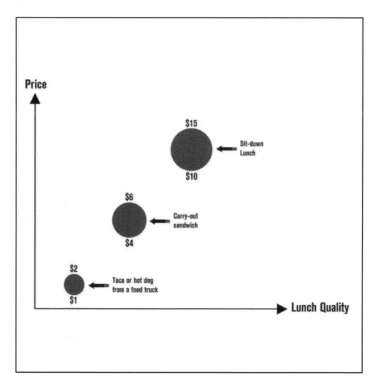

For the same product, customers will have different price ranges at different quality levels. Each price range will be associated with a particular quality level. For instance, although I consider a price range of $4 to $6 to be reasonable for a sandwich or a fast food meal, I do not mind spending more money, say $10 to $15, occasionally for a sit-down lunch. My budget allows it. On the other hand, my acceptable price range is much lower, only $1 to $2 when I want to purchase a quick hot dog or a taco from a food truck. A consumer's range of reasonable prices may shift as the available choices in a product category change or the person's own wherewithal and tastes evolve. Figure 3.1 summarizes these ranges.

For the manager, the customer's knowledge about the range of reasonable prices for different quality levels in the product category is a critical piece of information. Once these ranges are understood across the quality spectrum, the manager can use it for pricing decisions in four important ways.

1) The customer's range of reasonable prices provides the path of least resistance for setting a good price and varying prices using promotions.

Some researchers refer to the range of reasonable prices as "normative" prices[60] because they are what customers expect to pay and consider to be the fair price range for the product. Once the target customers' range is known, setting or keeping the product's price within this range is tantamount to minimizing the importance of price from the customer's purchase decision. When a product's price is within the reasonable range, it is less likely to be a hurdle to making the purchase.

Many, or even most customers may still not buy the company's product; but their choice will be based on the assessment of its other aspects, not its price. Returning to my sandwich example, once I see a sandwich in the $4-$6 range, I will consider its other attributes such as the type of bread, the ingredients, and the number of calories, in deciding whether to buy the sandwich or to pass. Its price will be insignificant in my purchase decision because I have already deemed it as reasonable. The value of the range of reasonable prices lies in the fact that it drives the importance customers give to price relative to other attributes. Stay within this range, and customers will turn their attention to other product features; go outside this range, and suddenly price becomes the focus.

The range of reasonable prices also gives the manager guidance about how much leeway they have for changing prices. As a general principle, it makes sense to set the product's list price or regular price at the higher end of the range of reasonable prices to increase profit margin. After that, to offer "good deals" to customers, the manager can periodically run price promotions ensuring that the price is lowered to a value below the range of reasonable prices. We will touch upon useful psychological principles for designing effective price promotions throughout this book.

2) The customer is insensitive to price changes within the range of reasonable prices.

An important implication of the range of reasonable prices is that customers will be relatively insensitive to price changes as long as the "before" and "after" prices remain within the range. What's more, customers wrongly believe they have good price knowledge and will be able to discern even small changes[61]. Together, these two processes lead to complacency that managers can harness by raising prices confidently.

Pricing experts have coined many names for the range of reasonable prices. These include "the zone of indifference," "acceptable price range," and "the latitude of price acceptance[62]." Research shows that the range of reasonable prices can be wide or narrow depending on the product and the consumer. In the original study where this concept was discovered, the range of reasonable prices for grocery products was around 4 to 5% on each side of the product's average price, making the total range around 10% of the category's average price. As an example, if the average price of a 24 oz. box of breakfast cereal across all brands is $4, the customer's range of reasonable prices for customers is $3.80 to $4.20, a range of $0.40. Other studies have shown that the range is far bigger, as much as 15% to 20% for discretionary purchases. The range also depends on the magnitude of price as shown in Figure 3.1. If the price itself is a small value, the range will be small. As the magnitude of price increases, the band becomes correspondingly bigger [63]. Figure 3.1 shows how the range of reasonable prices expands as the magnitude of price increases.

3) Shifting the price to the high end of the range of reasonable prices is an effective pricing strategy.

Imagine a company sells breakfast cereal, and the manager knows that the target customers' range of reasonable prices for breakfast cereal is $3.80 to $4.20. Where should they price the cereal? The company would be better off by setting the cereal's price at the higher end of the range, say at $4.15 or $4.19, to earn the highest price and profit margin. With these prices, the product will remain within the consumer's range of reasonable prices, avoiding any concern that the breakfast cereal is expensive. On the other hand, pricing below the range is not always a good idea. Some pricing researchers have argued that falling below the range raises concerns that the seller is somehow cutting corners, and the product's quality may be suspect[64].

Companies like Panera Bread, Chipotle, and Torchy's Tacos have used the range of reasonable prices of their target customers cleverly in recent years. When pricing their menus, they deliberately price their items at substantially higher (and we would expect, more profitable) levels than competitors such as Taco Bell or McDonald's. For instance, Chipotle's burritos are priced at $6.50 to $7.50, well above the $3 to $5 range of Taco Bell[65]. These prices remain within the higher limit of reasonable prices for Chipotle's target customers so that they will use product attributes such as quality of ingredients, location, customer experience, and others in choosing which burrito to buy for lunch. In head-to-head comparisons, Chipotle will come out the winner within the reasonable price range.

4) Varying quantity instead of price is an effective pricing strategy.

In the consumer packaged goods industry, for products like breakfast cereals, cookies, and potato chips, input costs fluctuate a lot and are difficult to manage. Changing prices frequently is risky because of the potential for consumer confusion. There is also the possibility that updated prices might exceed shoppers' range of reasonable prices, causing them to switch to another product. Managers want to keep prices steady and stay within the reasonable price range yet maintain their profit margins when input costs are rising. Companies accomplish these conflicting goals by keeping list prices relatively stable and changing the product's packaging. They vary the quantity of the product sold to consumers. Thus, while the product's visible "package price" remains unchanged, the price that the customer pays per unit weight or unit volume fluctuates with input costs. Some pricing practitioners refer to changing prices by changing the product's quantity as the "Boil the Frog" pricing method to acknowledge that the gradual quantity changes remain unnoticed by most shoppers.

In the words of consumer analyst Marcia Mogelonsky, "They're raising the prices a little, and shrinking the boxes a little. If you're running through the supermarket, you don't necessarily notice that your cereal box is an ounce or two smaller. That's how they're controlling the prices." Through their public relations messaging, reputable companies are often upfront about using Boil the Frog pricing as a core part of their pricing strategy. For example, a Unilever spokeswoman explained the rationale behind this decision as follows: "Like other companies, Unilever is working to mitigate the impact of these rising commodity costs through hedging, product reformulation and cost savings programs. We have chosen to reduce package sizes as one of our responses to these dramatic input cost increases[66]."

How should a digital marketing agency price its services?

Consider a digital marketing agency that provides a range of services to the healthcare industry. The services include website design and maintenance, SEO, social media and email marketing, and app development. The company wished to enter a new customer segment and offer these services to medium-sized hospitals. It did not have a good understanding of what prices would be reasonable to charge for this particular customer segment. (This is a common pricing issue faced by companies; the customer's valuation of the product or service can be dramatically different depending on the segment). Among the issues it considered was whether to offer a la carte pricing or price bundles and how much to charge for its offerings.

In assessing how competitors priced their offerings to the medium-sized hospital segment, the marketing agency quickly discovered that virtually all the key players only offered solution packages. No one offered à la carte services. What's more, they all required annual contracts. The analysis also found that the range of reasonable prices for the medium-sized hospitals was much larger and centered around a much higher average than what the agency's managers expected or that of its other healthcare customers.

Armed with this information, the company put together a pricing schedule for hospitals that was in line with the prices of its competitors. It took care to remain within the clients' range of reasonable prices but priced its services a little higher than the average because it wanted to be perceived as a premium seller. Armed with the research and a better understanding of customer price perceptions, the agency was able to charge substantially higher prices than initial estimates.

There are two main lessons to learn from this case study. First, even for the same offering, the range of reasonable prices can differ dramatically for different customer segments. The second lesson is that the company must conduct careful price-focused competitor analysis at the outset, and then periodically, to understand competitors' prices and what prices customers consider as reasonable. Without these insights, the digital marketing agency would have needlessly underpriced its services, devalued its brand, and perhaps even inadvertently started a price war with its competitors.

How to Measure the Customer's Range of Reasonable Prices

The range of reasonable prices alleviates the manager's anxiety that every price increase will be noticed and will have adverse effects. It also provides managers with useful, practical guidance about where they should price, how much leeway they have before price increases are noticed, and how low they have to go when offering discounts before they make an impression.

One way to find the customer's range of reasonable prices is by trial and error. The seller can keep raising the prices periodically until suddenly, they will observe a sharp drop-off in sales. At this point, they may surmise that the price has exceeded the high end of the customers' range of reasonable prices. On the other hand, if the seller keeps lowering their prices, sales will take off when prices stray too low, below the reasonable range into the "screaming deal" range. Alternatively, and counterintuitively, sales could drop off a cliff at low-price levels, if customers become suspicious of the product's quality.

As should be obvious, it is inadvisable to use a trial and error method of raising or lowering prices to discover your product's range of reasonable prices for two reasons. First, the method is fraught with risk, and the possibility of costly missteps. Second, a simpler, structured survey-based method will provide the same information without any shenanigans. Here's how you can evaluate your customer's range of reasonable prices:

1) Start with a clear definition of the product category that makes sense to the customer.

Marketing scholars call this category a "goal-derived category."[67] Examples of such categories are "What to eat for lunch" for individual consumers and "Services to manage my company's digital marketing" for business customers.

2) Ask your customer to divide the product category into quality levels that they consider as having meaningful differences.

The responses will typically include 3-4 levels. Here's what a customer may come up with for the category of "what to eat for lunch":

- When I want a quick bite to eat, and don't want to spend too much, e.g., food truck or vending machine.
- For daily lunch to eat at my desk, e.g., a carry-out sandwich.
- Occasionally when I want to take my full lunch hour and sit down and eat in a restaurant.

For the digital marketing agency in the B2B domain, customers in its medium-sized hospital segment fell into three categories based on their needs. They were those who wanted full service, those who were interested in a limited set of marketing services without any bells-and-whistles like app development, and a third group who only wanted the bare-bones services of email marketing and website management. Using this information, the agency created three different solution bundles for its customers.

3) For each level of quality, ask your customers the question, "What is the range of prices you consider to be reasonable and would be willing to pay?"

The digital agency called marketing executives at a dozen of its prospective customers and asked them about pricing schedules they had received from competitors. While a few were non-committal, most customers had little hesitation in sharing this information with the agency. As you can imagine, this was valuable information, which the agency obtained by just picking up the phone and asking clients.

4) Use the values provided by the customer to establish the range of reasonable prices by level of quality and create a graph.

Figure 3.1 provides one example of such a graph. It shows that the individual considers $1-2 to be a reasonable price range for a taco or hot dog from a food truck, $4-6 for a carry-out sandwich, and $10-15 for a sit-down lunch. With this systematic and relatively straightforward method, you will be able to obtain your customer's range of reasonable prices.

How Customers Assess Product Value Using Price and Quality

Value is not made of money, but a tender balance of expectation and longing. – Barbara Kingsolver.

The Emery model is a descriptive framework developed by pricing expert Fred Emery in 1969[68]. It explains how consumers form subjective judgments of a product's value from objective information about its price and quality. This paradigm is now known as the *Behavioral Pricing Approach*[69]. The Emery model also distinguishes between value judgment processes of motivated and unmotivated consumers.

Decades before cognitive psychologists developed the triple-code memory model, Emery anticipated the practical difficulty consumers would have with encoding, storing, and recalling correct price values, and explained how they would deal with it. Emery's model is just as insightful today for managers in understanding how consumers form and use price knowledge for decision making. The Emery model is graphically described in Figure 3.2 for consumers who make value assessments thoughtfully, and in Figure 3.3 for those who are relatively unmotivated and take cognitive shortcuts to assess value. It distinguishes between the objective values of the product's price and its quality and its subjective, unquantified levels as perceived and used by the consumer in decision making. It is the subjective price and quality which are mapped to each other to form judgments of how good or bad of a value the product is. Let's use the example of a LED light bulb to demonstrate how the Emery model works.

Imagine a LED light bulb with a price-tag of $3. Let's say it is sold by a brand that is new to the consumer called Kangaroo. The bulb is 60W equivalent (consuming approximately 9 watts of electricity) and has an expected life of 20,000 hours. Its objective quality is therefore 20,000 hours of expected life, and its objective price is $3. Is this bulb a good value or poor value?

According to Emery, to answer this question and assess the bulb's value, the consumer does not use the objective price or objective quality information directly. Instead, by recalling previous buying experiences, knowledge of the prices and quality levels of other LED light bulbs, if any, and information obtained from external sources such as product displays, websites, ads, and so on, the consumer converts the objective values into subjective judgments of price and quality. In Emery's words, *"price judgments are relative, not absolute; relative to what is known of other prices as well as being relative to the significance attached to the associated use-values."*

Subjective price and quality judgments of consumers are *ordered categories* in the consumer's mind. The consumer may consider a price of $1 (or less) as a 'cheap price' for the LED bulb, around $3 as a 'reasonable price,' and around $5 as a 'very high price.' In Figure 3.2, this is shown by the inward movement from the objective price line to the subjective price line. According to Emery, when making value judgments before buying decisions, consumers don't think in terms of actual prices, but in terms of subjective prices. This is also the case with quality. The consumer may translate a tested life of 5,000 hours (the objective quality level) into a subjective judgment of 'bad quality' for the LED bulb, 10,000 hours into 'average quality,' and 20,000 hours into 'excellent quality.' Any available knowledge about the brand, combined with thought and effort put into the assessment, will serve to recalibrate the consumer's translation of the bulb's objective quality into its subjective quality. For instance, a well-known brand that the consumer is comfortable with may be able to get away with a lower level of objective quality while a new or less known brand will be judged more harshly. If a new model having a life of 30,000 hours comes out in the future, this will become the excellent quality standard. The lower-life products will be recalibrated to be consistent.

Figure 3.2 The Emery model: How motivated customers trade-off price and quality to form judgments of the product's value.

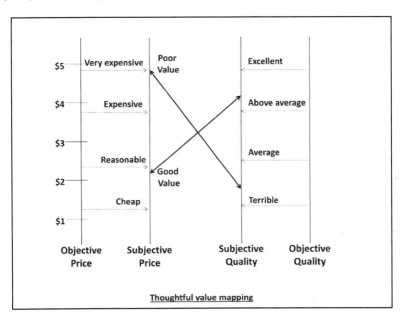

Thoughtful value mapping

In the final step of the Kangaroo LED bulb's value assessment, the consumer compares its subjective price with its subjective quality and arrives at a judgment of value. In our example, the $3–20,000-hour life LED light bulb is seen as, "this bulb has a *reasonable price,* and it has *above average quality,*" which in turn is translated to, "this bulb is a *good value.*" Contrarily, if the bulb were priced at $5 and had a tested life of only 5,000 hours, it would be "very expensive and terrible quality." It would be assessed as, "this bulb is poor value."

The Emery model also explains how customers form judgments of a product's value when they are unmotivated, not knowledgeable, and are relying on mental shortcuts. At such times, instead of trying to ascertain the product's objective quality and mapping it to a subjective level, customers simply use the information in the product's price to infer its subjective quality.

Figure 3.3 The Emery model: How unmotivated customers make inferences of value using their subjective knowledge of price.

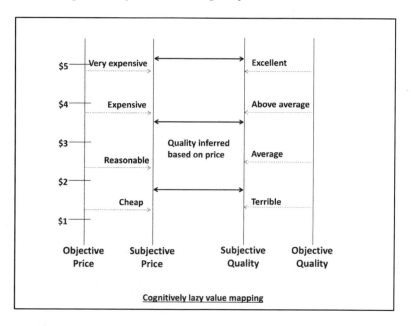

Cognitively lazy value mapping

If the bulb's price is $5, for example, instead of finding out its tested life, converting it to a subjective quality judgment and then mapping it to a subjective price, they will simply infer that the bulb must be of high quality (see Figure 3.3). On the other hand, if the bulb costs $1, it will be regarded as a poor-quality bulb. In such instances, the informational value of the price is the primary influence on customer perceptions.

Even in today's world where neuroscience, artificial intelligence, and advanced analytics are commonly used for pricing, the simplicity and descriptive power of the Emery model are compelling. Here we will consider three of the most important implications of the Emery model.

1) The Emery model's predictions coincide with the findings on the price knowledge of shoppers. It suggests it is more useful to understand the range of subjective prices that customers consider to be reasonable rather than trying to find precise reference prices. As an example, based on their experience of booking hotel rooms over years

or decades, the target customer may view prices below $50 per night as indicative of cheap hotel rooms, $51-100 as average priced, $101-200 as "above average" priced, and any room that is priced above $200 per night as expensive. Emery's model provides the key insight that because of the imprecision of subjective knowledge, customers will not be as sensitive to specific prices or price changes as managers tend to believe. They will be relatively unaffected by small price changes *as long as* these changes remain within the range of subjective price knowledge.

2) It is important for managers to know which objective quality measures customers use to form their subjective judgments of quality. When I purchased my Toyota Prius, the vehicle's fuel-economy and Consumer Reports' rating of the car's reliability were both critical considerations. I combined these two objective measures of the Prius' quality to form my subjective judgment of quality. I didn't care about the color or the wheel size. Once the manager understands which quality measures are important to their target customers, they can take steps to manage quality perceptions. The same is true of price. If a product's price fluctuates very frequently, or over a very wide range, the consumer's subjective knowledge of its price may be shaky, and it may lead to the consumer delaying buying decisions or rejecting the product altogether in favor of competing products that have more stable prices. The manager must play an active role in influencing the target customer's subjective price perceptions.

3) Perhaps the most insightful and thought-provoking idea from the Emery model is that customers will use different methods to map subjective price and quality judgments onto each other to form an assessment of the product's value. The method depends on whether the evaluation is undertaken thoughtfully or whether an inference or heuristic is used. When customers use a shortcut, and use price to infer quality, high prices will contribute to a positive assessment of quality, and support rather than harm judgments of the product's value. In such cases, if the company cuts prices, or maintains low prices, customers may see these actions as markers of poor quality.

In a report that leaked over a decade ago, Walmart's advertising agency found that the store's reputation for low prices worked against it when it tried to sell products such as clothing, home décor, and electronics. The report concluded that "our low prices actually suggest low quality" and its competitor Target felt "like the 'new and improved,' while Wal-Mart often feels like the 'old and outdated[70].'" Other observers have associated Walmart's low prices with the exploitation of its employees[71]. Reinforcing the informational value of price from Chapter 2, cheap is not always a good thing, even when the essence of the brand is low prices. This is a crucial point that managers often overlook because it goes against the grain of their intuition. The Emery model redefines the manager's role as focusing beyond objective prices to grasping and influencing consumers' subjective perceptions of prices.

The Placebo Pricing Effect

> *In this world, you get what you pay for. – Kurt Vonnegut, Cat's Cradle.*

We began this chapter with an admonishment to managers to stop worrying that their customers have precise price knowledge or that they will notice even minute price increases and respond instantaneously. We saw that managers' concerns are not validated by psychological research. We will conclude this chapter with perhaps the most compelling demonstration of the power of high prices: their ability to transform lived consumer experience positively.

You may be familiar with the placebo effect in medicine. It is the medical phenomenon where an inactive substance like an inert sugar pill or distilled water improves a patient's health condition, sometimes substantially, just because the individual expects the substance to work. In a nutshell, the individual's beliefs and expectations about the efficacy of the substance lead to actual physiological and psychological results. The placebo effect is so robust and occurs so broadly throughout the world that the method of conducting double-blind, randomized, placebo-controlled trials is now considered by medical researchers and the FDA to be the gold standard to gauge the efficacy of a new drug[72]. A new drug has to show that it performs substantially better than a placebo before it is adopted for widespread use.

With respect to pricing, the good news is that the placebo effect also occurs with prices and provides the manager with a counterintuitive and powerful way to think about pricing decisions. It shows the ability of price to contribute to the product's actual quality, defined by its ability to effect behavioral change in consumers. For instance, when a drug has a higher price, it works more effectively on consumers who know its price, and vice versa. Behavioral economists call this phenomenon the *placebo pricing effect*.

Consider the following example of the placebo pricing effect. In one controlled experiment involving a purported test of the efficacy of an opioid analgesic, 85 percent of the patients who thought they were taking an expensive pain relieving medicine priced at $2.50 for each pill, reported a significant reduction in pain when they were administered electric shocks afterward. In comparison, only 61 percent of those who were taking cheaper pills that were discounted to 10 cents experienced reduced pain. In reality, everyone in the study took the same sugar pill. The researchers began their article as a letter to the editor of one of the most prestigious medical journals, JAMA, with this understated and awesome sentence: "It is possible that the therapeutic efficacy of medications is affected by commercial features such as lower prices[73]."

However, does this sort of placebo effect of prices occur for "normal" products that we consume every day? In a word, yes. In another study, two groups of participants drank an energy drink called SoBe Adrenaline Rush, which claimed to increase the drinker's mental acuity after consumption[74]. There was one difference between the two groups. One group paid $1.89 for the drink, its regular retail price. Just like the opioid study, those in the second group were told that the regular price of the drink was $1.89, but they would only have to pay $0.89 because the drink was purchased at a discount by their university. Afterward, participants solved several word jumble puzzles. The drink worked more effectively on participants when they paid $1.89

for it. These individuals were able to solve an average of 9.5 puzzles out of a maximum of fifteen puzzles within 30 minutes. In contrast, those who paid $0.89 for the Adrenaline Rush solved an average of 7.7 puzzles, or almost two puzzles less than the first group.

A third study went even further. It put consumers in a functional magnetic resonance imaging machine and scanned their brain activity while they were sipping wines they were told had different prices (e.g., $10 and $90) but was actually the same wine. The researchers found that "increasing the price of a wine increases subjective reports of flavor pleasantness as well as blood-oxygen-level-dependent activity in medial orbitofrontal cortex, an area that is widely thought to encode for experienced pleasantness during experiential tasks[75]." Consumers experienced more pleasure when drinking the $90 wine than when the same wine had a $10 price tag.

For managers, the placebo pricing effect has profound implications. Its occurrence turns the perspective of price as a reluctant sacrifice made by customers entirely on its head. Instead, it shows that price is not just an informational signal of quality (as we saw in Chapter 2), but it contributes to the customer's creation and experience of actual quality. People derive more real value from the product when they pay the price that the product deserves, even, or perhaps, because it is a high price even when the act of payment itself is painful. And the customers' derived value is degraded just because the product is offered at a low price, even when the price is low for idiosyncratic reasons (e.g., an institutional quantity discount allows the product to be offered at a lower price). Instead of thinking of price increases as burdens for customers, the placebo pricing effect shows that when they are deserved, high prices contribute to the authentic value experienced by customers. Giving customers discounts may seem like doing them a favor and improving their satisfaction. In reality, it may cause them physical pain and mental fog.

CHAPTER 4

Is It Worth the Price?

With all these forks in the roads of our path, why do so many choose to take the knife? – Anthony Liccione.

According to the NACJ framework, customers pass through a series of psychological states on their way to purchase. Price plays different roles at different points in these customer journeys. An important question that arises any time price enters into the equation is, "Is it worth the price?" In this chapter, we will examine the customer's decision making process and understand how they attempt to answer the question of worth. We will consider the role of decision heuristics and explore how concepts such as price thresholds, price points, and temporally reframing the price offer help answer the question of worth. We will also investigate how the ease of evaluation of price influences consumer decisions and consider ways by which managers can influence the weight customers give to price. This chapter concludes with a consideration of the psychology of pricing unique products like paintings. It highlights the importance of simplicity and fairness perceptions of buyers in the pricing process.

How Customers Make Purchase Decisions

These expensive, these is red bottoms, these is bloody shoes. Hit the store, I can get 'em both, I don't wanna choose." – Cardi B, Bodak Yellow.

Here's how I purchase table wine. Let's say I have run out of my stock of white wine and want to replenish it. On my next trip to the grocery store, I will take a detour to the wine section and browse through the shelves of Chardonnays and Pinot Grigios and white blends. I completely ignore all the other types of wines on that occasion. Because I usually shop in one of those vast grocery superstores, there are dozens of brands to choose from. To deal with the choice overload, I use the following purchase rule: *find the brand of white wine that is marked down the most (the one with the highest regular price) to a sale price of around $10.* As my purchase rule illustrates, when choosing wine for everyday drinking, I consider a price range of about $10 per bottle to be acceptable and want the best quality wine at that price. It also shows that I am not particularly loyal to any brand of wine.

Applying my purchase rule, if there are two bottles, one that is marked down from $13.99 to $9.99, and another that is marked down from $15.49 to $9.99, I will pick the second bottle, put it in my shopping cart, and I am done. I don't bother to look at the wine's brand or its vintage or where it originated from. Most of the time, I use this simple "highest price marked down to $10" rule to buy my bottle of white wine. I use this rule because it has well worked for me, and I have been able to purchase delicious white wine for a reasonable price. Because I use this rule, it usually takes me no more than a couple of minutes to choose the white wine from a product assortment that has hundreds of choices.

I am not alone in using a heuristic when making purchase decisions. Decision heuristics are simple decision strategies, commonly known as *rules of thumb* or *mental shortcuts*, that most consumers use to simplify their decision tasks. For example, when going to the grocery store, one shopper may decide to "stock up on Tide detergent since we're almost out." Another consumer may use the heuristic, "buy whichever peanut butter brand is on sale." A third one may employ "pick either Jif or Skippy, the peanut butter brand I did *not* buy last time (because I like variety)." The main reason for making and using such shopping rules is to speed up and simplify decision making while still ending up with a satisfactory choice[76].

For most buying decisions today, and that includes grocery purchases, customers have far too many options to choose from[77]. It is difficult to find any product category that suffers from a scarcity of choices. An average grocery store carries around 40,000 different items[78], with over a hundred different options of soups, cookies, toothpaste, shampoo, and cereal each[79]! Even when buying a car, Americans can choose from 275 different major automobile makes and models, with thousands of additional variations available in accessories and trims[80]. And the same is true for everything from breath mints and mutual funds to RVs and everything in between.

The only feasible thing that a grocery or car shopper can do is to use decision heuristics. Any complex decision strategy simply would not work. It would be impossible to go to the store, line up all the dozens of brands of peanut butter jars or Chardonnay bottles, make a list of all their features, and conduct a detailed multidimensional trade-off analysis to figure out which peanut butter or Chardonnay is the best one to buy. And then move on the bread, cheese, lunch-meat, and so on, and repeat this process over and over again. The sheer number of purchase decisions to be made, and the formidable amount of information that is available to make them makes any complex decision making strategy impossible to use in shopping decisions. Short-cuts are necessary.

For many people in many product categories, the decision heuristics they use are based on loyalty to brands. One of the fastest and least risky decision rules is to repurchase products you like, have experience with, and trust. Consumers' use of loyalty-based decision heuristics is one reason why strong brands can charge price premiums even when they are displayed next to identical store brands (often made in the same manufacturing plant with the same formulation) on the shelf.

However, not all decision heuristics are based on brand loyalty. As the story of my white wine choice illustrated, consumers' decision heuristics are often based on price. Price is an essential input into consumers' decision heuristics because it constrains the consumer's choices. Consumers, even very wealthy ones, have finite shopping budgets. As a result, prices sometimes limit but more often influence how much they purchase and which options they buy. As we will see throughout this chapter, the inclusion of price in consumers' decision heuristics provides significant opportunities for the manager.

Psychologists have found that decision heuristics simplify complex decision strategies in one or more of four ways that affect how prices are used in shopping decisions[81]:

1) The consumer examines fewer alternatives.

One mode of decision making simplification is to pare down the considered options. Instead of considering a dozen brands of peanut butter, the shopper limits their selection from a smaller set, of perhaps two or three brands. The larger, well-known brands benefit in this scenario. Alternatives with unusual prices (whether they are atypically high or atypically low) stand out and have a greater chance of being noticed but not necessarily considered. Brands with normal prices that the shopper is familiar have a greater chance of being favored. Inertia and habitual tendencies work in the incumbent and habitually purchased brands' favor and against upstart brands.

2) The consumer considers and examines fewer product features.

The second mode of decision simplification is to consider fewer attributes when making the decision. This is especially relevant in buying decisions because products have a virtually unlimited number of features. When using a decision heuristic, the consumer relies on a small number of features, often just one or two, to decide. In buying peanut butter, for instance, the consumer may use the brand name or whether the peanut butter is crunchy or creamy to choose which one to buy. Price often makes this short-list of features because of its aforementioned significance in decision heuristics.

3) The consumer relies on readily available feature values instead of retrieving them from memory.

When using decision heuristics, consumers are likely to home in on readily available information. Information provided at the point of purchase, whether it is a physical store or a web- or mobile-site is influential[82]. This is why supermarkets take so much trouble with sale signs, price tags, shelf-talkers, and in-store displays. We will discuss the effects of sales signs and other visual cues and how managers can use them in Chapter 7. Factors such as which reference prices are supplied, how prices are displayed, and which alternatives are placed next to each other at the point of purchase all matter.

4) The consumer simplifies the weights given to product features.

Instead of developing complex weighting schemes like weighting brand name by 15%, price by 40%, taste by 10%, and so on, the shopper will use simple schemes like "give equal weight to each feature." Coupled with the use of one or two features in the heuristic, the shopping decision becomes a trade-off between two product attributes. The consumer may trade-off brand versus price, quality versus price, or even simply based the decision on an evaluation of the product's price as being satisfactory or not, giving 100% weight to price.

In the domain of simplified shopping decisions, knowing which heuristics are popular among customers is crucial for the manager. With this knowledge, you can influence your product's appeal relative to your competitors' offerings, and even affect other aspects of the customer's buying behavior such as how much of the product they buy and what price they pay for it.

How Heuristics Influence the Customer's Decision

You are not your body and your hair-style, but your capacity for choosing well. If your choices are beautiful, so too you will be. – Epictetus, Discourses.

During the customer's decision journey, they routinely evaluate the worth of available product options at multiple stages. In the NACJ framework, the psychological states of *aware, explore, browse, review, search, evaluate* and *decide* all require the assessment of worth in one way or another. Consequently, assessing worth is a cornerstone of the customer's decision making on the road to purchase and consumption.

The consumer assesses the worth of a product in two fundamentally different ways[83]. The first method is a quick cursory evaluation, known as *option prescreening*, to assess whether to retain the product for further in-depth consideration or to summarily reject it and move on to other choices. Its main goal is to pare down the set of acceptable alternatives from an unmanageably large number to a small handful using a decision heuristic. The second form of worth evaluation is a deeper, more careful process in which the consumer assesses the remaining, pared-down set of alternatives carefully, engaging in cognitive processes of comparison and trading-off.

The two worth determination processes can occur at any time and place, not just when the consumer is on the cusp of a purchase. Price plays important roles in both worth assessment processes, providing managers with opportunities to gain an advantage over the competition and favor with the consumer. Let's explore these functions of price more carefully.

Prescreening processes

An initial cursory evaluation of the item's worth often conducted quickly and decisively within a second or two of exposure, is an essential stage-gate in many decision journeys. If your product doesn't make it through this first consumer gate, it will never reach the consumer's Instagram feed or the store's cash register. When browsing in a clothing store, for instance, one glance is often enough for a shopper to reject a whole rack of garments from further consideration[84]. The purpose of this rapid-fire evaluation is to decide whether to retain the product further for more in-depth assessment or to drop it in favor of other alternatives. Several decades ago, marketers coined the term "consideration set" to describe the relatively small number of options, between two to six, that consumers will consider in depth. The initial cursory assessment of the product's worth is essential for getting your product into the consumer's consideration set. Managerially, this challenge is critical when the consumer is in a search mode to fulfill a specific purchase goal.

As we saw earlier, in today's marketplaces, no consumer considers even a fraction of the available options meaningfully, which is why prescreening is so important. Consumers must, of necessity, use simple decision heuristics to drastically pare down the vast arrays of options that they encounter in every product category to a manageable handful. The surviving options become the consideration set and are given more thorough consideration.

Price threshold

During the prescreening process, the most common function of price is to serve as a *cut-off* or a *threshold*, dictating the product's inclusion or exclusion from the consumer's consideration set. Consider Amanda, who has decided she wants to "spend no more than $100" to buy a new summer dress before she embarks on that increasingly rare occurrence, a mall shopping trip. When she is browsing through displays of summer dresses in a mall store, the $100 price will serve as an *acceptability threshold* for Amanda. Any dress over $100 will be summarily rejected as unacceptable. Of course, Amanda's very likely to use other heuristics in conjunction with price to further simplify her selection task. For instance, she may have other criteria such as yellow, crinkled cotton, etc., in which case, her acceptability threshold is now "below $100, yellow, and made of crinkled cotton."

Price need not act only as an *upper-limit threshold* in the prescreening process. It can, and often does, serve as a *lower-limit threshold*. Take the example of Saul and Stephanie, who have been invited to a dinner party by their friends. On their way to the party, they may decide to take a bottle of wine as a gift and use their standing rule of "the wine we buy will be a gift, so it should cost at least $40" as the appropriate heuristic in selecting the gift. In this example, any wine that is priced *below* $40 will be eliminated from further consideration, while a wine that is just above $40 will be seen favorably.

And finally, prices can also act as a *preferred range threshold.* For instance, if Saul and Stephanie decided, "we want to give a Cabernet Sauvignon that is priced between $40 and $50," this would be an acceptable range that would drive their consideration set in the wine store.

For managers tasked with pricing decisions, consumers' price thresholds are meaningful in two ways. First, as the summer dress and the wine gift examples illustrate, the key to remaining in the consideration set is for the product's price to fall on the right side of the consumer's price threshold. It is useful to know what your target customers' price threshold is and how they use this threshold in their decision process. The second role of price thresholds is even more interesting and promising. You don't have to sit back and passively learn customers' thresholds; you can influence and actively create price thresholds for your customers to use. The cleverness of De Beers in the next case study provides a clinic in how to create a profitable and sustainable price threshold that influences consumer buying behavior.

De Beers and the Diamond Engagement Ring

A diamond is forever. – De Beers advertisement.

The ingenious marketing approach used by diamond seller De Beers over the past 80 plus years illustrates how game-changing creating a price threshold can be. The De Beers strategy unfolded in two stages. First, the company coined the slogan "A Diamond is Forever" in 1947, now widely regarded as the best advertising slogan of the twentieth century. In it, De Beers characterized a man's purchase and gifting of a diamond ring when proposing marriage to a woman as a timeless tradition[85]. It reinforced this message repeatedly over the years until eventually it was widely known and accepted as the conventional behavior of every American man. And as cultural norms changed, jewelry companies marketed diamonds in this way just as aggressively to the LGBTQ community[86].

The extraordinary statistics tell the story of how successful De Beers turned out to be. In the late 1930s, before De Beers created the slogan and the "engagement = diamond ring" emotional connection, only about 10% of engagement rings contained diamonds because of the expense involved. Other stones such as sapphires and rubies were equally common. However, by 2000, the number of engagement rings with diamonds had gone up to 80%. In late twentieth-century America, across age, race, social class, sexual orientation, and geography, most people considered a diamond ring to be synonymous with an engagement ring. The "A Diamond is Forever" message, sustained by De Beers over decades through mass media, succeeded in changing what was an atypical and unusual purchase without any social or religious significance into a conventional one that is expected of every individual who wants to propose marriage to their partner.

How much should a diamond engagement ring cost?

The "A Diamond is Forever" message, while successful, does not answer the question of how much the engagement ring should cost, sowing doubt and confusion in potential buyers. And if we know one thing about consumer decisions, it is that doubt and confusion are bad for action. They delay purchase. For De Beers, providing a concrete and substantial price threshold to the eager fiancé was essential to prevent them from pinching pennies and buying a ring with a small or poorly-cut diamond. How to create a universally applicable price threshold that consumers can understand and agree with? A ridiculously low price for one person would be a completely unaffordable price for another. It wouldn't make sense to say, "A diamond engagement ring should cost at least $X" because $X would be too high for some people and too low for others.

*A diamond engagement ring should cost about two months'
salary.*

This is where the ingenuity behind De Beers' marketing and the
role of psychological pricing comes into play. The company designed
another inspired marketing message in the 1980s that circumvented a
specific price point and provided a specific price threshold that ap-
plied to everyone regardless of their income. This time the ad showed
an attractive just-engaged woman called Jane Smith brandishing her
diamond ring. The tag-line read, "2 months' salary showed the future
Mrs. Smith what the future will be like." The subtext was that if Mr.
Smith proposed with a diamond ring that cost less than two months of
his salary, it should plant seeds of doubt in the lady's mind about the
intensity of his love and commitment to her.

What is particularly clever about a *seller-supplied price threshold* is
that it is substantial, flexible, and feasible all at once. It is not one fixed
value. Instead, it's a moving target that is geared to the customer's
wherewithal. If you are George Clooney, you spend $750,000 for an
engagement ring[87], but if you are a young person in your early twen-
ties working in your first entry-level job and focused on paying off
your student loans, you will spend $1,000-2,000. For both individuals,
it is a substantial amount of money that is dictated by the seller-supplied price threshold. Sales managers would call this price threshold a
stretch budget for the ring buyer.

This two-months-salary price threshold for engagement rings supplied to American consumers by De Beers remains firmly entrenched
today more than three decades later. Amid the emotional turmoil associated with the momentous decision of proposing marriage to a romantic partner and choosing an engagement ring, this price threshold
serves as a soothing heuristic that signals the ring purchase's nor-
malcy. Millions of individuals have decided which ring to buy using
this rule. According to the 2018 American Wedding Study conducted
by *Brides* magazine, the average price paid for an engagement ring in
the United States was $7,829, which works out to just over two
months' after-tax salary for the median wage earner[88].

How Price Points Influence Consumer Decisions

I am always interested in designing things that have a great price point attached to it. – Tony Burch.

Closely related to price thresholds is the concept of a *price point*. Although Urban Dictionary cynically defines the term as "bullshit speak for 'price,'" the truth is that price points influence consumers' buying behavior in many product categories and can be used to good effect by managers in their price-setting decisions.

In this book, we will define the price point as *the price level that is so well-known and well-accepted by consumers that they consider it to be the normal or usual price for the product.* As this definition suggests, the price point is usually a characteristic of the product category, not of an individual product or brand. When buying in the product category, consumers use the price point for making buying decisions with little or no cognitive effort. Around $5 for a meal, a dollar a day for news, coffee, and shaving, $1,000 for a computer, and $400 for a car payment are all popular price points in the United States.

Price points are influential for the simple reason that consumers prefer to buy products at the price point than at other higher or lower price levels. Consumer psychologist Robert Schindler aptly refers to price points as "inevitable wrinkles in demand curves[89]." Figure 4.1 illustrates this positive effect of price points on consumer demand.

In the hypothetical example shown in the figure, when the product's price increases from $3 to $4, and then again from $6 to $7, demand for the product increases instead of declining, as would be expected with normal price increases. $4 and $7 are price points for this product because they attract customers and increase demand.

Price points are found in almost every product category. The manager needs to know their value to set attractive prices. Deloitte consultant Georg Muller writes that in the apparel industry, consumers consider prices of $99, $149 and $199 to be noteworthy price points for outerwear jackets. Retailers leverage this consumer preference by offering several jackets to choose from at these price points[90]. These prices also tend to be popular promotional prices when retailers want to clear out jackets at the end of the winter season. For instance, a popular promotion on the Burlington Coat Factory site was branded men's jackets labeled with "Was $499.99, on clearance at $199.99[91]."

Figure 4.1 The positive value of a price point for shoppers.

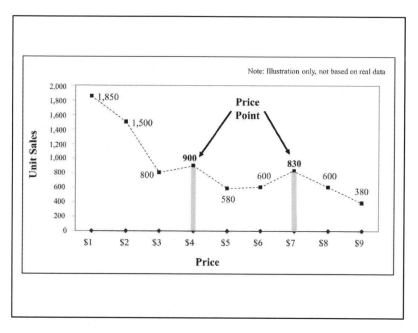

Another intriguing example of a counterintuitive but sharp price point comes from Prosecco sales in the United States. Prosecco is an Italian sparkling white wine, similar in taste and appearance to French champagne. But it is markedly lower in price. In the United States, prosecco has risen in popularity among wine drinkers and now accounts for about 20% of sparkling wine sales. Wine shoppers treat prosecco as a mid-tier-priced offering in their purchase decisions. Prosecco buyers have a tightly defined price point of around $13 for a bottle. In a 2018 report, Nielsen reported that 38% of prosecco sales occurred at the level of $13-$13.99. Even more interesting, this is the price point at which prosecco sales grew the fastest, 29% year-over-year in 2017. No other price level, higher or lower, was even close[92]. While the reason for this price point is not yet understood, what is clear is that American customers regard a $13 bottle of Prosecco positively.

In the fast food industry, $5 is widely regarded as a powerful price point for a meal. Most fast food operators sell a meal at this price point. Dairy Queen's 5 buck lunch, Subway's $5 footlong sandwich, McDonald's McPick $5 for 2 menu, KFC's $5 Fill Ups, Dunkin' Donuts' Go2 for 5 deals, and the Taco Bell $5 Chalupa Cravings Box are all based on this price point. As writer Brad Tuttle points out, "At a time when popular fast-casual chains are pushing the average dinner bill upward, the $5 price point is especially likely to get the attention of deal hunters. And that's why fast food customers are seeing more and more of the fiver[93]." This begs the question of how sellers discover price points in the first place.

Subway and the Five Dollar Price Point

It's not particularly complicated. $5 is a nice round, approachable, affordable-sounding number. – Brad Tuttle.

Price points are not always discovered through market research. The five dollars price point for a fast food meal is a case in point. Faced with slow business on the weekends in 2004, Stuart Frankel, the owner of two Subway locations in a Miami hospital, came up with an original idea for a price promotion. His brainwave was to sell all footlong sandwiches on his menu for a flat $5 price, but only on weekends. This was a substantial reduction from their regular prices, which were in the $6-$8 range. In launching this $5 promotion, Frankel wasn't thinking about how his customers would react, nor did he conduct any research. His straightforward reason was, "I like round numbers."

Once the promotion started in the two Miami Subways, sales took off. From stores that were deserted on weekends a few weeks earlier, customer lines extended beyond the doors, all drawn irresistibly to their favorite Subway footlongs. It was clear that Frankel had unknowingly struck a chord with his customers with the five dollar price. As writer Matthew Boyle observed, "Nobody, least of all Frankel, knew it at the time, but he had stumbled on a concept that has unexpectedly morphed from a short-term gimmick into a national phenomenon that has turbocharged Subway's performance[94]."

The lower price on the footlong sandwich increased ingredient costs in the restaurant's profit equation. However, the substantial sales increase (which rose by double digits) when combined with higher productivity of the sandwich artists (they were making more sandwiches in their shifts) led to Frankel still earning a profit on each sandwich sold at the $5 price. Subway's corporate employees eventually noticed these spikes in revenue and profit and tested the $5 price point, first in other Florida Subway stores, and eventually throughout the chain by 2008. The promotion continues to be successful even now, a decade later, though inflation has made it more difficult to implement in some parts of the country. Franchise owners revolt periodically against the $5 footlong promotion but keep having to bring it back because it draws customers to the store.

Unlike De Beers that deliberately created the "two-month salary" threshold, Frankel and his colleagues at Subway's headquarters accidentally discovered the power of the $5 price point in fast food. In trying to explain why the $5 price works so well, public relations expert Derek Farley observed, "If the consumer needs something that gives them permission to experiment with a brand, $5 is the magic number. It is consistently the threshold that reinforces the idea of a deal[95]." Brad Tuttle adds, "the $5 mark is widely regarded as a terrific restaurant deal when it covers an entire meal for one, or even better, a few people. This is especially the case compared to the typical $7 or $8 (or sometimes much more) a customer will spend to fill his belly at Chipotle [or] Panera Bread." This doesn't sound very scientific, but it works.

The main lesson from Subway's success is that although price points are often hidden, they already exist in the marketplace in every product category. Consumers do not have to be trained or habituated to accept the seller's offers at sharp price points. They are already receptive to this price level. When offered, they instinctively understand it's a reasonable price and accept it more readily than other prices, even lower ones. This is why price points tend to be persistent, lasting for years or decades, long after the sellers and the products themselves have changed beyond recognition.

The manager's job is two-fold here. First, the company's pricing culture needs to be creative and open to the discovery and exploitation of price points. Like Frankel, the manager should be willing to experiment to develop offers at different prices with the acknowledgment that some, or even most of these promotions, will fail to find price points. Second, once a compelling price point is discovered, the company's apparatus should be willing and able to convert it into an enduring price point at which something compelling is always on offer to consumers. Depending on the product category, this may involve creating limited-time promotional offers of single or bundled products at that price point, as well as everyday offers. The manager should find every way to allow their customers to make purchases at the price point regularly.

Temporally Reframing a Price Offer

Dwight: I don't understand why you would buy a policy? Michael: It's just the cost of a cup of coffee an hour. –The Office.

In an August 1960 newspaper advertisement, German typewriter seller Olympia offered its "world's finest" precision portable typewriter with the tag-line "IT'S YOURS... for just pennies a day." More than fifty years later, in a moving 2013 advertisement for UNICEF USA, a montage of distressed and hungry children in heart-wrenching conditions rolled on as film actress Alyssa Milano exhorted the viewer "to reach into your pocket and pull out 50 cents [a day] to save that child[96]." In another commercial, Gerber advised parents to start a Grow-Up life insurance plan for their infants for "just pennies a day."

Sellers and fundraisers have used pennies-a-day price offers for decades. It is a popular and effective way to quote a price. Magazine publishers first began promoting their subscriptions on a per-issue basis instead of an annual price back in the early 1980s. This move was fueled by field experiment results conducted by Time Magazine and other publishers. The companies tested response rates for solicitations that used per-issue price offers ($1 per issue) and compared them to solicitations using per-year price offers ($52 per year). They consistently found per-issue offers to be 10-40 percent more effective in enticing new subscribers. Even today, the *New Yorker*, the *Financial Times*, and the *Wall Street Journal* solicit new subscribers this way. "$1 per week for first ten weeks" is a widely-used promotional offer.

There is also considerable evidence from academic research that the pennies-a-day strategy works. Consumer psychologist John Gourville has found consistent support for its effectiveness in his research[97]. In one study, for instance, participants were asked to donate to a worthy cause through payroll deductions. When the request was framed as "an ongoing contribution of 85 cents per day," 52 percent of those asked agreed to donate. But when it was framed as "a total contribution of $300 per year," only 30 percent of respondents accepted.

What exactly is pennies-a-day price framing, and why does it work?

The pennies-a-day price offer is what consumer psychologists call "temporal reframing of the price." A larger total expense that the consumer will incur once is converted into a series of small daily or ongoing expenses *solely for the sales pitch*. In all the examples mentioned earlier, consumers wouldn't pay pennies every day by venmoing the seller. When the time comes to buy, they would pay the full price, or pay every month. In the case of the Olympia typewriter, for instance, its price in 1960 was $75 (approximately $625 in 2018 dollars). The buyer had to pay the full amount or make a down payment of $10-$15, and pay off the balance in monthly installments.

The purpose of the pennies-a-day price offer is to make the shopper think about how much buying the item will cost in terms of small daily chunks of money. This method works well when the buyer is evaluating a single alternative. The decision involved is to either take the seller's offer or to leave it, not choose between two different offers. Under such circumstances, consumer psychologists have found that consumers evaluate the price offer in two quick steps.

First, they recall comparable expenses to provide some context to the pricing offer's evaluation. For instance, when told that feeding a malnourished child in Burundi will cost you only about fifty cents per day, the shopper will recall other small expenses they may incur which cost about 50 cents such as drinking a cup of coffee at home. In some cases, the marketer may go a step further and make this comparison for the shopper explicitly.

Next, consumers assess the pennies-a-day offer relative to these expenses. If the offer seems similar, a psychological process known "assimilation" occurs where the individual deems the two expenditures to be similar and concludes it is reasonable to compare them. The shopper assimilates the pennies-a-day offer to the comparable offer: Feed a starving child in Burundi = drink a cup of coffee at home. However, if the offer is perceived as different, that is, if it doesn't share common features with the small expense, a process called "contrast" occurs. The individual rejects the possibility of comparison. Gourville describes the result of this assimilation versus contrast comparison as follows:

> "...both the PAD and the aggregate transactions may be judged as similar to their respective retrieved comparisons, which results in assimilation and category inclusion in both cases. Therefore, the PAD transaction takes on the characteristics of expenses such as coffee and lottery tickets—expenses typically thought of as trivial, affordable, and out-of-pocket. Similarly, the aggregate transaction takes on the characteristics of expenses such as airline tickets and appliances—expenses typically thought of as significant and somewhat unaffordable and that consumers generally look to avoid or delay. As a result, all else being equal, the PAD transaction should be perceived as a more attractive offering and lead to higher compliance than the financially equivalent aggregate transaction[98]."

Temporal reframing does not have to be done on a "per day" basis. Any shorter period is better than a longer period. For example, if a price per day is not viable, a price per week offer will be more effective than a per-month or per-year offer. Temporal reframing also works better under certain conditions. Research shows that reframed offers are more effective when[99]:

- *The seller uses even price endings instead of odd ones to communicate the reframed prices.* For instance, saying "Your health club membership is only $2.00 a day" is more appealing to customers than saying it's $1.99 a day. Customers see the product as higher quality and are more likely to purchase it when the reframed offer has an even price ending.

- *Products have high aggregate prices rather than something that costs little money.* Presenting a price offer that says "Your Netflix subscription costs $0.43 a day" is not as compelling as saying "Your car lease costs $8 a day" to consumers. In the Netflix subscription case, it will be more effective to offer the monthly price. Like most other things, pennies-a-day offers are susceptible to inflation.

- *Products have been sold with short temporal frames in the past.* Telling customers "Your health club membership is only $2 a day" works well but telling them "Your car insurance is only $2 a day" arouses suspicion. This is because consumers are used to thinking of car insurance payments in six-month or annual terms, whereas they think of gym membership prices in weekly or monthly terms.

- *Customers are less inclined to do mental math themselves.* For individuals who like doing the math in their heads to discover how much something costs per day or per use, providing reframed prices will backfire by making them feel misled by the seller.

When making a pennies-a-day price offer, the manager's task is clear: Frame the price offer as pennies-a-day (or with as small a temporal frame as makes sense) and provide a comparison expense which the consumer has no trouble believing is comparable to the price offer. The food company Kellogg's ran popular advertisements for its Corn Flakes cereal in the 1990s. The ads showed the shocked reactions of consumers when they were told that one serving of Corn Flakes with a half cup of skim or low-fat milk costs less than 25 cents.

One shopper responded, "You can't even buy a postage stamp for 25 cents anymore." Another responded, "Four bowls for a buck." Kellogg's didn't even have to provide the comparison; customers conjured it up themselves and used it to evaluate the price[100].

The bottom line is that a pennies-a-day offer works for *take it or leave it* offers because it makes the product seem affordable. It is especially effective when competitors selling the same product don't use this psychological pricing strategy.

Dollar Shave Club's Success With Pennies-A-Day Pricing

We're debuting a razor with 19 blades and 74 lubrication strips... Just kidding – no, we're not. – Pankaj Bhalla, Gillette's head of North American Grooming[101].

Men spent approximately $15 billion for razors and shaving supplies in 2015[102]. This market is intensely competitive, dominated by established consumer brands like Gillette and Schick for decades. The strategy of these major players has been to introduce increasingly complex razors with intricate features, more blades, and significantly higher prices every few years accompanied by an advertising blitz. Consumers responded by upgrading each time and increased their spending in the category.

The pricing model used by Gillette, Schick et al. has become notorious as the "razor-blade pricing model." The razor is priced low, even at a price that is significantly below cost. The company earns profits by selling blades over a lengthy period that the locked-in customers are forced to buy at extravagantly high prices. For example, a single Gillette Fusion 5 blade costs $3.75, and one Schick Hydro 5 blade is priced at $3.82[103]. The razor-blade pricing model has been so successful over the years that many other product categories including printers and ink cartridges, video game consoles and cartridges, and cellphones and data plans, have adopted it successfully.

Not surprisingly, many consumers resent razor-blade pricing. What's more, the customer journey to buy razor blades under this pricing is cumbersome. The consumer has to go to a store, seek out a cashier or salesperson to open the locked display case (the razors are too expensive to leave out), and spend $10 or more for a pack of blades every so often. Many consumers feel taken advantage of and forced to overspend on razor blades.

This is where the Dollar Shave Club came in. Abandoning the razor-blade pricing model that was standard in this industry, the company built its business model around a simple pennies-a-day pricing approach, combining it with a subscription to significantly improve the customer's purchase experience. The company launched in March 2012 with a social media video centered around the pricing claim, "For a dollar a month, we send high-quality razors right to your door." This value proposition, coupled with a humorous launch advertisement that went viral, and excellent customer service, led to the company's rapid growth.

The pennies-a-day subscription offer changed customers' shaving behavior. Instead of buying blade cartridges as needed, they received them regularly. It converted the discretionary and painful purchase process into a convenient and habitual replenishment delivered to the customer's home. It changed how buyers used razors, specifically how often they replaced cartridges. Because they were so inexpensive and delivered regularly, shavers used new cartridges more often.

From $6 million in revenue in 2012, sales of Dollar Shave Club grew to $250 million by 2016. At this point, Unilever acquired the company for $1 billion. Dollar Shave Club still uses a pennies-a-day subscription pricing even though the company is now part of a stable of established consumer brands owned by a large conglomerate[105]. Monthly replacements cost $1 for the standard 2-blade cartridge — more expensive choices of blades that rival Gillette's Fusion 5 cost $6 to $9. Still, Dollar Shave Club's prices are substantially lower than comparable Gillette or Schick products[104].

The main lesson from Dollar Shave Club's success is that for low-priced, frequently purchased and frequently used products, pennies-a-day pricing combined with a subscription offers a compelling value to consumers, especially when entrenched incumbents use complicated razor-blade pricing that generates resentment. Online retailers like Amazon have adopted pennies-a-day subscription pricing widely with their "Subscribe and Save" marketing programs, where the customer receives a discount of up to 15% for signing up to receive consumable products like non-perishable groceries, cosmetics, toilet paper, and cleaning supplies periodically[106].

The Ease of Evaluating Prices

Now she pays the price, nothing comes without a price, without some blood, just a little sacrifice. – Marguerite, Come One, Come All, Chorus.

Imagine the following scenario. You are out shopping at a farmer's market on a beautiful spring weekend. As you walk past a farm-stand devoted to healthful ancient grains, you see an eye-catching one-pound package of locally-grown organic quinoa. The package looks expensive, made of hand-sewn sackcloth, like something you would find in a Georgian-era market if you were Elizabeth Bennet out shopping with Mr. Darcy. Its price tag says $11.79. Is this a good price for the quinoa? And more importantly, assuming you're interested in purchasing it, how much weight will you give the price in your buying decision compared to its packaging, the fact that the quinoa is locally sourced and sustainable, or some other aspect?

Surprisingly, the answer does not depend on your knowledge of quinoa prices. Instead, it depends on how easy or difficult the stand-owner makes it for you to evaluate the quinoa's price. To understand why this is the case, consider the following question asked to undergraduate students in a controlled laboratory experiment[107]:

"Imagine that you are a music major and are looking for a specialized music dictionary in a used-book store to use for your studies. Let's say you have planned to spend between $10 and $50 for your purchase. You come across a dictionary which looks brand new, and it has 10,000 entries in it. How much would you be willing to pay for it?"

On average, study participants said they would be willing to pay $24 for this dictionary. Another group from this same undergraduate pool was given a somewhat different scenario. The dictionary they saw had a torn cover but was otherwise whole. It had 20,000 musical entries. Participants were willing to pay $20 on average for this dictionary. These two were the "separate evaluation" study conditions because participants only saw one dictionary and evaluated their willingness-to-pay for it.

There was also a third group in the study. Unlike the first two groups, these people saw both music dictionaries side-by-side. What do you think they were willing to pay in this "joint evaluation" task? Not surprisingly, they were willing to pay more for the torn music dictionary with 20,000 entries ($27) than the brand new dictionary with 10,000 entries ($19).

Consumer psychologists call this phenomenon a *preference reversal* because the relative valuations of the two dictionaries changed depending on whether the individuals evaluated them separately or side-by-side. For psychological pricing, a more appropriate phrase is a *willingness to pay reversal.* When evaluating individually, people were willing to pay more for the dictionary with fewer entries but which is in pristine condition. When evaluated together, their economic valuation was higher for the dictionary with double the number of entries even though its cover was torn.

Why did consumers reverse their willingness to pay?

The answer lies in the fact that consumers find some product attributes easy to make sense of and use in their decision making on their own but have difficulty with others. For instance, it's easy to say that a torn dictionary is terrible or that a brand new one is good in and of itself. The number of entries in a music dictionary, not so much. How is one to know how many entries is a good number for a music dictionary?

What's more, people tend to give greater weight to attributes that are easy to evaluate and make sense of in their decision making. This is why, when considered separately, potential buyers were willing to pay more for the brand new music dictionary than the dictionary with the torn cover. They did not give much weight to the number of entries in the standalone decisions because they had no basis for determining whether the entries were high or low.

This problem disappeared when consumers could compare the two dictionaries side by side. Now they could easily discern the importance of the number of entries because they had two values to compare. The relative insignificance of the dictionary's appearance compared to the number of entries in the dictionary was readily evident. Accordingly, buyers were now willing to pay much more money for the dictionary with 20,000 entries and the torn cover.

How can managers use this effect?

Pricing managers can draw a valuable lesson from the ease of evaluability heuristic. As we saw in Chapter 3, most consumers have inadequate knowledge about specific product prices. Relative to other features, a product's price tends to be more challenging to make sense of during the buying decision, especially when no guidance is given. This problem intensifies for items that are purchased infrequently, for brand new products where the customer doesn't have experience, and products which consumers don't care much about. As consumer psychologist Christopher Hsee points out[108]:

> "What determines whether an attribute is hard or easy to evaluate independently? My speculation is that it depends on how much knowledge the evaluator has about that attribute, especially about the value distribution of that attribute. An attribute will be hard to evaluate independently if the evaluator does not know its distribution information, such as the possible values of the attribute, its best and worst values, and so forth. Without such knowledge, the evaluator will not know where a given value on the attribute lies in relation to other values on the attribute and hence will not know how to evaluate it."

Returning to the organic quinoa package on the farm-stand priced at $11.79, a casual shopper will find it very difficult to ascertain whether this is a good price. To further downplay the significance of price, a savvy farm-stand owner could highlight quinoa's nutritional properties, provide a detailed explanation about how it was grown emphasizing its farm-to-table credentials, or paint enticing images of ancient Inca farmers harvesting this "Mother Grain" in the Andes mountains six thousand years ago[109]. These features would all be relatively easy to evaluate by shoppers on their own. Just like the brand new music dictionary in the study, focusing attention on such features would drive up customers' willingness to pay, making the $11.79 price appear reasonable. As an aside, this is the essence of branding strategy where the marketer develops and reinforces positive associations for the brand that consumers deem as valuable and worth paying extra money for when compared to a similar unbranded alternative.

On the other hand, what if, for some reason, the farm-stand owner wanted the shopper to pay more attention to the quinoa's price instead of its other features? More broadly, how can a manager make a product's price easier to evaluate for their customer? They need to provide the customer with concrete assistance in making sense of the price. The farm-stand owner might place a sign which says, "Quinoa of this quality typically costs $10-$20 per pound," implying that the quinoa on offer is very reasonably priced. Alternatively, simply providing a regular higher price, say $14.99, and indicating the "today only" sale price is $11.79 would produce a similar effect. Providing a single comparison price or a range of prices would make it much easier for shoppers to evaluate and use the quinoa's price in their decision.

This approach is commonly used by companies when introducing expensive products and services. Apple has been a skilled exponent of this method for more than a decade. In 2006, when Steve Jobs introduced portable speakers called *iPod Hi-Fi* at a launch event, he began by showing a competitor's product and explaining, "This Bose product costs over a thousand dollars... And we are delivering audio quality that is absolutely competitive with these products with the new iPod Hi-Fi and we're going to price it at $349." Twelve years later, at its HomePod product launch, Apple's Senior Vice President Phil Schiller said, "Typically Wi-Fi speakers of this quality sell for $300 to $500. And a smart speaker may cost you $100 to $200. So it's not unreasonable for a HomePod to be priced in the range of $400 to $700.

So we're really excited to tell you that HomePod is going to be priced for $349[110]." In both cases, and at many other Apple product launches, the company's executives are careful to educate the audience about prices before revealing the new Apple product's price.

In other contexts, companies may embark on a longer-term project of making their customers knowledgeable about prices and features of the product or service. Over the last two decades, the exchange-traded fund industry, led by discount brokerage firms Vanguard and Fidelity, and supported by numerous personal finance bloggers and advisors, have educated individual investors about the significance of high expense ratios and frontloads on fund performance[111]. Their goal is to help customers make informed fund choices in their retirement and personal investment accounts that takes prices into account.

The psychology behind consumers' ease of evaluation teaches an important lesson to managers. You should have a clear sense of how easily you want your customers to process your product's price and how much weight you want price to have in their buying decisions. Only then can you pick the appropriate price communication approach to influence your customers.

How to present your product's price relative to competitors' prices

The ease with which price can be evaluated also has important ramifications on how to present your offer relative to competitors' offers. If you have a lower price than your competitor for items of comparable quality, you will want to use communication methods that show the two offers side-by-side, much like the Apple executives when they introduce new products at launch events. For instance, you may run a direct comparison advertisement (as long as it is legal in your country to do so) where prices (your lower price and your competitor's higher price) are the focus of attention. You will also want to make such comparisons through direct mail, email campaigns, social media, and elsewhere. This will make prices easy to evaluate and increase their weight in customers' decision making, favoring your offer.

On the other hand, if your price is significantly higher than your competitor's price, you want to let price remain a relatively difficult-to-evaluate attribute when compared to others. You want your target customers to see your offer in a stand-alone fashion (the "separate evaluation" mode from the study), and preferably not think of the competitor's product during the evaluation. Shining the light on aesthetic attributes of the product (e.g., styling, shape, color, ingredient quality, etc.), service (friendliness of staff, ambiance, reliability, etc.), and so on, and mentioning price incidentally, or in a way to highlight its consistency with the rest of the offer will be useful in this situation. Luxury brands like Hermès, Burberry, and Cartier follow this approach, preferring to showcase their products in their own stores to benefit from the separate evaluation mode of shoppers.

The Psychology of Pricing Unique Products

If you are asked to give a reliable estimate of the price of a [painting] without seeing it, ask what the size is of the work, which technique the maker used, and for what price the maker may have sold artworks to museums. – Olav Velthuis.

Throughout this book, we have seen time and again that setting the price for any product is a tricky business that can have unintended positive or negative consequences for the seller. The challenge is even greater when pricing unique products like artworks, handicrafts, bespoke garments, and other labor-intensive, creative items. In such cases, the best thing the seller can do is to use a structured, repeatable method that brings some order to the potential chaos.

Most of the time, when setting prices, managers consider production costs and account for a reasonable profit. However, it makes little sense to price a painting based on the cost of paint, canvas, and paintbrush wear and tear. Another approach to use would be to accost the buyer, ascertain the product's value to them, and use this information to set the price. Also not feasible. For unique products, a further pricing challenge is that customer value differs dramatically from one individual to the next, and even at different times for the same person. This is why, when pricing unique products, the buyer's perceptions of simplicity and fairness are critical, and individual customer value takes the back seat.

Before the widespread adoption of fixed prices and price tags, prices of unique products were fluid and determined by bargaining. (We'll consider price fluidity and its consequences in detail in Chapter 6). You will experience this process today if you buy a carpet in Morocco[112]. After a lengthy ritual that involves drinking mint tea and inspecting dozens of carpets, the seller talks up the buyer's chosen carpet ("museum quality") and quotes an astronomical price. The buyer, if they're savvy, counters with a much lower number. Through the bargaining process that follows, the product's value is established, as is its price. Such a process makes sense because each carpet's value is unique to each buyer.

How artists price their paintings: The size-based method

Shouldn't paintings be priced the same way? Few products are more unique or more individualized in their value to potential buyers than a painting. The buyer of a painting derives *aesthetic value* based on their ineffable appreciation of it, *social value* from the status its possession provides, and *investment value* based on estimates of future appreciation[113]. It turns out that the most popular pricing method in the art world is a surprisingly standardized procedure, and it teaches us the importance of simplicity and fairness perceptions of customers in pricing decisions. The pricing method uses the painting's size as a primary driver of its price. Artists employ two versions of size-based pricing[114]: *Square-inch pricing* and *linear-inch pricing*.

The square-inch pricing method takes the height (h) and width (w) of the painting and multiplies it by the artist's reputation factor (r). The formula used is: h x w x r = price. Linear-inch pricing adds the painting's height and width and then multiples it with an appropriate reputation factor. In this case, the formula is: (h + w) x r = price.

The most obvious difference between the two methods is the role of the painting's size. With the square-inch method, the price difference between a smaller and a larger painting is much greater than it is with the linear-inch method. Similarly, the value of the reputation factor is smaller if the same artist uses the square-inch method instead of the linear-inch method. An example is helpful here to illustrate these differences. In Table 4.1, the artist's reputation factors are set so that the large painting's price is the same using both methods.

Table 4.1 Calculating a painting's price using the size-based method.

Variables	Large painting	Small painting
Painting size	18 inches x 24 inches	6 inches x 9 inches
Square-inch Reputation factor	$1.50	$1.50
Square-inch price	$648	$81
Linear-inch reputation factor	$15.4	$15.4
Linear-inch price	$648	$231

The second important variable in the size-based pricing method is the reputation factor. As should be clear, it is the artist's reputation factor that dictates the painting's final price. In theory, someone who uses a reputation factor of 15 will price their paintings at ten times the price of someone who uses a reputation factor of 1.5. In practice, however, because artists look to each other for clues about what they should charge, the reputation factor used tends to be rather homogeneous[115], especially when a peer group of artists using use the square-inch pricing method.

The main advantage of size-based pricing lies in the perceptions of simplicity and fairness it creates. It can be explained easily to a potential buyer. As art business consultant Maria Brophy points out, *"A couple of years ago when a collector would ask, "how is Drew's artwork priced?" I didn't have a good answer ... Now when someone asks, I can confidently say, "we charge $1.50 per square inch plus frame costs."* [116]*"*

How do artists determine their reputation factor?

This is where subjectivity and the role of peers come into play. Here are explanations given by four artists about how they decided what reputation factor to use for pricing their paintings:

- "Why $11? I'll be honest; it just feels right to me at this point." – Brad Blackman

- "Within a few minutes of number crunching, I was able to deduce, "Oh, she's charging $1.5 per square inch." And then you can decide from there what your work can garner comparatively." – Amira Rahim, paraphrased.

- I price smaller paintings at $1 per square inch so as to be affordable... and larger paintings at $1.50 to $2 per square inch.. because they'll appeal only to serious art collectors. – Cedar Lee, paraphrased.

- I'm not a mathematician, I'm an artist. Therefore, I price my works according to what I FEEL that I should charge. It's all about a mix of common sense (I know that good sense is not that common) and flip of the coin. – Jose, Wetcanvas

Admiring Art/ Martino Pietropoli/ Unsplash

What the size-based pricing method means for art buyers

The widespread use of size-based pricing means that buyers are likely to find a better value (strictly in dollar terms) in smaller-sized paintings. The value differential will be greater when artists use square-inch pricing. Second, they are likely to find more homogeneous prices for paintings than they should expect, meaning that there will be many paintings available from different artists at prices of $200, $500, $900, and so on. These are not price points in the sense of consumer-preferred prices that we saw earlier in this chapter. These are prices that sellers converge on based on using the same pricing method for their unique products. This should make the selection process easier for potential art buyers by framing the purchase decision as "Which $500 painting should I buy?" instead of "Is this painting worth $500?"

And third, the role of haggling is minimized. The idea behind size-based pricing is precisely to get away from bargaining over a painting's price. Even though paintings are very much like carpets in their individualized value to buyers, they are priced very differently. Because of fixed prices, the buyer is likely to find something they adore for a steal or be shocked at the price of a painting they didn't like.

The size-based pricing method used by contemporary artists to price their work provides an excellent lesson about the importance of consistency and communicability in pricing decisions. Even for a unique product whose value is entirely subjective, non-comparable, and wildly divergent across consumer tastes, using a cookie-cutter pricing method with a dash of subjectivity (the reputation factor) makes sense. We'll let artist Amira Rahim have the last word on the virtues of using the size-based pricing method for paintings[117]:

> "The most sound approach I've found has been to charge by size. This keeps it fairly consistent and makes the most sense to your customers. It also helps you ascertain the price of a painting pretty quickly and objectively, which is important as you start to produce more and more work."

CHAPTER 5

The Price in Context

*Charge 'em for the lice, extra for the mice, two percent for looking in
the mirror twice, here a little slice, there a little cut, three percent for
sleeping with the window shut. When it comes to fixing prices, there
are a lot of tricks I knows.*

— Les Miserables, Thenardier, Master of the House.

In the previous chapter, we considered the role of price in decision
heuristics employed by consumers. We also considered how managers could use this information to influence buying decisions. In
most customer journeys, decision heuristics take consumers only part
of the way on the path to the final choice and purchase. For example,
for consequential decisions like choosing a college, buying a vehicle,
or even purchasing a new mattress, prescreening heuristics such as
price thresholds and price points serve as powerful decision aids.
They help consumers to make the decision task manageable, by narrowing down the number of alternatives and forming a consideration
set. After that, in the next step of the sequential choice process, the
person further narrows down the consideration set to select one of
the remaining alternatives for purchase. For managers, this is the critical second and final step in the customers' purchase decision making

process. When this process is over, you want your product to be the *last product standing that the customer is handing over their credit card to buy.*

At this later stage of decision making, customers are willing to go beyond the use of mental short-cuts and examine the remaining product alternatives in more depth. They are willing to stop being cognitive misers and to do the hard work of thinking. Instead of a quick way to eliminate choices or judge the suitability of a product, price becomes a significant product attribute to the consumer at this decision stage. It is comparable to other product attributes in many ways, but distinct in one crucial way. The distinction is this. Whereas all other product attributes provide benefits to the consumer, price represents the financial sacrifice incurred to receive those benefits.

In its role as a product attribute, price is usually *traded off* against other product attributes in the consumer's buying decision. The basic equation at play is, "if you want more benefits, you'll have to shell out more money." For consumers, this begs the question, "Is this extra increase in quality worth this extra money?" As we will see throughout this chapter, the customer's price-quality trade-off is the fundamental psychological process that managers need to understand and try to influence to tilt the customer's buying decision in their favor.

In this chapter, we will consider the role of price in influencing the customer's value perceptions. We begin by considering budget-based decisions and investigate how to build and manage product lines that provide customers with different options of price and quality. Then, we will review the research on how to influence customer choice within the product line and introduce four famous psychological pricing nudges, the attraction effect, the similarity effect, the compromise effect, and the influence of incidental prices. This chapter will conclude by investigating the question of whether all-inclusive prices or itemized (also known as partitioned) prices are more attractive to consumers and why.

Budget-Based Decision Making

I was greeted by quite the crew, this Louis Vuitton and some Jimmy Choo...I said, Baby, there's a Walmart a block away, and I don't think they sell these brands... I'm afraid my baby's got champagne taste on a beer budget." – Home Free, Champagne Taste (on a Beer Budget).

Many purchases start with a budget that is real or implied. Consumers have a pretty good idea of which alternatives are feasible based on how much they are willing to spend on a particular occasion. Given their budget and prior experience, they also have a sense of the product quality they may expect to receive at the price they are willing to pay. For example, John may decide he wants to eat a fast food hamburger and fries for lunch and spend around $6 to $8 for his meal, drinks not included. John knows he's probably not going to be fed by Bobby Flay, eat on delicate china, or have Wagyu beef or vine-ripened heirloom tomatoes in his burger at this price point. But he does expect a clean restaurant, hot and tasty food, and quick, friendly service. John's outlook illustrates the core trade-off customers must make in budget-based decisions. They start by answering the question, *"How much do I want to spend for my purchase?"* followed by *"What should I expect to get in return?"* The corresponding product features and quality that they will receive in return is fairly well-defined and known based on prior experience. We will call such consumer decisions as *budget-based decisions.*

When customers make budget-based decisions, the manager really to provide four things to the customer to close the sale and satisfy them: (1) an adequate number of product alternatives that vary in price and quality to choose from, (2) a reasonable correspondence between price and quality for each alternative that seems fair to the customer, (3) price differentials between the alternatives that reflect relative differences in prices, not absolute differences, and (4) for products with taste-based features like flavors, colors, scents, melodies, etc., multiple options of taste-based features to choose from. For example, if you're going to run a frozen yogurt store, you have got to offer a dozen flavors or more, not just vanilla. Let us consider each factor in more detail.

111

use
to set
price

(1) Provide customers with an adequate number of alternatives that vary in price and quality to choose from.

When customers desire products with different levels of price and quality and have particular tastes, the best approach for the company is to offer them a choice using a line of products. Economists call this as vertical differentiation. Most product lines contain at least three levels of price and quality, and may have four or five levels, with multiple alternatives within each level. In pricing, we call such lines as "good-better-best" product lines to reflect the quality range covered and the associated fact that there will be significant variations in prices. The fundamental idea behind good-better-best product lines is to offer customers choices and let them choose the price-quality level they desire for themselves. Figure 5.1 illustrates the Good-Better-Best product line.

Figure 5.1 The Good-Better-Best product line.

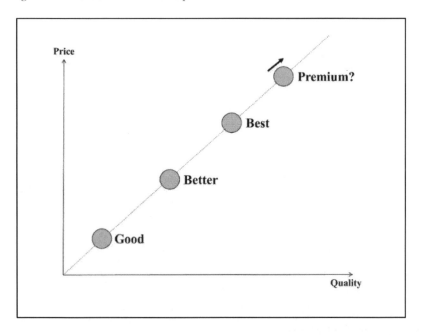

Note that the term "Good" is used euphemistically in this framework. When we say *good* here, we really mean to say the *cheapest and lowest quality*. Depending on industry conventions and the seller's

value proposition, other SFW terms for this option inc
bargain, low-cost, affordable, or economy option. The *bett*
the one with the medium price and medium quality in th
line. For many sellers, the better option is the bread-and-butt
ing. It is the item in the product line which sells the most and
most profitable. For instance, Toyota's biggest sellers are its mid-line
Corollas and Camrys, while it sells relatively smaller numbers of the
economy Yarises and the high-priced Avalons[118]. The *best* option in
the company's product line is typically the option that has the highest
quality and price that the seller offers. Many product lines may include a fourth *premium* product and even a fifth *super-premium* product. The goal of the best, premium, and other higher-end options is to
help the company build a reliable and reputable brand and boost its
brand image to gain pricing power for all its products. Sometimes
these offerings serve as decoys, as we will see later in this chapter.

Here are some examples of currently and recently available good-
better-best product lines, with the caveat that companies are always
tweaking their product lines in response to customer, competitor, and
market responses. In many cases, the escalation in features is evident
as we move up the line.

- *United Airlines*: Basic Economy, Economy, Economy-plus, Busi-
  ness class, First class.
- *Mercedes Sedans*: C-class ($40,000+), E-class ($53,000+), S-class
  ($90,000+).
- *LinkedIn*: Basic (Free), Career ($29.99/ month), Business
  ($47.99/ month), Sales ($64.99/ month), Recruiter ($99.95/
  month).
- *Procter & Gamble detergent brands*: Era ($.15/load of laundry),
  Cheer ($.26/load), Tide ($.40/ load), Tide Plus ($.64/ load).
- *Typical Bar, Club, or Pub*: Rail drink ($6; unbranded liquor), Call
  drink ($8-10; mid-tier liquor brand), Top-shelf drink ($13+; pre-
  mium liquor brands).
- *Shell Gasoline*: Regular (87 octane), Plus (89 octane), V-Power
  (91 octane).

- *Disney World park tickets*: Base ticket (entry into one park per day), Park Hopper (visit multiple parks each day), Park Hopper Plus (additional admissions to other activities and waterparks).
- *Dropbox Cloud Storage*: Basic (Free), Plus ($8.25/ month), Professional ($16.58/ month).
- *Dunkin' Donuts breakfast sandwiches*: Egg & Cheese Wake-up Wrap ($1), Egg & Cheese on English Muffin ($1.50), Egg & Cheese on Croissant ($2.50).

The company systematically offers different versions of the product so that customers can choose for themselves which one is appropriate for them based on this budget, how much they value the product and the level of benefits they want on a purchase occasion. This choice helps customers stick with the seller and make budget-based decisions every time. On a particular morning, if I am feeling skint, I will make do with the one-buck Wake-up Wrap and a hot coffee at Dunkin' Donuts. If I'm feeling flush, I will splurge for the croissant sandwich and a cappuccino.

(2) Ensure that the level of quality corresponds to the product's price throughout the line.

The second important property of good-better-best product lines is that customers should be able to discern differences in price and quality of the alternatives in the line readily. The products in a seller's product-line are substitutes and can potentially cannibalize one another[119]. From a psychological pricing perspective, customers making budget-based decisions should be able to pick their preferred option without hesitation. Many of the same people fly in United Business class when they are flying for work and purchase an economy-plus or economy seat when they are traveling for pleasure and paying out of their pocket. But it's all good; the frequent flyer miles keep adding up.

Not all budget-based choices have the same degree of ease or difficulty when choosing an item from the product line. Depending on the product, consumers will be able to decide what constitutes quality either based on just one attribute (e.g., the thickness of a trash bag) or a combination of many different characteristics which may themselves involve trade-offs. For instance, when purchasing a smartphone, screen size, and weight both matter, but they are usually correlated negatively. The manager's primary objective should be to make it easy for customers to choose the product with the price and quality level they want, avoiding confusion and potential indecision. For this reason, providing more than four or five levels of price and quality in the product line is inadvisable. Most product lines have three to five levels, including all the product line examples shown previously.

Another important consideration in designing and marketing the product line is that it should encourage *asymmetric trading up* by customers. The phrase *asymmetric trading up* sounds like bombastic jargon. In fact, it is a highly useful concept for managers that are making pricing decisions. It means when they're in the final stages of their purchase decision and about to choose an alternative, the pricing structure should be such that more customers are tempted to upgrade from the good option to the better option, or from the better to the best one, than to downgrade to a cheaper alternative than they origi-nally planned to buy. If you are a revenue management manager at United Airlines, you want more of your economy class flyers to wonder, should I spend the extra $45 to get more legroom in economy-plus, than saying to themselves, let me save $35 and fly in basic economy at the back of the plane even if I have to relinquish my carryon bag. To accomplish asymmetric trading up, companies usually ramp up the amount of value perceived by customers for higher priced options in the product line relative to lower-priced choices. There are many ways to pull this off.

The perceived value of the more expensive alternatives can be boosted by making them scarce. Business class airline seats, for instance, are far fewer in number than economy seats. (We will see a lot more of scarcity pricing in Chapter 7). A second way is to provide augmented features for expensive options that certain types of customers crave or find indispensable. Disney World's Park Hopper ticket provides the much-desired flexibility of taking in highlights from multiple theme parks in a single day that all-adults groups value. Families with children, in contrast, would find it much harder to park-hop. It's not surprising that Park Hopper tickets command a hefty 50% premium or more when compared to a single park ticket[120]. A third way to encourage asymmetric trading up is to provide significantly more functional benefits in the higher-end product options. Dropbox's free version called "Dropbox Basic" offers 2 gigabytes of cloud storage, which is barely enough to save half an hour of video. Its plus version, which costs $9.99 per month, provides two terabytes of storage, a thousand times as much. We will consider trading up in greater detail a little later in this chapter.

(3) Price differentials should reflect relative differences in prices, not absolute differences.

Humans are hard-wired to process incoming stimuli such as sound, light, taste, smell, and for our purposes, prices, and the differences between them in a non-linear way. Our ability to discriminate between stimuli depends on the level of the stimulus' initial intensity. The Weber-Fechner law, dating back to the 1860s, postulates that the stronger the initial stimulus, the greater the change in its intensity has to be for the individual to notice the change. Pricing expert Kent Monroe translated this psychophysical law into the pricing realm this way: *The differences in prices between products [in a product line] should reflect relative differences rather than absolute differences*[121]. In practical terms, the implication is that prices of the good, better, and best products cannot be equidistant if the manager wants to maximize perceptions of differences between them and prevent higher-priced options from being devalued and lower-priced options to be overvalued. The prices of the good and better options need to be closer together, and the prices of the better and best options need to be further apart from one another. To apply the Weber-Fechner law, and derive prices of the items in a product line is straightforward. The following four-step method is used to calculate price differentials to apply this principle and achieve maximal discrimination in the line:

Step 1: Determine P_{max} and P_{min}, the highest and lowest prices in the product line.

Step 2: Determine n, the number of alternatives in the product line.

Step 3: Calculate Weber's constant k = $(P_{max}/P_{min})^{\wedge}(1/(n-1))$

Step 4: Use the equation: $P_j = P_{min}*(k^{\wedge}(j-1))$ to calculate prices of each product in the line (except the highest and the lowest-priced products that you already know).

Let's consider an example to demonstrate how this method works. Imagine that a brand of vacuum cleaners has a product line with five products. Its cheapest vacuum cleaner is priced at $100, and its most expensive option costs $500. The brand manager wants to determine what the prices of the other three vacuum cleaners in the product line should be. The simplistic, equidistant pricing approach is shown in the left panel of Figure 5.2.

Figure 5.2 Price differentials in a product line.

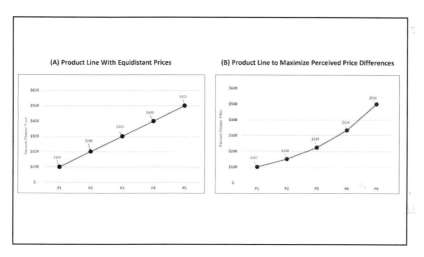

The prices are equidistant throughout the product line here. There is a price differential of $100 between consecutive products in the line, which means that the three mid-tier vacuums are priced at $200, $300, and $400, bookended by $100 at the low end, and $500 at the high end. We would price this way if we decided to ignore the Weber-Fechner law. The problem is that equidistant pricing will result in the highest-priced options appearing too similar to each other in price. This pricing will be likely to draw customers towards the $400, or even the $300 alternative, at the expense of the $500 vacuum cleaner.

To avoid this problem and to maximize perceptions of price differences in the line, the lower prices must be set closer together, and the higher prices further apart by using the four-step approach. The result of applying the method is shown in the right panel of Figure 5.2. (I encourage you to work out the numbers for yourself). Now, instead of $200, the second-cheapest vacuum cleaner is priced at $150. At the high end of the line, the second-most expensive vacuum cleaner is priced at $334 instead of $400. The $500 version is no longer in jeopardy of being confused with the second-most expensive version. The prices in this product line will be perceived as maximally different from one another by customers.

(4) Provide customers with multiple choices in taste-based features at every level of price and quality.

Most products have taste-based features that matter to buyers. Take the example of yogurt. Even with the same amount of sugar and milk-fat, one person may prefer strawberry yogurt, a second one may go for vanilla, while peach may be a third consumer's favorite flavor. From an accounting perspective, cost differences to produce these different flavors may be significant. From an operations perspective, manufacturing a variety of flavors escalates complexity when compared to producing just one or two flavors. Yet having these choices is important to consumers. Economists call this offering as *horizontal differentiation*. Customers want variety or they may reject the brand simply because it does not carry a certain flavor that they prefer.

Considering consumers' willingness to pay, academic research has shown that consumers make the distinction between product line attributes (the differences in quality) and taste-based attributes during decision making. They give greater economic weight to line attributes and little or no weight to taste-based attributes. In other words, consumers expect prices to be different across the product line but expect taste-based choices given a particular quality level to have the same price. For example, customers will be fine with paying more for yogurt made with organic milk than yogurt made with regular whole milk. However, they will expect the strawberry, vanilla, and lemon flavors of organic yogurt to cost the same[122].

It's not surprising that Mercedes C-class sedans come in a variety of 11 different colors, its E-class sedans have 12 colors, and S-class sedans come in 14 different colors. Not to mention numerous other line feature augmentations such as different types of alloy wheels, seats that provide massage, heated and cooled cupholders, rear seat entertainment system, and so on. While it is hard to persuade customers to spend more for a different color, Mercedes sedan customers have to shell out extra money to add many of these line features that clearly enhance quality, providing opportunities for trading up.

Not all taste-based choices are inter-changeable or substitutes. When they're choosing between Netflix, Hulu and HBO, for instance, consumers want large assortments of movies, TV shows, and original content to choose from. In 2016, many aficionados were outraged that Netflix's library of movies shrunk from 6,500 movies two years earlier to 4,330 movies[123]! Everyone's taste is different, and in this case, the content provider must cover all its bases, offering a wide selection of foreign movies, arthouse movies, classics, blockbusters, and exclusive content to choose from. People want a large choice assortment to be able to seek variety in their content consumption.

At first blush, well-constructed product lines are those that appear simple to the consumer and easy to navigate and choose from. But when the customer engages further, these product lines turn out to be complex and tempting, enticing customers not only to trade up to the next item in the line but to augment their chosen product with additional features and to pay extra money for these additions. Product lines that create the illusion of simplicity but are really complex, with ample opportunities to trade up are win-wins for sellers. They deliver a customized product that the customer feels good about and enjoys using after purchase. And they generate the highest possible revenue for the company from the company plus sales of high-margin augmentations. The manager has two distinct but interrelated imperatives when pricing a product line: *you want to deliver greatest possible value to your customers regardless of the product they choose from your product* line. *At the same time, you want to influence your customers' choices in ways that are mutually beneficial to the customer and your company.*

Influencing Customer Choice Within the Product Line

One cannot live without inconsistency. – Carl Jung.

With good-better-best product lines, in addition to the four tasks discussed at length in the previous section, another crucial managerial objective is to motivate customers to trade up from the good option to the better option, and from better option to the best option. Well-constructed and well-managed good-better-best product lines create the ~~illusion of self-determined choice.~~ But by using a combination of subtle and overt influence methods, the manager encourages customers to purchase a more expensive and higher-value option than the one they had in mind to begin with.

This is evident in the grocery store, where the good version is typically advertised in newspaper ads and signs to bring price-conscious or deal-seeking customers into the store. For example, my local grocery store often runs a promotion for boneless pork loin at $1.00 per pound (regular price = $1.89 per pound). This is the *good* version of the grocery store's pork product line. Enticed by the offer, when shoppers reach the meat case to buy the advertised pork loin, they encounter the thicker-cut (the better version), and pasture raised organic pork chops (the best version). Both these superior quality products are displayed prominently right next to the advertised boneless pork loin. In this lineup, the pork loin loses its charm for those shoppers who are not price-sensitive, and they will place a more expensive (and profitable to the store) product in their shopping cart.

Note that these shoppers would not have gone to the store to buy one of the more expensive versions. They went for the low-priced alternative and made up their mind to buy either the better or best versions of the product line at the point of purchase. Kent Harrison, marketing VP of Tyson Fresh Meats describes the manager's logic in this way[124]: *"Retailers must make sure to stock their case with a variety of choices, to give consumers the option of moving up to the next tier of quality, which will also be an opportunity for the retailer to gain higher total dollar sales."* And even better, the higher revenues are usually accompanied by significantly higher profit margins on sales of the better or best options.

Some cynics or marketing skeptics may call this approach *bait-and-switch* and question the ethics behind it. These criticisms are unfounded. I want to emphasize that managerial price actions such as the one described here are entirely ethical and are a part of effective pricing strategy execution. With this approach, customers are not hoodwinked or taken advantage of in any way. The advertised deal is legitimate and is available for the shopper if they choose to buy it.

As discussed in Chapter 1, customers are volitional decision makers, and they are in control of which pork-loin to buy throughout the shopping process, whether it is the advertised deal, the thick-cut version or the pasture-raised one. They will receive good value from whichever option they choose, but the quality will be higher for the more expensive alternatives. The role of price, and specifically the purpose of running the promotion, is to motivate the customer to visit the store instead of going to a competitor. Once the customer is in the store, the seller has the opportunity to engage their attention and put more alternatives in front of them, including ones that higher in price and quality. Which item from the product line the customer ultimately buys is entirely up to them.

Trading up is boosted by customers changing their minds at the point of purchase

Once customers have made up their minds to buy a product and are on the cusp of making a purchase, it is much easier to influence their decision about which specific alternative to buy. This is because individuals routinely change their minds at the point of purchase and end up making an impulsive choice[125]. Often, the decision context itself encourages the customer's trading up behavior. For example, if your employer is paying for your airline ticket and gives you free rein, upgrading to premium economy or business class is an easy decision to make for a long-haul flight. Similarly, if you are at a bar and having a great time with your friends, splurging on a top-shelf drink instead of your regular rail drink feels like a natural upgrade. Many consumers justify the expensive choice to themselves in other ways by generating careful and logical reasons –"I do not buy a new car every day, so I might as well opt for the pricier version with the bigger engine and the all-wheel drive" or "I am having a great time, I might as well splurge and make it a night to remember[126]."

Pricing expert Rafi Mohammed provides the example of Southwest Airlines introducing a Business Select[127] fare in which customers paid $10 to $30 more than the base fare, and received amenities such as priority boarding, faster passage through security lines, and a coupon for an alcoholic drink during the flight. In evaluating the introduction of this *best* option offered by Southwest Airlines, Mohammed estimated that it increased the airline's revenue by approximately $100 million and operating profit by 10% in the year after it was introduced[128]. United Airlines routinely offers the opportunity to purchase cabin upgrades or specific amenities like Priority Boarding to customers when they purchase the ticket and when they check-in for a flight.

When customers trade up, the company earns a higher profit margin.

From a company's perspective, there is a significant upside to influencing customers to choose an option that is higher in price and quality than they originally planned to buy. As mentioned earlier, in most cases, the good option or the better option in the product line is the company's core product, its bread-and-butter. For instance, close to 90% of passengers fly in the economy cabin. Full-service airlines earn most of their revenue from these customers. Similarly, a majority of vehicle buyers purchase the base version of the car or truck, and a majority of travelers book the standard room on a hotel property. These lower-priced options are sold to the company's core customers, covering its costs and allowing it to stay in business from one year to the next. Not surprisingly, managers are conservative about pricing these options. They cannot afford to lose their core business, so they usually restrict price increases for these products to the detriment of profit margins.

When offering the higher-priced options, however, such pricing conservatism is not necessary. Customers who are interested in more expensive choices are often less price sensitive customers. They are more concerned with non-price factors such as appearance, comfort, status, style, and performance. Companies can, therefore, sell higher-priced options in their product line at higher profit margins. For airline seats, an economy ticket on a New York–London flight may cost around $900; the premium economy tickets are priced at $1,800 to $1,900 while a business class ticket costs $4,000-5,000[129]. The additional cost of offering the marginally more legroom, better meals, and free alcoholic beverages in the premium economy and business classes is not proportionally higher. The airlines make significantly higher profits from the premium seats[130].

Four Famous Psychological Pricing Nudges to Influence Customer Choice

> *The irrationality of a thing is no argument against its existence, rather a condition of it. – Friedrich Nietzsche.*

At the final stage of the decision making process, the consumer commonly asks one of two questions. If the alternative is being evaluated by itself, the question typically asked is, "Is this product's quality worth this price?" Let's say James is thinking about what to do during an upcoming one-week vacation and is considering whether to shell out $1,000 for a week-long cruise to the Bahamas. He's not considering any alternative travel option. If he doesn't take the cruise, he'll probably stay at home and staycation. Assuming he can afford it, James will trade-off spending the $1,000 for the cruise against his overall pleasure and enjoyment of the experience, and the emotional value of the memories created from going on the cruise. In these types of decisions, the consumer's question is about the value offered by one particular product in exchange for the asking price. The trade-off is between the price paid and the benefits received from the product.

In a different type of a decision, if the consumer has already formed a consideration set of options, and there are multiple alternatives to choose from, their question will be slightly different. They will ask, "Which product shall I buy? Product A, the high price–high-quality option, or Product B, the low price–low-quality option?" (or of course, C, or D... depending on the number of alternatives in their consideration set). In these types of decisions, the consumer's question is one of choosing where to land on the good-better-best product line, with explicit trade-offs to be considered between the available options.

In this section, we will examine four different ways by which managers can influence consumers' answers to these two important questions, (1) "Is this product worth its price?" and (2) "Shall I buy the high price–high quality option or the low price–low quality option?" In helping consumers answer these questions, the manager must always keep one fundamental point front and center in their mind: *The answers to both questions are influenced by the decision making context, and there are aspects of the consumer's decision making context that the manager can control.* In other words, customers will come up with dramatically different answers to the questions depending on the other available alternatives and their prices. Under one set of conditions, the customer will answer the question, "Is the product worth its price?" with a "yes." Under a different set of circumstances, they will answer "no." Similarly, in one context, the customer will choose the higher price, higher quality alternative (e.g., Tide, Pepsi, the leading national brand) and in another context, the same person will choose the lower price, lower quality alternative (e.g., Gain, the economy store brand).

The manager can design and orchestrate the decision context to tilt the consumer's choice in a way that is favorable to the company. This idea is now famously called *nudging* by behavioral economists, but it has a long history that precedes the use of this term[131]. We will consider four famous psychological pricing nudges in this section. Note that in the discussion that follows, we focus on the aggregate response of consumers to the decision context. Not every person is going to behave in the predicted way, but enough will, so that there is a significant difference on outcome measures such as the number of sales, market share, and profit when a particular set of choices is offered to customers.

Nudging customers to purchase high-margin jewelry

A few years ago, I worked with an entrepreneur (let's call her Hilda) who designed and sold jewelry through limited-time events called trunk shows at upscale boutique stores. At the time, Hilda was starting out and only had two items to sell, a $100 bracelet and a $400 jewelry set that included a more elegant bracelet, earrings, and a chain. In the past, she had tried to sell the earrings and chain separately but didn't have much success, so she bundled them into a single set. The top panel of Figure 5.3 illustrates Hilda's product line. When we considered her costs, it was clear that the bracelet was by far the most expensive item to manufacture, and Hilda made very little money from its sales. On the other hand, the $400 jewelry set was much more profitable because of the lower costs of making the earrings and chain.

Hilda had a problem that many managers face with their good-better-best product lines. The low-priced products are more popular, but the company makes more money on the high-priced products in the product line. When Hilda displayed the bracelet and the jewelry set side-by-side at trunk shows, almost every customer purchased the bracelet, and hardly anyone bought the set. When asked why, her customers told her the set was too expensive, and they did not want to spend $400. In response to this customer feedback, Hilda was considering lowering the set's $400 price by around 20%. However, this would have meant essentially destroying her profit, so it wasn't a smart pricing move.

What Hilda did instead was to use one of the most popular and widely known psychological pricing tricks known to marketers today. She added a decoy or an artificially expensive item to her product line. Some pricing experts also call the decoy item as an anchor[132]. Specifically, Hilda designed a slightly more elaborate version of the jewelry set, studding the pieces with a few extra precious stones. She set its price at a stratospheric and totally unreasonable level of $2,500.

Figure 5.3 Selling jewelry at upscale boutique stores with the attraction effect.

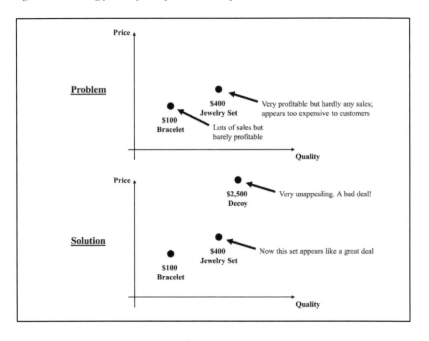

The bottom panel of Figure 5.3 illustrates Hilda's new product line. When the three choices were displayed side-by-side at trunk shows, the $2,500 set appeared to be a poor value to everyone who saw it. However, by creating this perception, it performed its job brilliantly. It made the $400 jewelry set that Hilda wanted to sell appear to be a terrific value. Once she introduced the decoy, sales of her $400 set jumped. In fact, in the trunk shows over the next two months, she sold more $400 sets than $100 bracelets, which was an amazing turnaround. Introducing the $2,500 set had another fringe benefit for Hilda. It raised the stature of her fledgling jewelry brand. After all, anyone with the chutzpah to sell jewelry worth thousands of dollars must be an accomplished designer, right?

Decoys are used today in virtually every industry. An upscale restaurant sells a $140 hamburger topped with foie gras and black truffle. Few people order this menu item, but its value lies in making everything else on the menu appear to be a great deal[133]. Swiss luxury watchmaker Hublot sells a one million dollar Black Caviar watch. Software companies sell prominent but unaffordably priced enterprise "all-in" software that few customers have the budget for. Fully-loaded and prominently advertised farm equipment may cost three or four times as much as the base model of the machine that most farmers purchase.

Publications like *the Economist* and *BusinessWeek* offer two or three subscription choices side-by-side[134]. The digital and the print versions are clearly inferior to the All Access subscription that includes both digital and print, yet all three are priced the same. To any customer who still remains oblivious, the publisher places a "BEST VALUE" banner on top of the All Access offer to make sure even they don't miss comparing the target option with the decoys.

The popularity of decoys is based on the fact that they are a straightforward and inexpensive pricing cue to increase sales of high-margin products in the product line. If your company does not use decoys strategically to promote the sales of the highly profitable products in your product line, you should consider doing so.

Using decoys in a choice set is just one nudge to influence customer choice. Other nudges are equally effective in making one option stand out in a choice set and increase the customer's preference and willingness-to-pay for it. We will consider four of these nudges that are particularly useful in psychological pricing activities.

1) The Attraction effect

The case we just saw is an example of the *attraction effect*. When the consumer is given three alternatives, and two of them involve distinct trade-offs in price and quality (the $100 bracelet or the $400 set), but the third one is clearly inferior to one of the two (the $2,500 set vs. the $400 set) but not the other, consumers gravitate disproportionately towards the superior, dominating option (the $400 set). This is what happened with Hilda's product line. Because the inferiority arises from the mismatch between price and quality, the power of this effect lies in the fact that the marketer has a considerable degree of latitude in constructing the inferior option. In Hilda's case, she decided to offer the $2,500 set as a decoy because she wanted to increase sales of her $400 jewelry set. What if she wanted to sell more of the $100 bracelets instead? She could have introduced a decoy that was closer to the $100 item. A bracelet priced at $300 that was just slightly higher in quality than the $100 version would have made the $100 bracelet seem like a steal and boosted its sales.

2) The Similarity effect

To understand the ~~similarity effect,~~ let's consider the case of a neighborhood brasserie which sells a roast chicken entrée for $18 and a Ribeye steak entrée for $25 on its "nightly specials" menu. The restaurant owner's problem is that even though the chicken has a lower price, she makes far more profit from selling it than she does by selling steak to her customers. With she sells a ribeye steak to a patron, she barely breaks even. Her customers prefer the ribeye, and that is by far the most popular item ordered each night. What should the owner do? Figure 5.4 illustrates how the similarity effect works.

Figure 5.4 Increasing sales of the chicken entrée with the similarity effect.

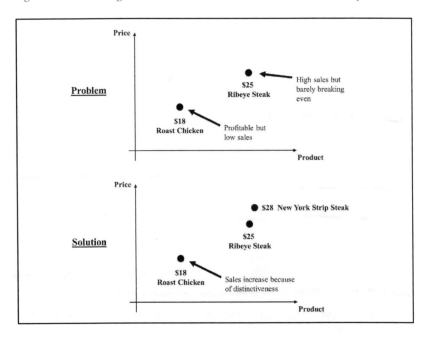

One solution to this problem is to offer a second steak entrée, say a New York Strip steak for $28, as a nightly special. According to the similarity effect, having two steak entrees on the menu but just one chicken entrée will nudge the customers' preference towards the chicken because this is ~~the option which appears unique and dissimilar to~~ the other two specials. Here the shift in customer preference comes from the similarity or lack thereof among the choices offered by the seller.

3) The Compromise Effect

Let's stay with the same brasserie and take on another of the owner's problems to understand the *compromise effect*. On the restaurant's dessert menu, the owner has an assortment of three gelato flavors for $4 and a blueberry cheesecake for $9. Both desserts are delicious but haven't sold well. The issue mentioned in many feedback forms is by the time they get to dessert, the patrons are stuffed. Most people don't order dessert, and those who do, order the gelato. Virtually no one orders the $9 blueberry cheesecake. While she makes some profit from selling the gelato, what the brasserie owner wants is to increase the ticket amount by getting people to spend more on desserts.

How can the brasserie owner use the composition of her dessert assortment to boost dessert sales? According to the compromise effect, she should introduce a third dessert at a mid-price point, for instance, a $6 slice of chocolate cake topped with raspberry compote. Such an addition will be immediately more popular, and diners will gravitate towards the "middle" choice to avoid buying either the cheap option or the expensive one.

When they have a middle choice, people tend to shy away from extreme alternatives. (As an aside, this is also one reason why middle-tier items in a product line tend to be more popular). Notice that in the compromise effect, each of the three options is a good value, delivering the commensurate level of quality for its respective price. The change in behavior occurs due to the customers' natural preference for moderate options, and aversion for extreme choices. The main lesson from the compromise effect for managers is to provide choices to customers that are mid-tier. In essence, this nudge is an argument in favor of offering a good-better-best line instead of a good-best line. Figure 5.5 illustrates the compromise effect.

Figure 5.5 Increasing sales of dessert with the compromise effect.

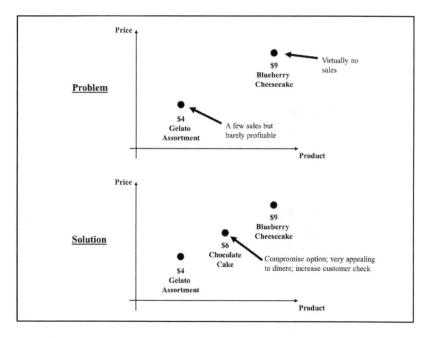

4) Effects of Incidental prices

The three nudges we have considered so far are about consumers making comparisons to related products or services in the choice set that provided diagnostic price information. What about entirely un-related prices from a different product category that the consumer has no interest in? Imagine that you own a boutique where you sell stylish pieces of jewelry from a young, up-and-coming designer like Hilda, in a display case. You want to support this designer and do anything you can to boost her sales. In a display case adjacent to Hilda's jewelry, you have the option of showcasing either Louis Vuitton and Hermès bags, retailing for $1,000 to $5,000 apiece, or Louis Vuitton and Hermès scarves ranging in price $100 to $500. Which should you choose if your goal is to increase jewelry sales of the relatively unknown designer? This is where the fascinating research on *incidental prices* comes in. It shows that completely unrelated prices influence the willingness to pay of consumers for an item in the vicinity of the target product. The higher the incidental prices that the customer is exposed to at the point of purchase, the higher will be their willingness to pay for the target item[135]. Figure 5.6 illustrates this idea graphically.

Figure 5.6 Using the influence of incidental prices to sell jewelry.

The authors of the incidental prices study call these prices "irrelevant anchors." They may be irrelevant from the customer's perspective because the effect is caused by unintentional exposure to the prices of products that are of little interest to them. However, incidental prices are very much relevant to the seller. Their influence suggests that sellers should use more nuanced and carefully plotted display strategies or other high price cues to boost customer valuation of target products. For instance, a seller may judiciously organize shelf or store displays in such a way that the target product having higher revenue and margin potential is given the center stage and is placed next to the most expensive unrelated products with prominently shown high price tags. The same idea also applies to side-by-side online displays. Returning to the question about what which item should you place in the display case next to the target jewelry case, expensive bags or less-expensive scarves? By now, the answer should be clear. You should place Louis Vuitton and Hermès bags costing several thousand dollars apiece next to the young designer's jewelry case.

In this section, we saw four psychological pricing nudges that involved composing product assortments strategically to influence the customer's preference for a target product. The *attraction effect*, the *similarity effect*, the *compromise effect*, and *incidental prices* all provide managers with opportunities to make relatively small changes to the customer's decision environment at the point of purchase and affect their choice.

Do Customers Prefer an All-Inclusive Price or an Itemized List of Prices?

> *Well, he hands you a nickel, he hands you a dime, he asks you with a grin if you're havin' a good time, then he fines you every time you slam the door, I ain't gonna work for Maggie's brother no more.* – Bob Dylan, Maggie's Farm.

In making pricing decisions, one aspect that often gets overlooked or is given little consideration by the manager: *how to present the price to the customer*. Should the product's final price be presented to customers as one total amount, inclusive of all items? Or should the price be broken up into an itemized list where each charge is described separately? Does this difference matter in how customers respond to and evaluate the price? These are the questions we will try to answer in this section.

Consider the case of a couple who is planning to get married in the summer. They are still not sure where to go for their honeymoon. Costco Travel lists a seven-day vacation package to Hawaii that seems perfect for an amazing honeymoon. It includes a four-star hotel room in Kauai, airfare for two, and the use of a rental car for a week. Costco can quote the price for this travel package as *all-inclusive*, $4,500, or it can itemize the price of each component: Hotel = $2,500, two airline tickets = $1,500, and rental car = $500. This latter method, where the total price is divided into two or more mandatory parts and presented to customers as an itemized list is called as *partitioned pricing*[136]. We will define partitioned pricing as *a method of presenting the price offer to the customer in which the seller unilaterally and arbitrarily divides the total price of a product into two or more separate mandatory components.* Each mandatory component has a specific label attached to it, which often, but not always, explains the reason for the charge.

Managers must decide whether to use all-inclusive pricing or partitioned pricing in many industries. For example, an airline can assess a fuel surcharge and checked-in luggage charge separately and list it below the base ticket price in the fare quote or make it part of the ticket price, hiding the line items from customers. When listed separately on international flights, some airlines even invent vague names for such surcharges like "carrier-imposed fees" with a total that can amount to a value that is greater than the base fare[137].

An online retailer can price a pair of shoes at $144.95 and quote its shipping charges as an additional $7.95 separately. Alternatively, it can offer the shoes at $152.90, including shipping in the price. Like many upscale resorts, the Grand Cayman Beach Resort charges a mandatory resort fee of $50 per room per night that appears as a separate line item on the bill. The cable company Xfinity lists the price for its bundled programming, and various mandatory surcharges such as Broadcast TV fee, Regional Sports fee, Universal Connectivity Charge, and Regulatory Recovery Fee separately on the bill[138].

In all these examples, there is one core or base product (the airline ticket, pair of shoes, resort room, cable TV programming) and there are additional mandatory charges that the customer must pay to make the purchase (fuel surcharge and checked-in luggage charge, shipping and handling fee, resort fee, and Universal Connectivity Charge, respectively).

Partitioned pricing is not price bundling

Before considering whether partitioned pricing works, we must understand the difference between partitioned pricing and price bundling. Partitioned pricing, our focus here, is a method of communicating mandatory price items to customers. Price bundling, on the other hand, is an incentive offered to customers, where the combined price of multiple items is lower than individual prices, to encourage greater purchases. In all the examples of partitioned pricing we just saw, customers do not receive any discount for purchasing the separately listed items. They pay the same total amount for the product whether the price is presented as all-inclusive or is partitioned. The issue is one of *price presentation*, not of price promotion. With partitioned pricing, they have no choice about buying only one part of the product and rejecting partitioned prices. They must purchase the entire product or walk away. For example, shipping and handling is mandatory when purchasing shoes from the online retailer and must be paid for whether the charge is included in the price of shoes or is presented separately.

Another difference is that all price components are associated with the purchase of a single product in partitioned pricing. In price bundling, customers receive a discount for buying the bundle, and they often (but not always) have the opportunity to buy the items in the bundle separately. For instance, the Quarter Pounder with Cheese® Combo Meal at McDonald's is a price bundle because it costs less to buy as a bundle than the separate prices of the QPC, fries, and drink that make up the bundle. But you could buy the QPC burger alone if you wish and leave out the fries if you are on a diet (although in that case, you probably shouldn't eat the QPC either).

This is the critical question that managers must answer about partitioned pricing: *"If my company sells a base product with mandatory surcharges or complementary products, which way of presenting the total price to the customer is better, an all-inclusive price quote or a partitioned price quote providing an itemized list?"*

The benefits of all-inclusive prices

Presenting prices to customers as all-inclusive has some obvious advantages. First, all-inclusive prices are simple prices to communicate and explain because there's a single number involved. Where price communication is concerned, as we have seen before in the case of unique products, simplicity is beneficial. All-inclusive prices also help the manager to build a compelling story about the brand and contribute to a strong value proposition. For example, dollar stores have created an entire retail category based on the simplicity of a one-dollar price. Southwest Airlines has invented and trademarked the concept of "Transfarency®" which it defines as "the philosophy in which customers are treated honestly and fairly, and low fares actually stay low—no unexpected bag fees, change fees, or hidden fees[139]." Transfarency® is a key building block of Southwest's price image and brand and is a powerful way to execute its value proposition.

All-inclusive prices are also easy for customers to comprehend and use. In our honeymooners' example, if the couple is told that their one-week Hawaii honeymoon is going to cost $4,500 all-inclusive, it is much easier for them to decide whether they want to go or not based on their wedding budget. The clarity associated with the all-inclusive price also increases the customers' satisfaction with the company's pricing, even if they think the price is too high and therefore unaffordable.

Intriguingly for managers, despite being simpler, all-inclusive prices make it easier to hide information about costs and profit margins. The opacity of all-inclusive prices occurs because the differences in costs and profit margins associated with the different components can be used to make the overall product appear to be a good value. For instance, the $4,500 price tag for the Hawaii vacation package includes a car rental which has a lower-than-average price, and a hotel room, which has an above-average price, when compared to other honeymoon destinations like the Florida Keys or the Caribbean. Because of this, consumers may not realize they've paid too much when they are presented with all-inclusive prices. The company can use the variations in the different components of the product to create an offer that signals good value to the customer while maintaining healthy profit margins.

The online retailer Zappos uses all-inclusive pricing successfully as part of its overall branding strategy, benefiting from the advantages of all-inclusive pricing. It offers fast shipping and the ability to return purchased items without any hassles as part of the product's price. Both features are essential for online shoppers who can confidently order a shoe in multiple sizes, keep the one that fits and return the others[140]. What's more, some customers hate paying extra for shipping and will simply abandon their online shopping cart when a shipping charge comes up, no matter how small it is[141]. Zappos' simple all-in pricing is particularly attractive to such people. Sandals Resorts and Priceline are two other companies which have used all-inclusive pricing prominently as a differentiator to great effect in their respective industries for long periods.

On the flip side, when consumers are confronted with partitioned prices, they often express outrage at not having the choice to decline the surcharge. For example, TripAdvisor reviews of the Grand Cayman Resort, which has a mandatory resort fee of $50 per room per night, often refer to this fee negatively. Here's a review posted by user Kendal_UK:

> "When you pay ~$300 a night for a room you expect a few things to be included and you certainly don't expect the hotel to try and charge you for use of a "newspaper" (never saw this) or use of one of maybe five "floating relaxation platforms" ... umm you're a beach resort that's why we came... If it's a mandatory charge then include it in the room rate, it seems like just an excuse to make yourself look better on room comparison sites, or maybe it's a clever trick you've devised to avoid paying a % of this money to Marriott International."

Partitioned prices are more effective than all-inclusive prices

Despite the simplicity and clarity of all-inclusive prices, there are significant advantages to using partitioned prices, which *makes them the superior method of presenting prices to consumers where it is feasible to do so.* Pricing experts have observed that because of the superiority, "for most online shopping, as well as many important purchases such as cellular phone services, cable television, and travel, partitioned prices are now the norm, rather than all-inclusive prices[142]." Here's an example where understanding the science behind psychological pricing and observing the performance of companies that practice the pricing method goes against the grain of intuition which suggests that consumers should hate partitioned prices so much that they are ineffective for managers to use. But as we will see, this is not the case.

Why have partitioned prices become the norm? Their greatest appeal lies in increasing the product's perceived value by lowering the customer's estimate of how much it costs. Customers may complain about having to pay the mandatory surcharge on review sites, but research shows that they fixate on the base price and underestimate the magnitude of the surcharge when making buying decisions. For the Costco Hawaii package, for example, when prices are listed separately, the consumer will attend to the hotel's price of $2,500 and underweight the airline tickets and rental car when adding them up. Instead of calculating the actual package value of $4,500, they may come up with a value that is somewhere between $2,500 and $4,500 and perceive the vacation to be a more attractive deal than it really is.

Research also shows that this underestimation of partitioned prices by consumers is a reliable effect. It occurs in different settings. In one of the most-cited and earliest controlled laboratory studies on this issue[143], participants were asked to choose between telephones and were assigned to one of three conditions. While the identical phone was shown to all participants, in the *all-inclusive price* condition, the phone cost "$82.90, including shipping and handling." Its cost was expressed as "$69.95 plus $12.95 for shipping and handling" in the *partitioned dollar price* condition and the *partitioned percentage price* condition, it was "$69.95 plus 18.5% of the price for shipping and handling." Participants in all three conditions were later asked to recall the phone's price.

Those given the all-inclusive price recalled $83.90 (slightly higher than the actual price), the partitioned dollar price group recalled $80.36, and the partitioned percentage price group recalled $75.43. In other words, both groups given partitioned prices recalled lower prices than those given all-inclusive prices. The study's authors concluded that approximately a quarter of the study participants who saw partitioned prices completely ignored the surcharge when recalling the telephone's price afterward, and 55% failed to fully account for the surcharge. In a meta-analysis of 43 studies, researchers found that partitioned pricing leads to an average of 9% increase in customer preference when compared to all-inclusive pricing[144].

In another study, the buyers' bids were higher in eBay auctions that listed shipping and handling costs separately instead of offering free shipping[145]. A third study showed that consumers are more sensitive to product prices than they are to the amount of the sales tax they would have to pay on the purchase[146]. These findings have led some researchers to claim that everything being the same, partitioned pricing increases consumer demand relative to all-inclusive pricing, which also means sellers have higher pricing power when using partitioned pricing[147]. This is the power of partitioning prices in a nutshell.

Behavioral economics research on partitioned pricing provides six critical insights to managers. First, even though all the surcharges are neatly listed on the bill, invoice, or website, and in that sense, they are more visible and transparent than an all-inclusive price, consumers underestimate the total amount of the surcharges. Partitioned prices create the *illusion of transparency*. Consumers tend to mentally process the base price more thoroughly than they process the ancillary prices.

The second insight is that the harder the company makes it for the consumer to work out the calculations in their head to determine the total price, the lower is the consumer's estimate of the total price. Instead of listing all the surcharges as dollar amounts, listing them as percentages serves to enhance customers' perceptions of value.

Third, partitioned prices have a peculiar benefit that managers should be aware of. When prices are partitioned, they focus the consumer's attention on the product's secondary attributes that are tagged with distinct prices which might otherwise have been overlooked[148]. This effect is especially useful for managers selling niche products with specific secondary features that are superior to those offered by the market leader.

For example, if the Costco Travel package to Hawaii is sold using partitioned prices instead of one all-inclusive price, potential buyers will be more likely to consider the offers of the airline and the rental car company in the package more closely, weighing their respective quality to a greater extent, instead of just focusing on the hotel. This effect of partitioned prices is beneficial if the product excels on secondary features, and the company wants to use them as differentiators. For instance, if the Hawaii package includes airline tickets from a reputed, high-quality airline, potential buyers will be more likely to notice this and lean towards purchasing the package if the price is partitioned instead of all-inclusive.

The fourth practical benefit of using partitioned pricing is that they make the product appear to be an excellent deal when it is being compared to its alternatives. This issue is significant in online and mobile shopping where customers compare different offers side-by-side before making a choice. This is one reason why hotels decouple their room rate from resort fees, and partition other charges such as parking, internet access, and breakfast, even when such charges are mandatory.

Imagine what would happen if one hotel combined all these charges and quoted an all-inclusive price while its competitors partitioned its prices? The hotel with all-inclusive prices would appear far more expensive than its competitors and would be relegated to the bottom in consumers' online searches sorted on price. Even when one major player starts using partitioned pricing consistently, the advantage gained in consumer consideration and preference forces competitors to adopt the same method. Very quickly, using partitioned pricing becomes the norm[149].

Fifth, when they use partitioned pricing, managers enjoy new degrees of freedom for designing price promotions, price discriminating between customer groups, and taking opportunistic advantage of revenue-earning opportunities. The sale of frequent flier award airline tickets for international travel is a case in point. As described earlier, when customers buy international tickets, many airlines charge ambiguous carrier-imposed fees, which often constitute a significant part of the total ticket price. When frequent fliers want to redeem their miles for an international airline ticket, they still have to pay the surcharge in addition to government taxes and fees. Calling it "carrier-imposed confusion," a *Wall Street Journal* reporter pointed out that,

"The "free" ticket you buy with miles may require an additional $400, $500 or more—most of that pocketed by the airline.[150]"

Sixth, when presented with a partitioned price offer, customers care about the value of the components and their corresponding prices. Research has shown that perceptions of fairness and transparency play an important role in how consumers evaluate the offer. When a partitioned price has two components, customers prefer the higher price component to be associated with the higher-value benefit and vice versa[151]. If an eBay seller charges separately for shipping and handling, customers prefer that the product cost more and the shipping fee cost less. Similarly, the room rate at a resort should be higher than the resort fee, the pizza should have a higher price than the delivery service charge, and the airline ticket price should be higher than the carrier-imposed surcharge, for the best customer response to partitioned prices.

The main lesson from considering the choice between all-inclusive pricing versus partitioned pricing for presenting prices is this. Managers should use all-inclusive pricing when the goal is to highlight the simplicity and clarity of the offer's price as a key differentiator to attract customers who value these qualities and are enraged by surcharges. However, partitioned pricing will work better if the manager wants to create an illusion of transparency and increase the chances that customers will underestimate the offer's total price, or if they want to get customers to pay attention to the product's secondary attributes, and to be competitive when customers make direct price comparisons between the different available offers in the marketplace.

CHAPTER 6

Negotiating Price

Let every eye negotiate for itself and trust no agent.

— William Shakespeare, Much Ado About Nothing.

In business-to-business settings, prices have always been fluid and negotiable. For more than a century now, by contrast, most consumer goods and services, especially everyday purchases, have been sold using posted fixed prices without allowing customers to haggle. The introduction of fixed prices goes even further back. Business historian James Morris discovered that by as early as 1830, many country store proprietors in the United States were using a single-price system for selling essential commodities such as salt, flour, and sugar[152]. From these early beginnings, in one product category after another, merchants and retailers transitioned from negotiated prices to fixed prices between 1860 and 1920. The main reason for this shift was convenience. As stores became larger, carried more products and served more customers, fixed prices sped up purchase transactions by an order of magnitude or greater. Speed became increasingly significant as branded, standardized products became common in American stores[153].

Almost Every Price is Negotiable

No one will get a bargain he does not ask for. – French Proverb.

We have come full circle. Today, fixed posted prices remain little more than a crumbling tradition, sustained only by consumers' inertia and their ingrained reticence to haggle. The price of virtually every product, from a car or a vacation package to a ham or a bruised banana in a supermarket, or a double espresso in a coffee shop is, more often than not, negotiable[154]. The only hurdle to fluid prices is that in most cases, the consumer must initiate the negotiation process with the seller by stepping up and asking to pay a lower amount than what the price tag says. Few individual consumers know that it is ok to haggle in supermarkets, department stores, or coffee shops. Among those that know, only a minority dare or bother to do so.

Technology-driven pricing and changing cultural norms both favor the eventual abandonment of stable, fixed prices, and the adoption of negotiated prices. On the technology front, there is a strong push for customized prices due to the widespread adoption of price optimization software. Consider the similarities between today's algorithm-based customized prices and prices established through bargaining a century and a half ago. According to historian Steven Gelber:

> "Prior to the 20th century, consumption was almost always a personal transaction between a vendor (who was often also the producer) and a buyer, both of whom were likely to know each other as individuals in a unique interpersonal relationship. That broader knowledge of the other complexified the commercial relationship because it triggered feelings that transcended the simple exchange of value. Knowing that the other person was, for example, wealthy or strapped for cash, had a large family or was living alone, was a member of one or another socio-ethnic subculture, and so forth all altered the power relationship in the deal, and virtually every purchase was indeed a deal. Because the price for any item was established at the time of its sale through negotiation, that price often reflected not only the strict exchange value of the item to each party, but possibly also the constraints of ingroup sympathy, the opportunism of out-group antipathy, or particular knowledge of the other person's strengths or vulnerabilities[155]."

142

Today's buyers and sellers have "deep knowledge" of each other

Exactly the same type and degree of personal information that Gelber refers to are available to buyers and sellers today. In the 1800s, they learned about each other through a life-long interpersonal relationship. Today, they know these things through the collection of comprehensive attitudinal and behavioral consumer data by the company, and from intense online research conducted by the customer. We are reverting to the "deep knowledge" of the pre-industrial era insofar as understanding the momentary value of a purchase transaction is concerned. To give one example, today, when consumers conduct repeated searches for a particular airfare within a short window of time, they are likely to encounter increased prices on the sites of online travel agencies[156]. The seller learns something specific about the customer's needs and motivations from their observed behavior and adjusts its price quote instantaneously.

There is a second practical reason why customized pricing favors bargaining between buyer and seller during purchase transactions. When companies adopt customized pricing strategies, their pricing schedules become more complex, with many more acceptable price levels for each product and different types and amounts of incentives on offer. For instance, a company may vary the discounts it offers its customers, changing them to 5%, 10%, 12.5%, 15%, and so on depending on time, popularity, etc. and then rotate through these discount levels for the products or services in its product line or catalog.

Relative to simple, steady prices, a complex and unstable price schedule creates more opportunities and a greater openness to negotiating prices. If something was selling for a 20% discount yesterday and today's discount is only 10%, many consumers will think it is perfectly reasonable to ask the store clerk for yesterday's 20% off price. The insertion of online intermediaries in many consumer product categories further encourages customers to negotiate. These entities are less invested in maintaining the product's brand image and are more open to offering on-the-spot discounts to move inventory or close the sale. They don't have the same emotional reluctance to vary prices that a manufacturer who owns the brand and is concerned about its price image may have.

The "Marie Kondo effect" on bargaining by customers

Separately, spurred on by the Great Recession of 2008-2009, cultural trends encouraging frugality and minimalism have become very popular[157]. Just witness the Marie Kondo mania of early 2019 where ideas on tidying up developed by the Japanese organization and de-cluttering consultant spread like wildfire in the American mainstream culture[158]. Movements that support frugality, minimalism, and decluttering are based on the principles that consumers should make purchase decisions carefully, buy and consume less, and use every avenue at their disposal to pay the least amount and get the most value for their money when making purchases.

The widespread acceptance of such an *extreme value mindset* means that consumers want to play an active role in establishing prices. More consumers are becoming amenable to bargaining, even in product categories where everyone viewed prices as fixed until recently. For example, one woman recounted her surprise on the *Make Love, Not Debt* blog: "I was in line at the deli counter behind a tiny, sweet old lady [at a large chain grocery store]. She pointed at a small end of a ham in the display and asked the clerk to weigh it for her. It was about half a pound. What happened next floored me. "Will you sell it to me for half price?" she asked the clerk. "Yes," he said, and wrapped it up for her." Similar experiences occur in upscale stores, as the *New York Times* reported in this 2009 article:

> "Scott Stuart was at the Bloomingdale's store in Manhattan when a salesman sidled up to him, said a private sale was underway and offered him a discount on the slacks he was inspecting. That was last autumn, and in the months since, he has been inundated with similar discount offers. If a salesman does not make one, he has learned to ask. "In another market, I would have found it very inappropriate" to ask for a discount, said Mr. Stuart, a bankruptcy lawyer who works in New York and Chicago. "In this market, I'm finding it incredibly appropriate"[159]."

Personal finance bloggers have refined the idea of "bargain when you buy anything" even further by trying different haggling methods in different settings and then sharing those that work with their readers. For example, on the personal finance blog *Wisebread*, Kyle James provides suggestions for how to haggle in grocery stores: "The keys to negotiating at the grocery store are always to be polite and have a friendly conversation rather than be demanding. Throw in a legitimate reason to ask for that discount, and you stand a great chance of saving money on your next trip[160]." With each passing year, more and more consumers haggle when they are shopping for groceries, buying a cup of coffee, booking a hotel room, or purchasing jewelry[161]. The consumer inertia and reticence to negotiate pointed out earlier in this chapter is receding slowly but steadily.

In the NACJ framework, *negotiating* is a distinct psychological and behavioral consumer state that is commonly preceded by the states of *deciding* and *evaluating* and followed by *buying* and *using*. When the customer is in the *negotiating* state, they are close to opening their wallet and buying the product, but they are not quite there yet. They want to make sure they get the best possible deal the seller can offer them.

In this chapter, we will consider some ways in which psychological pricing can be used to involve customers in deciding the final price. Behavioral economists call these methods *participative pricing* to acknowledge that customers play an active role in the pricing decision[162]. *Pay What You Want* pricing, where the customer is in complete control and decides how much to pay, is the most extreme form of participative pricing. We will look at the business logic behind this method, its results for sellers, and cases where it is successful. Another participative pricing method is *Name Your Own Price*, in which the seller has more control over the final price. We will study its logic and customers' response to it. This chapter concludes by considering the psychology of frequent price changes and how they affect customer decision making. The case of Uber's surge pricing provides insights into customer reactions and potential solutions to the problems that arise from fluctuating prices.

The Pay What You Want (PWYW) Pricing Strategy

I can literally remember a couple of kids - local kids walked into our store in Clayton, Mo. And they walked up to the counter kind of laughing. And they said, I'll have three smoothies and two roast beef sandwiches. And here's my dad's credit card. Put three bucks on it.
— Ron Shaich, Founder of Panera Bread[163].

The most extreme form of participative pricing is to put the customer in the driver's seat by letting them decide how much they want to pay for the product. Many managers are interested in considering this pricing method, called *Pay What You Want* (PWYW) pricing or *elective pricing* by academics. At first blush, it appears to be a promising approach that demonstrates real put-your-money-where-your-mouth-is customer focus. What can be a more authentic way to acknowledge the customer's power in the relationship? PWYW pricing capitalizes on the culturally universal psychological norm of reciprocity, an individual's obligation to respond to positive behavior directed at them with corresponding positive behavior[164]. This is one reason why PWYW pricing is often considered by non-profits or used as a way to supplement charity-based revenue models or charity promotions.

PWYW pricing works as follows. The seller provides a good quality product to its customers and lets them consume or experience it. In a restaurant that uses PWYW pricing, for instance, the patron orders and enjoys the meal. The buyer is then given complete discretion to pay what they want for the product. The company does not send any invoices or present any bills. In some cases, it may proffer a suggested price to the consumer to serve as a reference price[165]. But, by and large, the customer pays if they want to and as much as they want to. And they don't pay anything if they feel so inclined. PWYW pricing has been adopted in many industries, including restaurants, video games, museums, orchestras, online music, software, movie theaters, and even advertising agencies[166].

Illustration by Shirin Abvabi

The business logic behind PWYW pricing is three-fold. Its first benefit is that by using it, the seller conveys authentic confidence in its offerings that is very hard to replicate any other way. Using PWYW pricing signals to the customer, "We are so sure you will like our product that you will pay a fair price for it." Second, because of its relative rarity as a pricing strategy, PWYW pricing creates instant differentiation from competitors. When every other all-you-can-eat restaurant charges a fixed price, the one that uses PWYW pricing is distinctive and memorable. Startups love it for this reason. PWYW pricing is also popular in non-profits when the buyer's payment is a charitable donation, and where revenue from PWYW sales is supplemented with other methods that sustain the business including volunteer labor, money donations from other sources, subsidized inputs, and so on[167].

The third benefit of PWYW pricing is that it empowers customers. This pricing method communicates that the business trusts them. This is a valuable signal in the current business environment, where a low degree of trust is the norm[168]. In exchange, the seller gives up control entirely to the customer to assess the product's economic value. From the customer's perspective, this way of pricing forces them to think of the company in relational terms and not kill the goose that lays golden eggs. For instance, they could skip out of paying and get free food today, but this will increase the chances of the PWYW restaurant going out of business. PWYW pricing is value-based pricing in its purest and most unilateral form.

The transfer of pricing power from the business to the customer required by PWYW pricing is a double-edged sword. If a significant number of customers choose not to think relationally, and underpay significantly, the business quickly falls into dire financial straits[169]. When a seller uses PWYW pricing, it needs to establish some boundaries to tackle the problem of freeloading patrons head-on. At one Denver-based PWYW restaurant, the owner warns non-payers the first time. If they continue to underpay, they are banned from returning. Some conscientious customers also have trouble with PWYW pricing. The downside of empowering customers is that they are forced to do the cognitive work to figure out what the fair price for the product or service should be. Some customers may feel confused or conflicted about the appropriate price to pay, or uncomfortable with having to engage in such a transaction and stay away altogether.

What happens when businesses adopt PWYW pricing?

In October 2016, when a new restaurant opened in Guiyang China, the owners decided to use PWYW pricing as a trial inducement strategy. Their motives relied on the aforementioned "give-and-take" logic of expected reciprocity. The restaurant had just opened its doors and wanted to encourage as many customers to try it as quickly as possible. It launched with a PWYW price promotion for a limited time. Customers could order as much food and drink as they liked and pay whatever they wanted after the meal. No questions asked. Like most trial pricing offers, the restaurant expected to lose some money in the beginning but earn it back when satisfied customers returned and paid full price during future visits.

This was the restaurant owners' theory anyway. What transpired was an unmitigated disaster. Within a week of opening, the restaurant had lost over 100,000 RMB (around $15,000 at the time), a substantial portion of the owners' total capital. Even worse, the day after the PWYW promotion ended, not a single person showed up to eat there at the regular menu price, leaving the restaurant owners heartbroken. The owner pathetically concluded: "If our food or service was the problem, then that would be one thing. But according to customer feedback, our dishes are both filling and tasty. It's just that the payments don't match up with the evaluations[170]." Other restaurants in China have tried PWYW pricing with similar results. One restauranteur who wanted to restore "a long-lost sense of trust in Chinese society" lost 250,000 RMB (or $37,500) in the first three months of operating his PWYW restaurant[171].

In Europe, a rigorously conducted field experiment by marketing professors in a Frankfurt Germany restaurant found that when the operator replaced the 8.99 Euro price for its lunch buffet with PWYW pricing for two weeks, customers paid an average of 19% less money. In the different setting of a movie theater, ticket revenues per customer dropped by 28% when fixed prices were replaced with PWYW prices. In a café, however, customers paid 10% more for cappuccinos and espressos under the PWYW price compared to the fixed price. On balance, just like the Chinese restaurants, PWYW pricing led to lower earnings per customer but more customer visits in Germany. Closer to home, in the United States, restaurant chain Panera Bread has repeatedly tried PWYW pricing in some of its stores but has not been consistently successful.

The evidence suggests that despite its potential benefits in achieving differentiation and empowering customers, PWYW pricing is far too risky to use as a general pricing strategy. Managers interested in adopting it as a primary pricing strategy should do so with caution and after proper due diligence. Running limited tests or field experiments to ascertain its suitability first is advisable.

Special cases where PWYW pricing schemes are successful

Despite the negative assessment as a broad pricing method, there are some specialized instances where PWYW pricing has been shown to work well. Let's consider each of these special cases to understand the boundaries within which to consider PWYW pricing as a viable pricing method.

1) To boost last-minute sales to fill empty capacity. Hotels, airlines, and even the Indianapolis zoo, vary their prices frequently and in a wide range in response to fluctuations in consumer demand. When demand is high, either because of seasonal or idiosyncratic factors, prices rise. It is during periods of low demand that PWYW pricing can be useful to attract customer attention and utilize perishable spare capacity. The Tricycle theater in Kilburn England is an exemplar of this pricing approach[172]. It makes PWYW tickets available only for some of the performances and restricts purchase to the day of the event. This allows the theater to fill any remaining seats with thrifty people who buy PWYW tickets at lower than regular prices but does not steal away sales of full-paying customers who are intolerant of the uncertainty and unwilling to wait until the end.

2) Where customers have an entrenched relationship with the business or are communally-minded. As the Chinese restaurant PWYW failures demonstrated, PWYW pricing can be ineffective for new companies as a way to induce trial and build buzz. This is because new customers have little attachment to the business or concern about its welfare. They tend to take advantage of PWYW pricing to get a deal while it is available and then move on to greener pastures afterward. Using the golden goose analogy again, new customers have not yet come to appreciate the goose's value, so they do not care if it perishes.

By contrast, when customers are regulars, know the owner, and have to hand over money face-to-face after a PWYW purchase, they are more likely to pay a reasonable price. Similarly, people who are communally-oriented (i.e., interested in the welfare and needs of others and in building reciprocal relationships) also tend to pay more[173]. For instance, the authors of the German field experiments described earlier credited the café's success with PWYW pricing to its chatty owner, who knew all his guests on a personal level. PWYW pricing was effective because the guests felt a connection to him and his café. Reciprocity worked well under these circumstances, and many regulars tended to pay more instead of less under PWYW pricing. Similarly, when the band Radiohead famously released its album "In Rainbows" digitally with a "digital tip jar," it was a financial win. The band ascribed this success to its existing base of loyal fans who were more than happy to pay a fair price although cutting out the intermediary helped as well[174].

Some experts argue that the success of a business that uses PWYW pricing such as a restaurant should be seen as an indicator of a local community's cohesion and willingness to support its members. When a community is tightly-knit, and people have strong relationships with each other and with the owners of a PWYW pricing restaurant, they will want to support the venture by paying fair or even high prices and subsidizing their less fortunate neighbors. PWYW pricing will thrive. In local communities, the PWYW pricing method is a way to advance a social movement, not just a pricing model[175].

3) When the seller's earnings are given to charity. In a 2010 paper in *Science*, a team of researchers led by Ayelet Gneezy conducted a field experiment selling souvenir photos after a roller-coaster ride using PWYW pricing. Some customers were told half the money they paid for their photograph would go to charity, while the others were told nothing. Without the charity explanation, customers only paid an average of $.92 when purchasing their photograph. In the charity condition, however, people paid $5.33[176]. For context, the regular fixed price for the photograph was $12.95. The authors deemed the incremental sales with PWYW pricing to be a success because far more people purchased the photograph than usual. The charity explanation can be made even more potent by changing the pricing method's name. In a study, when researchers called the PWYW offer a "Donate What You Want" offer, it boosted purchase rates and amounts paid by customers[177].

Research has also found it doesn't matter how much of the customer's payment is given to charity. Whether 1% of the PWYW price is donated to charity or 99%, people pay about the same[178]. A variation of charity contribution is reducing resource wastage. Restaurants all over the United Kingdom use PWYW pricing to sell food they would have thrown away. By doing this, they achieve two important goals concurrently. They generate incremental revenue and reduce food waste[179]. In the United States, several experimental restaurants have started using PWYW pricing recently to feed the needy and reduce food wastage. But these ventures are usually underwritten by religious organizations and philanthropists and are non-profits.

Using a high anchor price to guide customer decision making is helpful

One of the core psychological concerns about the PWYW pricing method is that it leaves customers to come up with the fair price they should pay. If you wish to use PWYW pricing, you should consider providing customers with guidance about the reasonable price. You may even want to provide a relatively high price as an anchor. In one study, researchers set up a glazed donut stand in an outdoor plaza and sold donuts by allowing customers to choose a price without any guidance ("Pay What You Want"), or by giving them a low anchor ("$0.25 or Pay What You Want") or a high anchor ("$1.75 or Pay What You Want")[180]. Customers paid $1.04 when the high anchor was given, but only $0.44 when the $0.25 low anchor was given. Without any anchor, they paid an average of $0.66 for a donut. Anchors, particularly high ones, can be used to boost the prices paid by customers with PWYW pricing.

We conclude that for most companies, PWYW pricing is too risky and unproven to employ as a broad-based, sustainable pricing strategy to price all products and services all the time. It is difficult to find a single for-profit company that uses PWYW pricing broadly and consistently to make money and thrive in the marketplace. However, as a niche pricing strategy that is employed for specific purposes such as filling excess capacity at the last minute, drawing in new customer segments, using up food (or other perishables) that would otherwise have gone to waste, or as a way to raise money for charity for a special event or for a limited time, PWYW pricing is an innovative and eye-catching pricing method that cuts through the noise and clutter in the marketplace. There are enough honest and decent people in the world to make this idealistic participative pricing scheme work in well-defined, narrow situations.

The Name Your Own Price (NYOP) Pricing Strategy

The first time I NYOP'd is a distant memory, but the rush of success felt after my price was accepted feels brand new every single time. – Christina Cross, travel blogger.

Another participative pricing method is Name Your Own Price (NYOP), made famous by Priceline in the late nineteen nineties and adopted by other sellers like online fashion retailer Garmentory, and eBay, with its "Best Offer" feature. In some respects, NYOP pricing is similar to PWYW pricing. Both involve active consumer participation in deciding the final price. But unlike PWYW pricing, the seller has more control in NYOP pricing over how the consumer makes the offer and what the final price paid is. The seller chooses the lowest price it is willing to accept and rejects the buyer's offer if it falls below this threshold. It also withholds information about the specific brand or product until after purchase to earn a higher profit. Because of these features, NYOP pricing is considerably more complex than PWYW pricing for both buyer and seller.

How does the Name Your Own Price pricing work?

NYOP pricing works as follows. (I have simplified the description somewhat for clarity of exposition). The seller provides information to the consumer about the products on offer but usually leaves some features or aspects hidden or unavailable. The best example is Priceline, where the consumer chooses the hotel quality (three-star, four-star, etc.) and location, like Houston's Galleria area. However, they cannot choose one particular hotel when naming their own price. On the side of sellers, hotels listing their properties on Priceline set the minimum prices they are willing to accept. Not surprisingly, this information remains hidden from the buyer. For instance, a hotel may set $80 per night as the minimum threshold price it is willing to accept.

The consumer names their own price by bidding for a four-star Houston-Galleria area hotel room. Priceline then randomly selects one of the listed four-star hotels and checks to see if the customer's bid price exceeds this hotel's threshold price. If yes, the transaction is consummated. The buyer's credit card is charged, and the non-refundable purchase is completed. Priceline earns the difference between the hotel's asking price and the customer's bid price. The customer is told the name of their four-star hotel for the stay.

If the customer's bid is below this first hotel's threshold, Priceline iterates through to the next four-star hotel on this list, and so on, until a hotel that has a lower acceptable price threshold than the customer's bid is found. If the customer bids below the thresholds of all four-star hotels in Houston's Galleria area that have partnered with Priceline, they don't get a room[181]. If they want to bid again right away, they will have to revise their search criteria in some way (e.g., look for a three-star hotel) or wait twenty-four hours to bid using the same criteria. This last constraint stops consumers from bidding strategically and encourages them to name a price they are really willing to pay.

Although NYOP pricing requires customer participation and gives them control over prices, it is far less transparent than PWYW pricing. Marketing experts call NYOP pricing an "opaque pricing model" for two reasons. First, the seller does not provide an initial offer to start the negotiation, although it may provide a high anchor such as the hotel room's regular price. Because of this, there is no explicit starting point the customer can use to begin the bidding process. Second, customers do not know the specific brand they will receive until after they have purchased and paid for the product[182]. For individuals with a strong brand preference, this is disconcerting at best, and unacceptable at worst.

The business appeal of Name Your Own Price pricing

Despite its relative complexity, NYOP pricing can be advantageous to businesses. First, just like PWYW pricing, because it is rare in the marketplace, this method acts as a differentiator. The differentiation is compelling for startups in crowded markets. For example, when online retailer Garmentory launched its site, it sold all its merchandise from small fashion boutiques only using NYOP pricing to attract attention and stand out from hordes of similar sellers. Second, because the prices and offers are relatively hidden, researchers have found that consumers incur substantial *frictional costs* when submitting incremental bids. In one study conducted in Germany, the frictional costs per bid ranged from 3.5 Euros for purchasing an MP3 player to 6.1 Euros for a PDA. (The study was done in 2003, hence the MP3 players)[183]. This burden increases the customer's commitment to the seller once they have begun buying from them. It locks customers in, and over time, it reduces price competition for the seller using NYOP pricing with other fixed price sellers.

Third, NYOP pricing provides an avenue to sell excess capacity or outdated inventory and earn reasonable revenue from these extra sales without hurting the core brand. When an upscale hotel sells its spare perishable inventory of rooms through Priceline, it is essentially shielding its brand from erosion. Only customers who don't care which hotel they stay at will avail of the lower NYOP price. Business travelers will choose to buy through regular channels and pay higher prices to benefit from the hotel's loyalty program. Thus, the hotel can discriminate between clearly distinct segments and price according to their respective valuations. What's more, some hotels may go a step further and design two different offers, a posted fixed-price offer to sell superior rooms through its own website and Online Travel Agencies, and a NYOP price offer for less desirable rooms (such as those with obstructed views, ones located next to the elevator, etc.) through other venues.

The challenges of Name Your Own Price for consumers

The promise of empowerment notwithstanding, NYOP pricing requires the consumer to perform considerable work. The process also snatches away significant aspects of choice from customers, which is a deal-breaker for those who want control over service features beyond price during purchase. And finally, consumers can collaborate and game a seller's NYOP pricing process by exchanging information about bids and outcomes with one another or bid in a coordinated way to discover price thresholds and the lowest successful bid prices[184]. For example, regular Priceline users share their bid amounts and whether they were successful or not on sites like Betterbidding.com.

Because of these drawbacks, the NYOP pricing method has failed to grow beyond a niche method in more than two decades since its introduction. Even Priceline, its earliest and most famous exponent, has curtailed its use, dropping NYOP pricing for airline tickets in 2016, and car rentals in 2018. Marketing experts attribute this retreat to the aforementioned weaknesses of the NYOP pricing method compounded by changing customer expectations and newer competitive options. In the words of Sam Shank, CEO of HotelTonight.com, "Today's booker isn't looking for a commoditized roof over their head. They're seeking unique and memorable experiences[185]." When Garmentory launched its business, it sold its merchandise exclusively using NYOP pricing to stand out in a crowded competitor field. But over time, it pivoted to offering mostly fixed prices, using the exclusivity of the boutiques available through its site as its core differentiator instead of NYOP pricing[186]. The bottom line is that although NYOP pricing sounds glamorous and compelling in theory, it has not yet been widely successful in practice. An ambitious and creative startup founder may yet crack the code of NYOP pricing.

The Psychology of Frequent Price Changes

It's definitely annoying. What exactly is making it go up and down?
– Aishia Senior.

Customers today have to deal with another new phenomenon in many industries – frequently changing prices. Until recently, most businesses changed their prices once or twice a year, usually when they printed new catalogs for customers. Even cutting-edge, upstart online retailers like Amazon did not change their prices all that much. One study analyzed book prices on Amazon over 449 days during 2003 and 2004 and found that a book's price on Amazon changed an average of once every 222 days[187]. In other words, Amazon changed its prices once every seven months or so in the early 2000s. Today, for many products, the retailer changes prices 7 or 8 times a day.

Frequency of price changes has increased significantly

A growing number of businesses use pricing optimization software that links the company's internal costs with data points about their customers' preferences and buying patterns to recommend pricing actions[188]. Much of this data sits in the cloud and is analyzed using sophisticated software. Additionally, many companies have started adopting dynamic pricing algorithms for setting prices. These methods calculate the best prices to charge in real time based on how much customers are buying, what competitors are charging, along with other market variables[189]. Because the pricing decisions are made by algorithms and exclude humans entirely, in theory, businesses can change prices every second, or even instantaneously, if they so choose.

For any enterprise, the biggest constraint to changing prices is *menu costs* – the costs associated with changing prices. Historically, changing prices was expensive and time-consuming. Price lists had to be re-calculated, typed up, and mailed to distributors and customers. New catalogs, labels, menus, and signs had to be printed. Press releases announcing the price changes had to be drafted and sent out[190]. These expenses forced companies to maintain prices for lengthy periods. Over the past few years, however, technology has drastically shifted the economics of changing prices. Menu costs have fallen dramatically. For many companies, it costs virtually nothing to change prices, putting pressure on managers to change prices frequently.

To add fuel to these fires, short-duration price promotions, flash sales, and daily deals have also all become very popular in the last few years. Many sellers see frequent price changes as a way of keeping customers on the hook and luring them back to the store or website. Using the logic that only the most price-sensitive customers will persevere, they see constant changes in price as a smart way to offer discounts selectively, increase customer engagement, and protect their profit margins[191]

It is not at all surprising, then, that everyone from movie theaters to Disney World and even restaurants and frequent flyer programs is changing their prices frequently[192]. Not to mention airlines and hotels, which have relied on frequent price changes as part of their business models for decades. Even on sites like Amazon and other online retailers, as noted earlier, it is now common for prices to change several times a day. But is this necessarily a good thing?

Why customers hate frequent price changes

In a nutshell, no. Sellers should make the *can-should* distinction in weighing the pros and cons of frequent price changes for customers. They should be cautious in separating their technological capabilities, which dictate how often they *can* change prices and their customers' preferences, manifested in how often they *should* change prices. Prices that fluctuate are like *flickering traffic lights to customers. They confuse, they frustrate, they annoy, and they stop customers in their tracks.*

Consumers find it hard to form a reference price. As we have seen earlier in this book, when consumers buy a product, they become knowledgeable about its prices over time[193]. They learn every time they shop or read or hear about prices through advertisements or social media. They form a reference price for the product over time.

This process is disrupted when a product's price constantly changes and fluctuates over a wide range. Many consumers find it hard to form a stable and coherent reference price because of the price volatility. Price transparency is lost, and they have difficulty working out what is driving the price changes, and if these changes make sense.

The buying decision becomes more complex. Under normal circumstances, when purchasing items like groceries, consumers use a relatively simple decision heuristic. They look at the item's price first, then they think of their reference price or range of acceptable prices to gauge whether it is cheap or expensive. They either buy the item or walk away based on this evaluation. (We saw this process play out in different ways in Chapters 4 and 5).

When prices change frequently, however, this process becomes infinitely more complex for consumers[194]. Now the reference price is no longer easily available. In deciding whether to buy, the person has to search at different places, try to remember what they paid last time, check when the price changed and by how much, and so on. What should have been a habitual, straightforward process taking less than a minute has suddenly become complicated and irksome.

Consumers delay purchase. In a complicated buying situation, consumers shift into the mode of questioning, "Should I buy now, or should I wait longer in case the price goes lower?" They do not know when to pull the trigger. Even when prices have dipped, for instance, they will wait for prices to go down even further and end up missing out on what would have been a great deal. Consumer psychology research shows that when decisions become complex, many people delay deciding or back out of it altogether[195]. For example, when the price of a jacket, handbag, or a pair of shoes goes up and down many times a day on an online retailer's site, the best option for many is to tune out and postpone the purchase. The following example from an *Associated Press* news story illustrates this perfectly[196]:

> "Take Aishia Senior, who recently watched the price on a coat she wanted rise and fall several times between $110 and $139 in a span of six hours on Amazon.com. She was so frustrated by the price fluctuations that she ended up not buying the coat on the site at all. "It's definitely annoying," said Senior, who

lives in New Haven, Connecticut. "What exactly is making it go up and down?""

Consumers fixate on prices and ignore other features. Another consequence of constantly changing prices is that it shifts the consumer's attention away from the product's features to its price[197]. As economist Julio Rotemberg observed, "...consumers use nominal price changes as a trigger for reflection about whether producers are fair or not[198]." We are hard-wired to pay attention to stimuli that change and to ignore the stimuli that remain stable[199]. When prices fluctuate constantly but the product's other features remain the same, consumers naturally turn their attention away from the functional and the experiential aspects of the product and focus their attention on price.

Nowhere is this phenomenon more evident in the marketplace than in the furniture category. Marketers have relied on constant sales for the past several years in this industry. Furniture-buyers used to base their purchase choice on factors like the furniture's quality, durability, and brand reputation before this trend began. But nowadays, influenced by the constant hype of sales, many furniture-buyers tend to focus much more on price.

What happens when people weight price too much? They often end up with lower-quality products or services that give them grief instead of providing them with pleasure and satisfaction. Instead of buying something once and using it for a long time, they have to keep replacing shoddy items that were purchased cheaply.

Sellers should make judicious and thoughtful price changes for good reasons

To avoid these problems, sellers need to embrace the idea that prices should be changed for well-considered reasons and with specific goals in mind, not arbitrarily just because it doesn't cost much to change prices. There are a number of legitimate reasons to change prices. For instance, many products are seasonal, and it makes sense to mark down sweaters in April and linen suits in October. Alternatively, a company may want to get rid of its remaining inventory and introduce new versions of its products. Companies like Apple, Sony,

Dell, and LG have to do this every year (or sometimes even more often) when they introduce a new generation of their electronic products. Other valid reasons for changing prices include rising raw material or labor costs, encouraging customers to try something new using limited-time price promotions, and rewarding regular customers with loyalty reward programs.

Another important consideration dictating the frequency of price changes is how often customers purchase the product. A useful rule of thumb is that the highest reasonable frequency of price change is one that mirrors customer purchase frequency. After all, if customers are not going to consider the product more than once or twice a month – this is typically how often many consumable goods such as toilet paper, laundry detergent, and dry goods are purchased[200], it makes little sense to change prices on an hourly basis.

Two other points about changing prices frequently are worth noting. First, as we saw in Chapter 2, how often a company changes prices is an important part of its price image. Prices that change too often are associated with discounters and low-quality vendors by many consumers, whereas prices that remain stable typically signal a premium seller[201]. Price change frequency should match the price image that the manager wants to cultivate for their brand. Second, when lowering prices, the firm should be diligent about explaining its reasons for the price drop publicly, not only to manage competitor reactions but also to avoid falling head-long into a costly price war[202]. The same is true of price increases.

Technology permits companies to make rapid-fire price changes, but customer reactions to such cavalier pricing actions may make quick fluctuations unproductive at best and inflict lasting damage to a company's bottom line at worst. Prices should be changed only as often as the company's tactical objectives and over-arching goals dictate. Next, we will consider Uber's surge pricing in more detail as a concrete case study of the benefits and pitfalls of frequently changing prices for a business and its customers.

The Psychology of Uber's Surge Pricing

I WILL NEVER USE YOUR COMPANY AGAIN! I AM OUT-RAGED AND DISGUSTED THAT YOU WOULD JACK UP YOUR CHARGES THAT MUCH BECAUSE OF A SNOWSTORM!!! – Anonymous Uber rider.

If you use ridesharing services like Uber or Lyft or food delivery services like DoorDash regularly, you have likely encountered surge pricing. Surge pricing is an excellent example of technological affordances and economic principles colliding to result in frequent price changes. Let's examine this pricing method from the perspective of customer psychology.

Earlier in this book, we saw that the market derives equilibrium prices for commodities such as electricity, coffee, and corn. The basic idea is that the fairest price for any product is the equilibrium price at which consumer demand matches the product's available supply[203]. If supply increases, the price should go down; if buyer demand increases, the price should rise. In addition to electricity and fine wine, the phenomenon occurs every year in the secondary market for Super Bowl tickets. Some people may spend thousands of dollars over face value while others may get an outstanding deal. It all depends on which teams are playing in the Super Bowl, the size of their respective fan bases, and how deep the teams' fans' pockets are[204].

Surge pricing used by Uber and other rideshare companies is based on this same logic of market equilibrium, and from a psychological perspective, one of *market-driven fairness*[205]. The idea behind surge pricing is to adjust prices of rides to match driver supply to rider demand at any given time. During periods of excessive demand when there are many more riders than drivers, or when there aren't enough drivers on the road and customer wait times are long, Uber increases its normal fares. They do this by using a *multiplier* whose value fluctuates, depending on the number of available drivers relative to rider demand. On a Friday evening in midtown Houston, for example, the surge fare may be twice the standard fare (in this case the multiplier is two). A few hours later, as fewer drivers remain on the streets, and many more bar-goers want to return home, the multiplier may increase to 4X or 5X. When surge pricing is in effect, Uber's riders are informed that their fares will be higher, and they have to agree to pay the amount. Only then is a driver dispatched to pick them up.

Surge pricing achieves two important objectives for Uber and its customers. The first goal is that it increases the supply of drivers. Lured by the ability to earn more, new drivers clock in, or drivers from other areas home in on the neighborhood with the surge price[206]. In one study conducted in collaboration with Uber, researchers found that surge pricing doubled the number of drivers during a busy period after a sold-out concert in New York City[207]. Another study found that because of the flexibility inherent in their work arrangement, Uber drivers are sensitive to price changes, increasing their hours in response to higher prices[208].

Second, surge pricing is an effective way to control customer demand and allocate available rides to those who place a higher economic value on them. Some Uber customers may deem the surge price to be unacceptable and find other means of transportation. Others who value the ride more will be willing to pay the surge price. What's more, research suggests that Uber's customers are relatively insensitive to surge prices. One large study involving over fifty million rides found customer demand was inelastic. For every 10 percent increase in price, customer demand only dropped by around 5 percent[209]. All of this makes sense from an economic standpoint. However, this logic bypasses the psychology of consumers entirely.

Not surprisingly, while economists have given ringing endorsements to surge pricing[210], customers have reacted with anger, frustration, and sometimes even outrage. The reasons for this mismatch have to do with the psychology of frequent price changes that seem unfair.

Uber's own low regular price makes its surge price seem exorbitant

When consumers use the Uber rideshare service, its standard price sets the reference point for what an Uber ride *should* cost. In most markets, this price is lower than the price of a taxicab or a limousine service. For example, one 2014 test found Uber to be cheaper than a taxi in all twenty-one cities that it considered[211]. Because of the low reference point established by the regular price, when Uber's surge price kicks in, it seems exorbitantly expensive by comparison, even with a low surge multiplier. After all, when a customer has just paid $13 on the way to a party, paying $47 three hours later for the same trip in reverse is bound to seem outrageous[212]. Customers are unable to convert the opportunity costs of having to wait for a lengthy period into dollars and cents.

Bolstering the power of the low reference point is the fact that virtually none of Uber's substitutes, whether it is taxicabs, buses, or the subway, use variable pricing. Consumers have fixed reference points for all of them, and strong expectations that prices will not change. What's more, prices of these alternatives are often significantly lower than Uber's surge prices, and not all of them have the same supply constraints. It's not surprising that stories of disgruntled customers' experiences, such as someone having to pay $14,400 for a twenty-minute ride go viral from time to time and generate a lot of negative publicity among Uber users[213].

Surge prices kick in at the worst possible time for riders

By its very design, Uber's surge pricing kicks in when demand is high when many of its customers are in dire need of the service. And perversely, the more intense the customers' desire for an Uber ride, the higher the surge price is likely to be. Different reasons fuel the desire for Uber rides (and the correspondingly high demand). Large numbers of people want to go out on Friday and Saturday nights, want trips to and from big concerts at around the same time and want to be shuttled to restaurants or other venues on special days like New Year's Eve and Valentine's Day. Many also need rides in the middle of a blizzard or a rainstorm just when few Uber drivers want to be out. It is natural for consumers to feel that Uber is taking advantage of them by ramping up prices when they are in direst need[214]. Explaining the rationale for surge pricing or finding that Uber's customers are relatively inelastic to price increases does not mitigate the inherent sense of injustice. It is not surprising that a Google search with the joint phrases "Uber surge pricing" and "price gouging" generates thousands of hits.

Drastic changes in surge prices create doubt and uncertainty

Compounding the perception problem is the fact that Uber's surge prices fluctuate drastically and all too often. One study found that in Washington DC, surge prices were 2.3 times the normal price at 1:54 pm on a Tuesday in March 2015 but had returned to normal levels just six minutes later. The study also reported that Uber surge prices changed so rapidly, that many changes occurred after every 3 to 5 minutes[215]. Surge prices are also location-specific and may be several times higher in one neighborhood than in another one that is a few streets away. As we have seen, when prices are volatile and fuzzy, many consumers simply stop trusting the company, because they don't know when to purchase and whether they are getting a good deal or getting fleeced.

It is not clear to customers how the surge price multiplier is calculated

Uber uses a sophisticated computational algorithm to figure out how high to raise its surge prices. For riders, the bad news is that the algorithm is a closely guarded secret and far too complicated to understand anyway[216]. This creates the sense that the surge multiplier calculation is a black box. Just as problematic for the consumer, in keeping with the economic theory on which surge pricing is based, there is no upper limit on how high prices can go. Figuring out the surge multiplier is like bidding in an auction: as long as there is an imbalance between supply and demand, the multiplier will keep rising, resulting in the possibility of some Uber riders paying obscene prices. Because of the lack of information or what journalism scholar Nick Diakopoulos has called *algorithmic accountability*, consumers feel powerless and disgruntled when confronted with surge pricing[217].

How can Uber improve its surge pricing method?

All the reasons for rider dissatisfaction have to do with the psychology behind surge pricing. Yet Uber's key differentiator (beyond regular low prices) is the flexibility and convenience it provides its customers. Surge pricing is essential to delivering these differentiated benefits. How can Uber use psychological pricing principles to address the most serious causes of rider dissatisfaction with surge pricing? Considering potential solutions to surge pricing is useful to us because it provides helpful guidance to managers working in other industries who have to deal with the challenges associated with frequently changing prices.

Cap the surge multiplier at a reasonable value and communicate it clearly to customers

As we saw earlier, rideshare users have little understanding of how surge prices change or how high they go. Rideshare users are more likely to express outrage when the multiplier starts rising beyond 5X. That is when the sense of unfairness and lack of synchronicity between customer value and the asking price starts to kick in. Surprisingly, Uber has tested multiplier values as high as 50X in Sweden[218]. Consumer outrage is virtually guaranteed at these levels, even from mild-mannered, easy-going people, because of the magnitude of the unfairness of such a price from a customer value standpoint.

An open-ended cap on the surge multiplier is counterproductive for the company for two important reasons. First, it creates the impression that Uber is out to exploit riders by extracting every single dollar it can. Second, the open-endedness produces uncertainty. The rider is at the mercy of circumstances; the graver the situation, the higher will be the multiplier. For instance, rideshare prices shot up during Hurricane Sandy and the 2016 New York City bombing[219]. It is telling that rideshare drivers do not like very high multipliers either. Not only do they feel embarrassed, but they also believe that they will have to compete with other drivers lured by high prices.

The solution to this problem is straightforward. If the company were to choose a reasonable cap, say 5X, and communicate that the surge price will never go higher, the policy would go a long way in reducing consumer angst and imposing constraints on what appears to be an unbridled pricing method. The idea of applying well-publicized caps or giving customers ranges within which prices will vary also applies to other situations where companies change prices frequently. Knowing the high price or the price range helps customers to evaluate current prices more effectively and make buying decisions confidently.

Reduce the volatility of price fluctuations and make price changes more transparent

Uber riders have vociferously complained that its surge prices fluctuate wildly from one moment to the next and vary considerably from one city block to the next[220]. This problem can be solved by reducing the frequency of price changes. We have played this tune many times before in this chapter, but it's worth playing again. *Just because technology allows a company to change prices instantaneously at little or no cost does not mean it is the best thing to do from the perspective of psychological pricing.* Fewer and more predictable price changes such as higher prices during rush hour or weekend nights and normal prices in late mornings and early afternoons will make the rider experience more predictable and comforting. Much of our discussion on *good-better-best pricing* in Chapter 5 also applies here where the regular ride (and price) is the good version, and service during busy and super-busy times are the better and best versions, respectively.

Explain the beneficial consequences of surge pricing to riders

In pricing terms, this suggestion has to do with explaining value clearly to customers because they have difficulty working out the economic benefits for themselves. Many riders only see the high price they are paying but fail to account for the significant benefits received in return. This is because it is very difficult to evaluate the economic or opportunity costs that the individual would have incurred for a long wait. To deal with customers' price-focused decision calculus, the manager should clearly articulate the benefits customers are receiving for the higher price.

Consider the major supermarket chain, Kroger. On each customer receipt, it prints a detailed accounting of savings the customer earned by using manufacturers' coupons, in-store promotions, and customer loyalty programs. The "You saved $X today" on the receipt ends the customer's grocery shopping transaction on a high note. Similarly, when Netflix increased its price in April 2019, it provided an explanation and underscored the value offered by its service: "Your monthly price is increasing to $12.99 on Wednesday, May 22, 2019. Why? We're hard at work improving Netflix so that you can have even more great TV shows and movies to enjoy. Here's to watching what you want, when you want, where you want."

Such explanations are even more important when higher surge prices are being charged. Going the extra mile and explaining to the rider that "Because of the surge price, you had to wait 30 minutes less this evening" or "It would have taken you 45 minutes to reach your destination had you taken a taxi, but it only took you 20 minutes today because you used us" with a text at the end of the trip can help to clarify the value of surge pricing to riders.

Rebrand surge pricing and call it something more consumer-friendly.

The phrase *surge pricing* is descriptive and accurate, but it likely originates from an economist's mind, not a marketer's imagination. The Merriam-Webster dictionary defines a surge as "to suddenly increase to an unusually high level[221]." From a customer perspective, surging is never a good thing for any price to do. It is natural that most people who are not trained as economists associate surge pricing with price gouging.

When marketers are challenged by a particular name's meaning or perception, they rebrand. Surge pricing could be replaced with a term that describes the method's benefits to riders instead of the rapid velocity with which prices increase. Alternative labels such as *convenience pricing* (it reduces rider wait time), *certainty pricing* (it provides certainty about getting the service and telling the rider in advance what they will pay before the ride) or *priority pricing* (it gives priority to riders who really need the service) are all more accurate and customer-friendly names for this pricing method than surge pricing. Whichever term is chosen, the "surge" label should be replaced because of the negative psychological connotations associated with it.

Uber's surge pricing offers a powerful example of how technology and economics have combined to create a sophisticated pricing approach involving frequent price changes, without letting customers participate effectively in the pricing process. It is rideshare service users who choose Uber over Lyft, a taxicab, or a bus, who experience the service, and who pay the asking price. It is vital to consider and manage their reactions to the pricing. Just because technology allows the company to raise prices without limit and change them every few minutes does not mean this is the best thing to do if the manager's goal is to influence, sell to, and satisfy customers.

CHAPTER 7

How Can I Get You to Buy?

Oh Mr. Tesco, I simply cannot resist your marvelous bargains.

– Gail Honeyman, Eleanor Oliphant is Completely Fine.

In the ebb and flow of most customer journeys, purchase represents a crucial milestone. Marketers expend tremendous resources in encouraging and guiding the consumer through the different pre-purchase decision making states such as *browse*, *search*, and *explore*, in the NACJ framework, and in maintaining a connection with the customer through the post-purchase states such as *share*, *bond*, and *review*. The marketer's actions in each of these states shapes the customer's relationship with the company. Yet, what ultimately counts are actual purchases. Every customer purchase contributes to the company's financial top line and bottom line and vouches for the effectiveness of the pricing strategy. All marketer actions have the ultimate ambition of getting the customer to purchase.

Figure 7.1 The transition from other psychological states to the buy state.

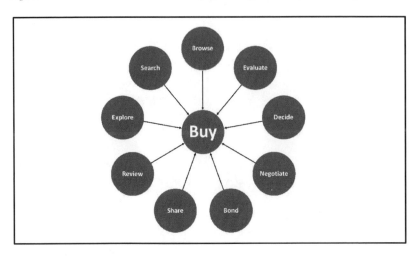

From the perspective of psychological pricing, the manager's goal is to transition the customer from the other psychological states in the NACJ framework to the *buy* state, as shown in Figure 7.1. Price plays a vital role in making this transition happen. In this chapter, we will consider how managers can use pricing actions effectively to close the sale and influence the acts of purchase and repurchase by the customer. We will discuss the roles played by point-of-purchase pricing tactics that include sale signs and other related visual cues, limited-time promotions, price-matching guarantees, and scarcity pricing in stimulating purchase. We will conclude the chapter by considering how sellers can use the goal gradient motivation of consumers to design loyalty reward programs that not only encourage customers to purchase but accelerate their purchases and re-engage them.

Marketers refer to the retailing environment, whether it is physically in a store or online, where the customer has the opportunity to complete the purchase transaction as the *point of purchase*. Customers are typically in the middle of their decision journeys when they get to the point of purchase. Some customers have conducted research beforehand, narrowed down options, and may even have a particular item in mind that they want to buy. Others are in the middle of a mood-repairing browsing episode without any clear purchase intentions. Still others have taken the cue from another customer's referral or review without making much of an effort to research the different options for themselves. Regardless of these differences in customer journeys, the question we will answer is, "what pricing tactics can the seller use at the point of purchase to encourage the customer to complete the purchase transaction?"

Sale Signs and Other Related Visual Cues

We're chemically programmed to respond to sales. There are hormones in our brain that activate when you see a sale. – Mark Ellwood[222].

In Chapter 2, we saw that charm prices are effective in communicating the seller's low price image to customers. In addition to price endings, amongst the most cost-effective methods to encourage customers to buy at the point of purchase is to employ "sale" signs or other signs conveying that prices are attractive. Examples of other signs include "Low Prices," "Bargains," "Great Deals Today," and "Priced to Save." Academic researchers call these signs *promotion signals* because they are meant to draw the attention of customers to the seller's current prices, create the impression that deals are available at the point of purchase, and hasten the customer's purchase[223].

One significant property of sale signs is that they are non-specific. They do not provide specific information about what is on sale, for how long, what the original or discounted prices are or how deep the discount is. Yet sale signs act as powerful visual cues that convey the seller's price is attractive and offers a good value when compared to competitors' price or even the seller's past or future prices[224]. They influence customers' decisions and increase demand[225]. The effect of sale signs occurs in the light of relatively poor price knowledge of customers that we covered extensively in Chapter 3. A customer may not know what the product's actual price is or whether the discounted price is substantially different from the original price, but they will respond viscerally to the idea that the item is on sale and that is a good deal. In the words of a store manager at HEB, a Texas-based supermarket chain:

"Occasionally we attach signs marked "Everyday Low Price" in front of two randomly selected brands in several product categories throughout our store, leaving their prices unchanged. Even though customers should be accustomed to these signs and realize that the prices are unchanged, sales typically double for those brands that have the signs attached to their displays. I'm just amazed[226]."

Another benefit of sale signs, compared to other methods of stimulating purchase, is that they can be used flexibly by the seller. Sale signs can be placed next to individual price-tags to draw the customer's attention to a particular price promotion. Or they can be displayed more generally to showcase entire product categories in the store that are on promotion. They can even be used as banners or window signs to signify that deals are to be found throughout the store.

Sale/ Photo by Justin Lim/ Unsplash

Sale signs work because they have been accompanied historically by actual price promotions. Most customers possess a strong and relatively accurate association between a sale sign and a price promotion. When they see a sale sign, many customers may simply use it as a proxy for a price cut or another price promotion and infer that the product is on sale. Their expectations that the on-sale product's price will be lower in the future are reduced. Sale signs help customers lean in favor of purchasing right away, instead of searching elsewhere, or postponing purchase to a later date.

Sale signs work best when they are used sparingly and legitimately by the seller. One study found that tacking sale signs on more than 30% of the frozen juice SKUs in a Chicago supermarket reduced consumer demand for the product category. Putting 20% of the items within a category on sale was enough to achieve the highest demand. Another study found a similar effect in a printed catalog. In this case, the downswing in demand occurred when more than 25% of the items in the catalog went on sale. The lesson from these studies is that managers should not use sale signs on more than 20-25% of the products they sell at any one time.

Blanket store-wide or site-wide sales ("Everything's on sale") are less effective in increasing demand that selective sales for a limited period. Managers should note that this finding does not apply to signs meant to create a favorable low price image for the store or the website as a whole, like Walmart's "Low prices. Every day. On everything" signs. But the advice of being cautious and using sales signs judiciously and accurately applies here.

Research also shows that when sales of the product that has the sale sign increases, at least some of that demand is "stolen" from alternatives that are not on sale. (After all, if the customer purchases the brand of frozen orange juice that is on sale, they are going to forgo other frozen orange juice brands that are not on sale). From the NACJ framework perspective, a sale sign not only transitions the customer from a pre-purchase state into the buy state, but it also influences the customer's purchase choice.

A robust finding from the behavioral economics research is that sellers should avoid using sales signs or related visual cues willy-nilly or in sneaky ways. The power of sale signs comes from the historical trust and credibility that has built up around this visual cue. Customers use them in their decision calculus only because they are true most of the time. When sellers try to game customers, either by making false claims about merchandise being on sale when it is not, or even worse, resorting to unethical practices like putting things on sale permanently, or using artificially inflated and meaningless initial prices and then offering equally dicey deep discounts off these values which are not really discounts at all, such schemes can backfire. Consider the experience of a consumer named Lauren Taylor Baker, recounted in the *Wall Street Journal*[227]:

> "Lauren Taylor Baker, a 31-year-old digital entrepreneur in Atlanta, says she used to get a thrill from finding a great bargain marked "final sale." "I have reached the end of the rainbow," she would tell herself. "It's the best price." But after several final-sale purchases she regretted, Ms. Baker says she feels burned and no longer believes a final-sale price is the lowest it will go. Now, she says, when shopping for something marked final sale, she ignores the original full price and evaluates it based on quality and fit. "I've trained myself to go into battle immediately," Ms. Baker says. "Who likes being held against a wall?"

As academic researchers Eric Anderson and Duncan Simester point out, "A firm's reputation may be irreparably damaged if consumers expect that a price cue signals a promoted price and later discover that the price is not discounted[228]." Numerous retailers like Kohl's, J.C. Penney, Zara, and Amazon have been sued successfully by consumers in recent years for using misleading or deceptive methods to communicate sales and comparative discounts[229].

And finally, sale signs and other visual cues of an attractive price only make sense if they are consistent with the company's pricing strategy and contribute positively to its brand equity. For ultra-premium brands, using sale signs without a plan will backfire. At luxury jeweler Tiffany & Co., internal marketing research showed that customers were put off when the chain started offering 20% off sales on items like pearl earrings and bracelets. According to one Tiffany executive, "We certainly don't engage in price promotion. We say, 'Here's the product and here's the price, and the price is justified[230].'" Similarly, brands like Chanel, Hermès and Louis Vuitton rarely use sales signs or other visual cues indicating attractive prices[231]. The success of their respective brands hinges on doing precisely the opposite to what sales signs do, which is to use cues to communicate scarcity and exclusivity.

Limited-Time Promotions

Regret is a censure of yourself for missing something beneficial. – Marcus Aurelius, Meditations.

When designing a price promotion, the manager makes several important decisions such as which products to promote, how much discount or other incentives to offer, whether to make special offers such as Buy One Get One and how to publicize the promotion. However, to get the customer to push the "Buy" button, perhaps the most important question of all is how long the promotion should run. Expiration terms influence *when* the customer makes the purchase. A carefully incorporated time restriction into the pricing offer, in and of itself, acts as an effective purchase trigger for customers.

In 2011, when daily deal promotion sites like Groupon and Living-Social were booming, I conducted a descriptive analysis of a Groupon promotion for a startup called Gourmet Prep Meals[232]. The company had launched just two months earlier and sold premium ready-to-cook meal kits throughout the Houston metro area when it ran a Groupon promotion. Its purpose was to gain exposure to new customers. The Groupon offered a deal of $25 worth of products for $12. The promotion ran at the end of September 2010, and the company sold over 600 Groupon vouchers. The vouchers were valid for a period of six months from October 1, 2010, to March 31, 2011. Among other things, we examined the rate of Groupon redemptions throughout the promotion in the study. Figure 7.2 shows the pattern of voucher redemptions.

Limited-time coupons redemptions have bimodal distributions

Academic research on limited-time promotions has found that the redemption pattern of customers follows a bimodal distribution[233]. As

Figure 7.2 shows, this is also what we found. In the first few weeks of the promotional period, a disproportionately high number of Groupon purchasers redeemed the voucher likely because it was top-of-mind (they had just purchased it). In addition to being top-of-mind, early redemption for a limited-time promotion is also driven by the fact that early redeemers are eager beavers. They are likely to be enthusiastic or curious about the seller's products and services and use the promotion as a way to try new things.

Figure 7.2 Rate of Groupon redemptions over the promotion period for Gourmet Prep Meals.

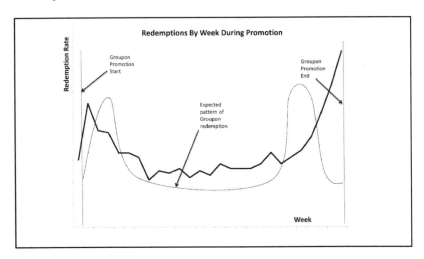

Once this customer group had redeemed their Groupons, the redemption rate dwindled, as seen in Figure 7.2. It picked up again towards the end in the last couple of weeks as many stragglers rushed to use their Groupons before they expired. The reason for this is that the regret from missing out on the deal, or what psychologists call "anticipatory regret," becomes salient for customers in the last stages of the promotion. Setting an expiration date is essential to trigger the psychological process of anticipatory regret, which in turn leads to purchase.

We found one more interesting result in the study. The second mode of the bimodal distribution (the customers' redemption rate just before expiration) was substantially higher than the first mode (i.e., buyers redeeming their Groupons in the initial phases of the promotion). The first mode had a redemption rate that was approximately three and a half times the rate during the promotion's middle period, whereas the second mode had a redemption rate that was almost five times higher than this baseline. Far more people redeemed their Groupon right before the promotion ended than when it started. The main takeaway from this study is that a price promotion should have an expiration date. Without a deadline, many customers will keep postponing the promoted item's purchase indefinitely.

Long duration or short duration?

While it is rarely wise to offer a promotion with an open-ended date, there is no single answer for how long the optimal duration of a limited-time promotion should be. Every seller should experiment with different durations to discover what works best for them, given their product and competitor markets. On the short end, a promotion like a flash sale may last only a few hours or a few days at most. On the long end, like Gourmet Meal Prep's Groupon, a customer may be able to avail of a promotion for several months before it expires.

The Groupon research finding on the bimodal distribution of redemption supports shorter duration promotions. After all, if many customers wait until the very end to redeem the promotion, a promotion that is of short duration will get them to redeem earlier and complete the purchase. The seller may even be able to run multiple short-duration promotions back-to-back to encourage more purchases and steal share from a competitor. However, there are other factors to consider.

In one study of coupons distributed through free-standing inserts in newspapers, researchers found that the promotion's optimal duration depended on the seller's brand strength and market share. Their recommendation was that to maximize profits, sellers having prominent brands and high market shares should use shorter duration promotions, whereas smaller, niche sellers should run limited-time promotions having longer durations[234]. Their logic was that more customers will gravitate towards the high-profile seller when its short-lived promotion is running, then still be able to turn to the smaller seller's offer.

Research has also shown that short-duration promotions are like double-edged swords where consumers consider economic and emotional repercussions of the limited time available for redemption. On the one hand, they favor customers pushing the Buy button by increasing the individual's anticipatory regret at missing out on the deal and creating a sense of urgency to buy. On the other hand, consumers are put out by the burden of inconvenience placed upon them by the seller. This lowers their evaluation of the promotional offer[235].

To deal with this potential downside, consumer psychologists suggest explaining to customers why the promotion has a short duration. For instance, saying something like "This flash sale offers a very high discount and will save you a lot of money, that's why we can only afford to run it for the next two hours" is a compelling explanation for customers who receive the short-fuse offer. Such an account delivers the dual benefits of increasing the promotion's attractiveness (unbelievable savings) and making customers who are offered the deal feel like they are insiders (we thought of you because you are valued).

The advertising effect of limited-time offers

Another point in favor of limited-time offers is that they have the unintended positive consequence of prompting full-price sales after the offer has expired. In one study conducted with an online ticket resale site, when researchers emailed customized offers to over 50,000 customers, relatively few people redeemed the offers. The redemption rate was an anemic 0.1 percent. However, far more offer recipients purchased full-price tickets from the site soon afterward. Receiving the offer brought the ticket resale site to customers' attention and prompted many of them to visit it and make a purchase. The authors concluded that "offers increase the expenditure for the individuals beyond the amount spent on the transactions where they are redeemed[236]." The study's authors also found significant *carry-over effects* such that customers who had received an offer purchased more from the seller after the offer had expired, and *spill-over effects* where these customers purchased from other categories beyond the one in the limited-time offer. Although we tend to think of price promotions as just short-term incentives, studies like this one show that their benefit also lies in informing, or even educating customers about the seller's offerings and bringing the seller's brand to the top-of-mind where future purchases are concerned. Essentially, price promotions function like advertisements, even when customers don't redeem the offer they have received.

Offers can go viral and generate social media buzz

Related to the advertising effect, sellers also benefit from short-lived offers by creating buzz in social media and increasing consumers' engagement with their brand. In Spring 2019, home-improvement chain Lowe's ran an elaborate one-day promotion that required customers to go to a Lowe's store, find a keyword on promotional banners it had specially put on display there, then text or go online to request a coupon using the keyword. Once they had done this, customers received a random Lowe's coupon valued at anywhere between $5 and $500 off any purchase. The coupon could be redeemed in a Lowe's store only on that day and did not have any other restrictions, essentially making it like money to spend in the store. The promotion energized customers and spread through social media like wildfire. Many customers forwarded the keyword to friends, who tried their luck at winning a high-value Lowe's coupon[237]. Other examples of buzzworthy limited-time offers include:

- ***Woot's Woot Off! promotions offering a $3 "Bag of Crap."*** Woot Off! promotions are run at random times on the online retailer's site. They last a day or two during which new items at really low prices are constantly listed after old ones sell out. At random times during this sale, Woot offers Bags of Crap, lovingly called BOCs. Each BOC contains an unpredictable assortment of merchandise for just $3. BOCs sell out within seconds, generating lots of good-natured smack talk, expressions of frustration and bragging on the seller's online community[238]. Its random occurrence and the high-value BOC deals make this promotion buzzworthy.

- ***Starbucks' reusable holiday cup promotion.*** On November 2, 2018, Starbucks offered a limited-edition reusable plastic cup in its stores. When customers brought back the cup throughout the holiday season, they got 50 cents off holiday beverages after 2 pm. The promotion was popular, generating intense social media buzz. Stores ran out of the reusable cups within hours[239]. On face value, the deal doesn't appear to be particularly compelling, yet its novelty and its basis in offering reusable and potentially collectible cups increased the promotion's social media appeal.

- ***Build-a-Bear Workshop's "pay your age" promotion.*** The toy company ran a one-day promotion on July 2, 2018. Loyalty program members could pay an amount equal to their age to purchase a stuffed animal from the retailer, resulting in a discount of over 50% in many cases. The result of this attractive offer was long lines at stores as customers waited for hours to purchase the toy. Many locations had to stop accepting customers because of overcrowding and crowd safety regulations. More than half a million people visited the retailer's stores, the highest store-traffic in the company's history[240].

These examples illustrate that buzzworthy promotions are of all types, but they typically run for a very short time, from a few seconds to a day or two at most. The seller tends to run out of the promoted item long before the scheduled end because they provide very generous incentives to the lucky few customers who manage to get them. While customers who miss out often express anger and frustration, the net benefit of these short-lived offers is to generate outsized store traffic, social media mentions, and engagement, and reach broad audiences long afterward.

Price-Matching Guarantees

> *Anything you can buy, I can buy cheaper. I can buy anything cheaper than you. – Annie Get Your Gun, Anything you can do.*

A price-matching guarantee is a formal promise given by the seller in writing, and publicized through advertising and in-store messaging, that if the customer finds a lower price for the same product at a competitor, the seller will match the price. A variation of the price-matching guarantee, called the price-beating guarantee, offers customers a payout, say 110% or 125%of the difference in prices if the customer finds a lower price.

The earliest instance of a price-matching guarantee appears in a Sears catalog that is over a century old[241]. Retailers have widely used price-matching guarantees since the 1980s. In recent years, as online shopping became popular along with customer practices like showrooming and the use of price comparison apps[242], and as physical stores found it difficult to compete with online retailers, price-matching guarantees have become increasingly important in the retailing industry. They are also common in other services industries such as online travel agencies, airlines, hotels, funeral services, and car dealerships.

A 2015 survey of retailers found that when asked about the tactics which brought in the most customers and sales, price-matching guarantees emerged as the second most effective pricing tactic behind free shipping[243]. Consumer electronics retailer Best Buy has attributed its turnaround since 2014, and particularly its ability to compete with Amazon, to offering a transparent price-matching guarantee to its customers. Best Buy CEO Hubert Joly pointed out, "Unless I match Amazon's prices, the customers are ours to lose[244]." The idea behind a price-matching guarantee is to assure potential customers they will get the best available deal at the retailer for a product they could buy elsewhere and persuade them to complete the purchase then and there. Here's how Best Buy words its *Price Match Guarantee*:

> "We won't be beat on price. We'll match the product prices of key online and local competitors. At the time of sale, we

price match all local retail competitors (including their online prices) and we price match products shipped from and sold by these major online retailers: Amazon.com, Crutchfield.com, Dell.com, HP.com, Newegg.com, and TigerDirect.com. We match BestBuy.com prices on in-store purchases and in-store prices on BestBuy.com purchases. If we lower our in-store or online price during the return and exchange period, we will match our lower price, upon request[245]."

Typified by this example, when offering a price-matching guarantee, the seller is careful to define the items to which the guarantee applies and does not apply and the set of competitors whose prices will be matched. For instance, retailers typically state that the price match only applies to identical products having the same brand, model number, size, weight, color, and quantity and only items that are immediately available for purchase at the competitor. The price-matching guarantee usually excludes products sold with contracts like cell phones, flash sales, items promoted through exclusive sales, prices offered to special customer groups, bundled offers, and financing offers where the seller's competitors may have other goals such as driving store footfalls, or rewarding loyal customers, and may be willing to take a loss on the sale.

Sellers also set other exclusions relevant to their business. For instance, Target also excludes pricing due to typographical errors by competitors, clearance sales, closeouts, doorbuster sales, and store-wide or category promotions[246], and Lowe's excludes the pricing of installation and labor. In most cases, the retailer's price-matching guarantee applies to regular prices of a well-defined set of competitors and tries to circumvent attempts at fraudulent or unreasonably opportunistic behavior by customers.

Decision variables to consider when designing a price-matching guarantee

Pricing experts have considered the most effective ways to design a price-matching guarantee offer and have concluded that there are many moving parts to the offer that must be considered. Among others, the decision variables that drive the design of a price-matching guarantee include[247]:

- **Type of guarantee:** Does the guarantee match the competitor's price, or is it a price-beating guarantee? If it is the latter, what is the extra incentive offered to customers who find a lower price (e.g., percentage of the difference, or percentage of the difference plus a fixed amount of money)?
- **Price used for comparison:** Does the guarantee refer to the advertised price (on the company's website, app, or in print advertising) or the actual price offered by the competitor? Does the guarantee include full price or price net of coupons, special offers, or customer negotiation?
- **Period of validity:** Is the guarantee only valid at the time of purchase, or does it specify a certain number of days afterward during which customer can discover a lower price? (This can have a significant impact on the price-matching guarantee's utilization because of seasonal and holiday sales which occur at the same times each year).
- **Seller's price:** Does the guarantee also apply to the seller's future price during the period of validity? In both online and offline channels? Does it include promotional pricing or original price only?
- **Specific restrictions imposed:** This includes the exclusions described earlier such as a list of specific competitors (physical and online sites), the geographical proximity (e.g., competitors to include only those within five miles of store location), in-stock merchandise only, and so on. This can be a lengthy list, and "defangs" the guarantee.
- **Implementation in the store:** Who will check the price evidence provided by the customer in the store, cashier, or store manager? What types of evidence are acceptable? What training will line employees require, and how will they be trained?

How price-matching guarantees work

Price-matching guarantees are meant to trigger purchase by customers who are on the cusp of buying. One controlled experimental study found that when the seller offered a price-matching guarantee to customers who were looking to buy a portable music system, 65.8% of customers stopped further search and made the purchase. Without a guarantee, only 40.8% of customers terminated their search[248]. Price-matching guarantees are fundamentally different from price promotions because their main function is to dissuade potential buyers from visiting other retailers, or even lengthening their decision making process. They assure customers to buy without actually offering a low price or an incentive to buy while conveying an image that the seller is concerned about their welfare.

To avail of the price-matching guarantee, customers must perform a significant amount of work. First, they must find and research prices for the identical product among all major sellers, then find lower offers if they exist, and finally provide evidence of the competitive offer to the retail employee. This process can be time-consuming and fruitless. It ensures that while the guarantee creates an aura of low prices and value for everyone, it delivers the most economical prices only to a small subset of the retailer's most price-sensitive shoppers who are willing to jump through all the hoops to get the lowest price. A price-matching guarantee is an effective form of price discrimination that puts the burden of action almost entirely on customers. As pricing expert Rafi Mohammed points out, "Under price-matching guarantees, consumers who play the game (by aggressively comparing prices before buying) will win, but those who don't will pay more[249]." On the positive side, however, price-matching guarantees encourage more customers to join the game and play.

Consumer psychology research shows that price-matching guarantees work on customers by changing the standard they use to evaluate prices in the final pre-purchase state. The guarantee raises customers' estimates of both the lowest and average prices in the market for the product they want to purchase. This, in turn, affects the seller's price image favorably. Customers view products and retailers that offer price-matching guarantees as less expensive. The positive perception that the retailer has low prices carries over to other products in the store, beyond those that the customer came in to buy. Just like sale signals, price-matching guarantees are more influential for customers whose price knowledge is sketchy. For instance, when customers don't know the range of market prices for the product, they have to rely on inferences derived from the price-matching guarantee. They are less likely to take the trouble to research prevailing prices or avail of the guarantee on offer[250]. On the other hand, when customers think that their fellow customers are actively monitoring prices and benefitting from the store's guarantee, they are more likely to believe that the store offers low prices even without first-hand experience of using the price-matching guarantee.

For sellers, offering a price-matching guarantee is a defensive strategy. In the retailing arena, in particular, many marketing experts see a price-matching guarantee as a hygiene factor instead of a real differentiator. Customers rarely choose a retailer because it offers a price-matching guarantee. Instead, they may decide to go to the retailer in the first place because of some other value differentiator such as an attractive choice assortment, strong reputation, the advice and service offered by frontline employees, ancillary services like installation, education, and repair, and so on. Once there, however, they will purchase because of the price-matching guarantee. Cliff Courtney, EVP of Zimmer Advertising points out, "*[Retailers] neglect to imagine that quality, or selection, or speed, or experience can trump incentives. People buy Starbucks when the coffee is free at work. They put four-figure rims on their cars when the car runs just fine without them. It's about value, not price.*"

The negative consequences of price-matching guarantees for consumers

Price-matching guarantees are not necessarily in the best interests of consumers. Research has found that beyond the psychological pricing objective of encouraging customers to buy, sellers also use price-matching guarantees as signals to their competitors to discourage them from competing on price. The unspoken message sent by a price-matching guarantee is, "If you try to undercut us on price, it's not going to work. We will respond immediately to the customers to whom low prices matter. It may be advantageous for both of us to compete on other factors." When they receive this message, competitors resort to fewer price promotions and maintain higher prices. Prices tend to be higher in markets where the significant sellers all use price-matching guarantees[251]. What's more, retailers that use price-matching guarantees often do not have the lowest prices. In one study of automotive tire retailers, 75% of sellers who offered a price-matching guarantee asked for a higher price for their product than a direct competitor who did not offer a guarantee[252].

Many sellers bypass the potentially corrosive effects of price-matching guarantees on their bottom lines by selling exclusive merchandise. For example, Best Buy offered a premium collection of laptops from brands such as Dell and Samsung Electronics that were only available in its stores[253]. The mattress industry is notorious for using different names and SKUs for what is essentially the same product. As Timothy Lee points out, "the popular Simmons Beautyrest line has different brand names at different stores. The *Beautyrest Recharge Allie* at Macy's is called the *Beautyrest Recharge Devonwood Luxury* at Sears, the *Recharge Signature Select Hartfield* at Mattress Firm, and the *Beautyrest Recharge Lyric Luxury* at US-Mattress.com. If customers don't realize these are names for the same mattress, it's harder for them to bargain effectively[254]." The work of customers to disentangle the different SKUs becomes much harder, and even then, the retailer may decline to honor the guarantee because the prices refer to seemingly different products.

The bottom line is that very few psychological pricing activities provide the same degree of assurance or push the customer to press the buy button as a carefully-defined price-matching guarantee. Instead of eroding the company's brand image and profit margin by offering a short-term discount, a price-matching guarantee offers an alternative method that burnishes the seller's brand, provides pricing power, and dissuades competitors from engaging in a price war.

Scarcity Pricing

The reason the top champagnes are not stratospherically expensive is that they are not scarce enough. – Gideon Rachman[255].

Scarcity pricing is defined as charging significantly higher prices to customers than the baseline prices by the same seller or comparable sellers to reflect the real or perceived scarcity of the product. In its most obvious form, scarcity pricing is a reaction by sellers to real supply scarcity. In commodity markets like electricity, for example, there is often an upper limit on supply. There are only so many turbines and solar panels to generate electricity in any given network. Demand, on the other hand, varies significantly, and often in predictable ways such as the time of day, the month of the year, the outside temperature, the condition of the economy, and so on. During periods of peak electricity demand, like hot summer days, the demand for electricity can quickly outstrip available supply. Under such conditions, many electric utilities adopt scarcity pricing. They raise prices for each kWh of electricity significantly during times of peak consumption to manage demand. They penalize business users for consuming during these times and try to shift some discretionary demand to off-peak times[256].

Pricing based on real scarcity also occurs frequently in consumer markets. Classical economist David Ricardo pointed this out over two centuries ago when he observed, "There are some commodities, the value of which is determined by their scarcity alone. No labour can increase the quantity of such goods, and therefore their value cannot be lowered by an increased supply... The value of [rare statues, pictures, and coins] is wholly independent of the quantity of labour originally necessary to produce them and varies with the varying wealth and inclinations of those who are desirous to possess them[257]."

To Ricardo's point, rare and hard-to-find items are expensive. They become even more expensive as they become rarer and harder-to-find, and demand and taste for them continue to increase. For instance, in January 2019, the owner of a Japanese restaurant chain paid over $3 million for a single 612-pound bluefin tuna, a critically endangered species of fish that is considered a delicacy. This worked out to a wholesale price of approximately \$4,900 per pound[258]. In contrast, the record high price was less than a quarter that amount or \$1,238 per pound just seven years earlier[259]. Prices of paintings by Impressionists like Monet, Degas and Renoir, wine bottles of exceptional vintage and pedigree, and real estate on Martha's Vineyard have all increased exponentially for the same reason.

For psychological pricing, however, perceived scarcity is far more exciting and promising as a practical tool for managers than real scarcity. Managers have little control over the real scarcity of products they sell, but they can undoubtedly influence their customers' perceptions of scarcity through their decisions, create a sense of urgency and propel them into the *purchase* state as quickly and as vigorously as possible. We will consider how controlling the product's availability can create a convincing illusion of scarcity and affect pricing and buying decisions.

Control availability of high-quality and desired items to create an illusion of scarcity

For high quality and relatively high-demand items, sellers often create an illusion of scarcity by deliberately limiting the amount of the products they sell so that they run out well before the customer demand diminishes. This approach creates a "rare = valuable" association for the brand in the customer's mind to get them to buy.

Take the example of Birkin bags, made by fashion brand Hermès. These bags sell at retail at prices ranging from \$10,000 at the low end to well over \$200,000. Even with such high prices, these bags are hard to buy. If an average customer wants to buy a Birkin bag, the only place they can do so is the secondary market, where the bags are routinely sold at multiples of Hermès' retail price. Each Hermès store receives only about two Birkin bags a week, and every single bag is spoken for months, if not years, in advance by customers who have established relationships with the store and who purchase regularly there. You cannot just pick up the phone and ask to be put on a waiting list for a Birkin bag at a Hermès store. According to a *New York Times* article:

"There was a waiting list at one point, but because so many people wanted these bags, a list simply became unmanageable," said a former employee, speaking anonymously because of the nondisclosure agreement he signed. Hermès refuses to comment on the method for bringing home a Birkin[260]."

Just like other domains of life, whether it is a romantic partner or deep dish pizza, people want what they cannot have even more desperately. A product's scarcity increases the consumer's arousal and desire for the product and makes them behave in relatively thoughtless, reactive ways instead of thinking through the ramifications of making the purchase carefully. The upshot is that consumers often tend to make purchases of scarce products impulsively[261]. What's more, these momentary effects that impel purchase are stronger among unmotivated customers. Perceived scarcity encourages purchase behaviors among the seller's relatively disinterested customers.

Consumer psychology research also shows that when the seller creates scarcity by restricting their product's supply (as opposed to real scarcity caused by demand outstripping supply in the marketplace), customers attribute a higher quality to the scarcely available products, and may even see them as prestigious and are willing to pay more for them[262]. A Birkin bag gains its prestige and price not just because it is a Hermès offering or because it is made with the most beautiful natural cowhide, but because it is virtually impossible to find.

In one classic study, when participants were given the option to choose from either a full and continuously replenished jar or a nearly empty jar, they liked and desired cookies from the nearly empty jar, even though the cookies were identical[263]. This consumer preference for scarce products is even stronger for products that are visibly and conspicuously consumed and affect the user's status. Let's introduce another brand that makes Birkin bags look like a generic store brand by comparison. Fashion brand Supreme's impressive growth story and large base of super-customers, many of whom build shrines to the brand in their homes illustrate the power of scarcity pricing.

The Supreme success story

Supreme originated as one small skating gear store in New York City in the late 1990s. By 2019, it has grown into a billion-dollar brand on the backs of its devoted customers around the world[264]. Ordinary Supreme products like t-shirts and hoodies routinely resell for hundreds, or even thousands, of dollars on the secondary market and many people make a living buying and then reselling them. Take the example of a t-shirt with Supreme's iconic logo (called the 'bogo' for 'box logo' by customers) from its Spring/ Summer 2014 collection that is comparable in appearance and quality to the regulation Hanes pocket tee shirt. A 3-pack of the Hanes tee shirt sells on Amazon for $7.96, while a Supreme shirt retailed for $32 in 2014 and currently sells on the secondary market for more than $1,500 apiece[265]. An important reason for the high prices of Supreme products is the brand's strategic use of scarcity as a core part of its branding and pricing strategy. A British super-customer named Boyd Hilton explained how he became enamored with Supreme:

> "The staff turned out to be thoroughly friendly and helpful, although when I naively enquired about the perfectly cool box logo Supreme T-shirts they were wearing, but which didn't seem to be on the shelves, I was brusquely told they weren't available. Undeterred, I visited the store pretty much bi-annually while on my freakishly frequent holidays to [New York City]... The staff began to recognise me, and eventually they let me buy one of the bogo tees held in the mysterious stockroom area behind the counter. I distinctly remember the special thrill of finally getting hold of a Supreme tee with the actual logo on it. It felt as symbolic of the glamour and excitement of New York as a Woody Allen film or an episode of Seinfeld[266]."

Figure 7.3 Customers lining up at a Supreme store for a Thursday morning drop

Every item the company sells, not just t-shirts, is made in limited quantities and is available for purchase only in a short window of opportunity during one of its Thursday "drops." While any given item is in limited supply, the company offers a range of merchandise. It further adds intrigue to its products by collaborating with other brands, celebrities, and designers in unpredictable and one-off ways. It often uses unlicensed images to provoke controversy, ropes in celebrities to model specific items, and so on. Then, on every Thursday at 11 am, it releases a small new batch of items, anointed with controversy and fueled by scarcity, to customers who stand in line for hours to buy a Supreme garment (see Figure 7.3).

Before each drop day, Supreme enthusiasts numbering in the thousands discuss their favorite to-be-released items on online venues like Facebook groups and subreddits. Not surprisingly, the hyped out items sell out quickly and reach astronomical prices in the secondary market. Scarcity, in addition to quality, is the cornerstone of the Supreme brand's value. From a pricing perspective, what makes the Supreme case even more impressive than Birkin bags is that these are ordinary everyday products like underwear and street clothes, purchased by everyday customers, that are transformed into objects of adoration and devotion by the brand's strategic cultivation of scarcity.

Other variations of scarcity-based pricing

Scarcity can also be used to fuel purchase activities beyond restricting product supply. Managers can combine scarcity-based pricing tactics with price promotions to encourage customers to purchase. In these cases, the seller's goal is to capitalize on the sense of urgency created by the combination of a compelling price offer and a small and limited window of opportunity that could close at any time (similar to the Woot Off! and the Lowe's promotion we saw earlier in this chapter).

Using scarcity restrictions. One effective way to combine price promotions and scarcity is to add a scarcity restriction to the offer. Scarcity restrictions can be vague such as "While supplies last" or "Limited quantities remain," or they can be specific such as "Limit X units per customer," and are added to a limited-time price promotion. Research has found that adding a scarcity restriction influences consumers by signaling that the deal is a valuable one. Scarcity restrictions act as "promoters of promotions[267]." In one study, when the vague restriction of "While stocks last" was combined with a *tensile claim* (stating the offer imprecisely such as, "Get *up to* 60% off regular prices"), consumers were likely to think the promotional offer was very informative and useful for their decision making. They believed they would save money if they availed of this vaguely-stated, scarce, short-lived offer[268]. The vagueness of the offer and the implied scarcity together motivates the customers from a *decide* psychological state to the *buy* state in the NACJ framework.

Offering limited-time promotions to highlight scarcity. A different, creative version of scarcity-based pricing offers low prices for a limited time and a limited assortment of products for a specific purpose. The Farmhouse Tavern in Toronto, which is open Thursday to Sunday, uses scarcity-based pricing to use up its stock of perishable food and open alcohol on Sunday nights, before its weekly three-day

194

hiatus. Starting at 6 pm every Sunday, the restaurant runs a "Fuck Mondays" promotion. The restaurant offers eight different food and drinks specials every hour. For example, during the 8 pm hour, short-rib pasta and the fish special may be on sale at half their regular price, but by 9 pm, the promotion is over. It is replaced with half-price glasses of wine from open bottles. As items run out, they are crossed off the restaurant's chalkboard menu. This pricing encourages customers to stay longer to sample different food and drink items. In the words of one customer, "That things could run out makes us order faster. That's part of the deal when you come out on a Sunday. It's a bit of a gamble.[269]"

Goal Gradient Motivation and Loyalty Reward Programs

There is no finish line. – Nike advertisement.

The concept of a goal gradient is based on a universal and straightforward motivational principle. We are hardwired to use the motivational resources at our disposal strategically to pursue and attain our goals. Once we choose a goal, the intensity of goal pursuit is not constant. In the early stages, when the goal is distant, motivation tends to be relatively lower. As we make progress and get closer to the finish line, we increase the intensity of our exertions[270]. (Nike's aphorism isn't psychologically accurate; there is a finish line, motivationally speaking). The closer to the final goal we get, the more intense the pursuit becomes. This principle is called the "goal gradient hypothesis" by psychologists to reflect the predictably changing intensity of motivation during goal pursuit. The phenomenon was first discovered in the behavior of rats over eighty years ago. Psychologist Clark Hull famously (and succinctly) observed, "Rats in a maze... run faster as they near the food box than at the beginning of the path[271]."

Let us consider how this phenomenon plays out in consumers' buying behavior and its implications for psychological pricing. In one academic study, researchers collaborated with a café to set up a customer rewards program. After enrollment, customers received a card which was stamped each time they purchased a coffee. (The study is from the pre-smartphone days before apps were available). After the customer collected ten stamps, they received free coffee. The authors tracked the purchase behavior of customers over a month while they were receiving rewards.

The study found that as customers collected more stamps on their card, they made subsequent coffee purchases more quickly. For example, the gap between the ninth and tenth coffee purchases was an average of 0.7 days faster than the difference between the first and second cup purchased. Study participants were either drinking more coffee as they got closer to the free coffee reward or switching coffee consumption from other vendors (or home) to this store. Regardless, they accelerated purchases by approximately 20 percent during the reward redemption journey. When the authors conducted back-of-the-envelope calculations, they estimated that on average, customers drank ten coffees in 24.6 days after accounting for the purchase acceleration fueled by goal gradient motivation. Without it and the resultant purchase acceleration, they would have taken nearly five days longer to make ten coffee purchases. The customers' goal gradient motivation was good for the coffee shop's unit sales. The authors did not report whether it was profitable or not because the seller had to give out an extra coffee without charge to achieve the purchase acceleration.

The psychological model behind this motivated behavior is called the *goal-distance model*. It states that the amount of effort the customer invests in making purchases is not constant, but is a function of their psychological goal distance, defined as the proportion of the total distance remaining to the goal. In the coffee shop study, getting free coffee was the goal. According to the goal-distance model, the activity involved must have two characteristics for goal gradient motivation to work.[272]

First, the customer must have a clearly framed goal with a well-defined starting point and an end-point. Loyalty programs fit the bill perfectly. Enrollment is the starting point for the goal, and the incentive received after completing specific tasks is the end-point, both of which are well-defined. What's more, after they've received the reward, the process resets, and the customer begins goal pursuit all over again. The second requirement is that the goal must be pleasant or what psychologists call an "approach goal[273]."

The goal-distance model states that the individual's degree of motivation to reach the *free purchase* finish line is dictated by two factors: (1) how far away they are from the finish line, and (2) how much progress they have already made towards it. Consider the number of coffees purchased at the store as a number line, and the customer as making progress along the line from zero coffees purchased to ten coffees purchased. The model says that the length of the number line (from start to finish), and where the person is on it both influence the customer's motivation. Motivation increases as the distance to the goal becomes smaller. Figure 7.4 shows this idea in graphic form.

Figure 7.4 How the customer's purchase changes with distance from the reward.

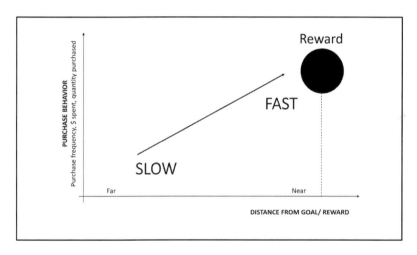

How managers benefit from consumers' goal gradient motivation

Many managers tend to think of loyalty rewards programs purely as a customer relationship management activity. But make no mistake. A loyalty rewards program is also a significant pricing activity. It offers incentives to customers in precise, targeted ways, such as in exchange for specific purchase or referral behaviors. There is far more to designing and implementing an effective loyalty rewards program than we can tackle here. However, for the particular purpose of encouraging purchases, the customer's goal gradient motivation can be harnessed with a well-designed loyalty rewards program. Here, we will consider four ways that customers' purchases are influenced by goal gradient motivation.

Create an illusion of progress towards the goal to gain momentum. During the process of goal pursuit, the customer's lowest motivation is in the beginning stages. That is when they will be the most sluggish buyers. What if the seller could bypass this phase and move to the speedier part of the goal gradient? One smart way to do this is by creating an illusion of progress toward the goal.

Managers designing a rewards program can create an illusion of progress by increasing the original distance to the reward and then completing early progress on the customer's behalf, essentially having the customer skip the sluggish part of the goal gradient. Here's how this idea works for the coffee shop rewards program described earlier. The program required the customer to make ten coffee purchases to receive free coffee. To create an illusion of progress, the offer is redesigned to "get a free coffee after twelve coffee purchases," with credit given to customers for the first two purchases at the outset by stamping two squares. Figure 7.5 shows this idea graphically.

In another study conducted at the same coffee shop, the researchers tested this idea and found that customers who were given the ten-stamp card (top panel in Figure 7.5) took an average of 15.6 days to buy ten coffees. However, those who were given the twelve-stamp card with two free stamps (bottom panel in Figure 7.5) took 12.7 days, or approximately 20 percent less time to buy the ten coffees. The coffee pricing and the reward requirements were the same for both groups. The only difference was the illusion of progress created by the two free stamps, which essentially jump-started the customers' goal gradient motivation and put them on a faster track to pursue the reward.

Figure 7.5 Using illusionary progress to bypass sluggish early motivation of the customer.

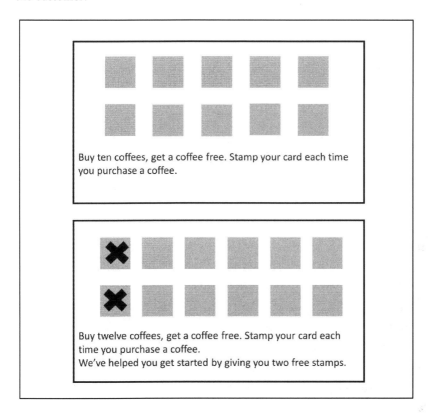

Identify and leverage positive aspects of the purchase to counterbalance the pain of payment. As we have seen throughout this book, one principal purpose of psychological pricing is to get customers excited and motivated to buy. We have also seen that prices are aversive stimuli for customers, signifying the financial sacrifice. An important lesson from goal gradient motivation is that, where possible, the purely aversive price stimulus needs to be tempered by combining it with a positive stimulus that provides a potential goal for customers. This is why rewarding the customer is so important a part of a price offer.

What's more, the rewards do not have to be expensive or even monetary. Typical rewards offered are cash back, free products or services, swag, and unique benefits such as higher levels of service. Even offering badges that confer status works. In one study conducted with users of a popular German Question & Answer community, researchers found that the number of contributions increased substantially as the user got closer to earning a purely nominal badge[274]. The badge cost nothing to the community organizer, and it influenced users' behavior significantly. Rewards add a positive approach goal to the pain of paying the price.

A related implication applies to high-priced items. Many customers pay off such items in installments rather than a lump-sum. Paying the balance off for a higher priced item can be explicitly highlighted as a goal by sellers, associating it with countdowns, fanfare, and other celebratory milestones and for instance, sending messages such as "Congratulations! You have already made ten payments. You only have two more payments to go, and then you will be paid off in full" activates the behavioral acceleration due to goal gradient motivation.

While paying the asked-for amount itself is aversive, paying off the full amount and reaching a zero balance is an approach goal that can induce the process of goal gradient motivation. Pricing a product in installments with a pay-off schedule instead of a single price can also achieve this purpose. Many companies that use installment pricing do not emphasize the goal-oriented nature of payments. Goal gradient motivation suggests that where possible, it may be fruitful do so.

Show progress towards the goal in ways that are easy to visualize for consumers. Easy visualization of goal progress is a potent way to harness the customer's goal gradient motivation. On the loyalty card, the visual impact of every stamp is what spurs progress. In research looking at this issue, one study found that when compared to either reporting progress towards a spending goal in dollar terms ("You have spent $400 towards the goal of $500 to earn the gift certificate") or in percentage terms ("You have completed 80% of your spending towards the rewards certificate"), showing progress visually using a progress bar displaying the amount of progress made towards the goal was more effective in motivating customers[275]. Consumers who can visualize the goal easily exert more effort and have higher goal commitment than those who find it hard to visualize their goal.

The recent trend towards gamification of loyalty rewards programs uses the power of visual display.

Reengage customers after they have earned a reward in creative ways. In the coffee shop study, one interesting finding was that customers who accelerated more strongly toward their first reward exhibited higher retention and faster program re-engagement. They were more enthused about obtaining their next reward after they got their first free coffee. Pursuing desirable rewards that one wants supports this process. Getting the customer started on the path towards their next reward as soon as they have earned the first one is equally important.

What's more, the same process applies to help others earn rewards. Several studies have looked at donations to charities and found evidence of *goal gradient helping*, which is that contribution rates increase as recipients approach their fundraising goals. As one study concluded, "people are not just more intense in pursuing their own goals when they draw closer to reaching those goals, but they also exert more effort when a person or organization [they support] is close to reaching their goals[276]." This makes a case for designing rewards programs that can be achieved through joint customer participation. For example, by making the same account easily accessible on multiple apps and allowing an unlimited number of gift cards to be associated with one account, Starbucks allows people to earn rewards through joint purchase activities. Like much of psychological pricing, the only limit to igniting the goal gradient motivation of customers is the manager's creativity and imagination.

END NOTES

Chapter 1 What is Psychological Pricing?

1. Throughout this book, whenever I use the word "product" alone, you should interpret it as generic shorthand for the phrase "products and services." This is because unless stated explicitly, all the concepts, ideas, and tools in this book apply equally to products and services.

2. Consider the case of the subscription-based movie ticketing company MoviePass, whose struggles have been attributed, in large part, to its pricing structure. For a detailed discussion, see Yoon, Eddie (2018). What MoviePass can teach us about the future of subscription businesses. Harvard Business Review.

3. Nance-Nash, Cheryl (2018). Is it cheaper to celebrate Valentine's day early (or late)? Deal News, February 9.

4. DelVecchio, Devon, Arun Lakshmanan, and H. Shanker Krishnan. (2009). The effects of discount location and frame on consumers' price estimates. Journal of Retailing, 85(3), 336-346.

5. Thomas, M., Simon, D. H., & Kadiyali, V. (2010). The price precision effect: Evidence from laboratory and market data. Marketing Science, 29(1), 175-190.

6. For price gouging during hurricanes, see Sorkin, Andrew Ross (2017). Hurricane price gouging is despicable, right? Not to some economists. New York Times, September 11. For Coke vending machines with variable pricing, see Leonhardt, David (2005). Why variable pricing fails at the vending machine. New York Times, June 27. For Olympics Games pricing, see Collinson, Patrick (2011). Are the 2012 Olympics ticket prices too expensive? The Guardian, January 7.

7. Cheng, L. L., & Monroe, K. B. (2013). An appraisal of behavioral price research (part 1): price as a physical stimulus. AMS Review, 3(3), 103-129.

8. For a good academic discussion of this issue, see Thaler, Richard (1980). Toward a positive theory of consumer choice. Journal of Economic Behavior & Organization 1(1), 39-60, and Sen, Amartya K.

203

(1977). Rational fools: A critique of the behavioral foundations of economic theory. Philosophy & Public Affairs, 6(4), 317-344.

9. Knutson, B., Rick, S., Wimmer, G. E., Prelec, D., & Loewenstein, G. (2007). Neural predictors of purchases. Neuron, 53(1), 147-156.

10. The Value Pricing Framework is discussed at length in Dholakia, Utpal (2017), How to Price Effectively: A Guide for Managers and Entrepreneurs.

11. The articles, Edelman, David C. (2010). Branding in the digital age, Harvard Business Review, 88(12), 62-69, and Edelman, David C., and Marc Singer (2015). Competing on customer journeys, Harvard Business Review, 93(11), 88-100, provide an excellent overview of the CDJ framework and its practical applications. The NACJ framework is described in Lee, L., Inman, J. J., Argo, J. J., Böttger, T., Dholakia, U., Gilbride, T., van Ittersum, K., Kahn, B., Kalra, A., Lehmann, D. R., & McAlister, L. M. (2018). From browsing to buying and beyond: The needs-adaptive shopper journey model. Journal of the Association for Consumer Research. 3(3), 277-93.

Chapter 2 Hidden Meanings in Price

12. Xinhua (2008). China sets Olympics record in weddings, as 300,000-plus couples tie knot. China Daily.

13. Clark, Dorie (2017). Why you should charge clients more than you think you're worth. Harvard Business Review.

14. This quote is taken from Chapter 1 of A. G. Lafley and Roger L. Martin. (2013), Playing to Win: How Strategy Really Works, Boston: Harvard Business School Press. See also, Lafley, A. G., Roger L. Martin, Jan W. Rivkin, and Nicolaj Siggelkow (2012). Bringing science to the art of strategy. Harvard Business Review.

15. Walter L. Baker, Michael V. Marn and Craig C. Zawada (2010), The Price Advantage, Second Edition. John Wiley & Sons. This quote appears on page 10 of the book, in a section aptly titled. The Nobility of Pricing Excellence.

16. Anderson and Simester cite the range of values after reviewing a number of price-ending studies. See Anderson, Eric T. and Simester, Duncan I. (2003). Effects of $9 price endings on retail sales: Evidence

from field experiments. Quantitative marketing and Economics, 1(1), 93-110. Their research reported results of field experiments that showed that prices ending with the digit 9 increased demand, and this effect was stronger for new products than for previously sold items.

17. Troy, Mike (2019), Why 99 Cents Only isn't a dollar store, Retail Leader.

18. See Stiving, Mark, and Russell S. Winer (1997). An empirical analysis of price endings with scanner data. Journal of Consumer Research, 24(1), 57-67.

19. The source for this list of symbolic meanings is Schindler, Robert (1991). Symbolic Meanings of a Price Ending. in NA - Advances in Consumer Research Volume 18, eds. Rebecca H. Holman and Michael R. Solomon, Provo, UT : Association for Consumer Research, 794-801. I have adapted and added to Schindler's list to make it current.

20. In Houston, many new upscale restaurants that have garnered a lot of buzz like Superica, B. B. Lemon, and Indianola use 2, 4, 6, and 8 price endings liberally throughout their menus.

21. Strulov-Shlain, Avner (2019). More than a penny's worth: Left-digit bias and firm pricing. Working paper, University of California, Berkeley.

22. Consumer psychologists Manoj Thomas and Vicki Morwitz call this the left-digit effect. See Thomas, Manoj, and Vicki Morwitz. (2005). Penny wise and pound foolish: the left-digit effect in price cognition. Journal of Consumer Research, 32(1), 54-64.

23. Schindler, Robert M. (2006). The 99-price ending as a signal of a low-price appeal. Journal of Retailing, 82(1), 71-77.

24. Salmon, Walter J., and Gwendolyn K. Ortmeyer (1993). Duncan Department Stores. Harvard Business School Publishing, 1-36.

25. Manning, Kenneth C., and David E. Sprott (2009). Price endings, left-digit effects, and choice. Journal of Consumer Research, 36(2), 328-335. Study 1 in this paper describes this finding.

26. Stiving, Mark (2000). Price-endings when prices signal quality. Management Science, 46(12), 1617-1629.

27. James, Kyle (2013). Learn to crack the price tag code at these major retailers. Rather-be-Shopping.com. See also Rapoport, Len (2017). Secret price codes that will save you money at Costco. Tough Nickel.

28. One such proponent is the consultant Ted Nicholas, who argues for using 7-ending prices.

29. Velthuis, Olav (2005), Talking prices: Symbolic meaning of prices in the market for contemporary art. Princeton University Press. The quote is from page 3.

30. Min, Chew Hui (2017). Mobile phone number with 10 eights auctioned for $24 million in China. The Straits Times, April 16.

31. Simmons, Lee C., and Robert M. Schindler (2003). Cultural superstitions and the price endings used in Chinese advertising. Journal of International Marketing, 11(2), 101-111.

32. Westjohn, Stanford A., Holger Roschk, and Peter Magnusson (2017). Eastern versus Western culture pricing strategy: Superstition, lucky numbers, and localization. Journal of International Marketing, 25(1), 72-90; Ngan, Henrique Fátima Boyol, Lianping Ren, and Grant O'Bree (2018). Lucky 8-ending–A case study on managerial price-ending beliefs in Macao. Journal of Hospitality and Tourism Management, 36, 22-30.

33. Haipeng (Allan) Chen and Daniel Levy and Avichai Snir (2017). End of 9-Endings and Price Perceptions. Working paper, MPRA.

34. Costco97 (2016). Hacking Costco: Decoding their price tags. September 28.

35. Kyle (2013). Learn to crack the price tag code at these major retailers. Rather-be-Shopping.com.

36. Mikkelson, David (2014). Big store price codes. Snopes, January 8.

37. The Krazy Coupon Lady (2019). 24 things every Costco shopper should know. March 20.

38. Pearlman, Alison (2018). Can I get a "McGangbang?" On the weird world of secret menus. Literary Hub.

39. Ramey, Corinne (2017). Can I have that burger with a side of peanut butter?, Wall Street Journal, May 16.

40. Forbes Magazine, The World's Most Powerful Brands 2018.

41. Burns, Will (2014). Walmart brand doubles down on 'live better' with commitment to American manufacturing. Forbes CMO Network, February 19.

42. Associated Press (2012). Why Walmart can pull off 'Everyday Low Prices' but everyone else keeps failing. Business Insider, September 3.

43. These brand associations are clearly described in Target's statement of its purpose and beliefs, available on its website. See also, Adamson, Allen (2010). The Target brand gets the simple things right (and a lot more). Forbes, October 27.

44. Zielke, Stephan (2010). How price image dimensions influence shopping intentions for different store formats. European Journal of Marketing, 44(6), 748-770.

45. Fonda, Daren (2018). Vanguard is losing battles on two fronts in fee wars. Barron's, September 11. Whitler, Kimberly (2018). Insight into the Vanguard brand: A top brand of the year in the Harris poll. Forbes, January 28.

46. Ng, Serena (2014). At P&G, new Tide comes in, old price goes up. Wall Street Journal. For Costco, see Tuttle, Brad (2018). Here's the real reason Costco will never stop selling $4.99 rotisserie chicken. Money Magazine, January 4; for Tesla, see Hardigree, Matt (2014). Why the pricey Tesla Model S is actually a great value. Jalopnik Reviews, September 4.

48. Sarkar, Ranju (2009). Parle-G, the price warrior. Rediff Business, May 4.

49. See for example Weinrich, Neal (2014). When is pricing information a trade secret? Berman Fink Van Horn blog, February 17.

50. Brown, Jennifer, Tanjim Hossain, and John Morgan (2010). Shrouded attributes and information suppression: Evidence from the field. The Quarterly Journal of Economics, 125(2), 859-876.

51. Davidson, Justin (2018). Why you should be in favor of congestion pricing in New York. New York Magazine, March 27.

52. Dholakia, Utpal (2015). The risks of changing your prices too often. Harvard Business Review.

Chapter 3 Knowing the Price

53. Marshall, Alfred (1890), Principles of Economics. London: Macmillan. For a pithy but interesting discussion about how neoclassical economics views consumer price knowledge, see Monroe, Kent B., and Angela Y. Lee (1999). Remembering versus knowing: Issues in buyers' processing of price information. Journal of the Academy of Marketing Science, 27(2), 20-225.

54. Dickson, Peter R., and Alan G. Sawyer (1990). The price knowledge and search of supermarket shoppers. Journal of Marketing, 54(3), 42-53.

55. Dehaene, Stanislas, and Laurent Cohen. (1995). Towards an anatomical and functional model of number processing. Mathematical Cognition, 1(1), 83-120. Dehaene's quote appears in Deheane, Stanislas (1992). Varieties of numerical abilities. Cognition, 44(1-2), 1-42.

56. Cantlon, Jessica F., Michael L. Platt, and Elizabeth M. Brannon.(2009). Beyond the number domain. Trends in Cognitive Sciences, 13(2), 83-91.

57. Bill Gates guessed the prices of five different grocery items including a box of Rice-A-Roni on an episode of the Ellen Show in February 2018.

58. Vanhuele, M., & Drèze, X. (2002). Measuring the Price Knowledge Shoppers Bring to the Store. Journal of Marketing, 66(4), 72-85.

59. Mayhew, Glenn E., and Russell S. Winer (1992) An empirical analysis of internal and external reference prices using scanner data, Journal of Consumer Research, 19(1), 62-70. This article provides excellent discussion about how shoppers use multiple reference prices when purchasing groceries in a supermarket. It provides empirical evidence to support this view.

60. See Bolton, Ruth N., and Katherine N. Lemon (1999). A dynamic model of customers' usage of services: Usage as an antecedent and consequence of satisfaction. Journal of Marketing Research, 171-186. This article introduces the concept of payment equity, which is the customer's evaluation of whether the prices are fair in relation to the benefits they are getting from the product. The authors call this the "evaluation of the fairness of the exchange."

61. Briesch, R. A., Krishnamurthi, L., Mazumdar, T., & Raj, S. P. (1997). A comparative analysis of reference price models. Journal of Consumer Research, 24(2), 202-214.

62. Kalyanaram, Gurumurthy, and John DC Little (1994). An empirical analysis of latitude of price acceptance in consumer package goods. Journal of Consumer Research 21(3), 408-418. This article covers the concept of the "latitude of price acceptance." The authors studying shopping decisions in the category of sweetened and unsweetened drinks and find that "presence of a region of price insensitivity around a reference price." As the average reference price increases, the latitude of price acceptance also increases, meaning the customers have a wider range in which they consider the product's price to be acceptable.

63. Monroe, K. B. (1973). Buyers' subjective perceptions of price. Journal of Marketing Research, 10(1), 70-80.

64. Monroe, K. B. (1971). The information content of prices: a preliminary model for estimating buyer response. Management Science, 17(8), B-519.

65. Available at: Fastfoodmenuprices.com

66. Both quotes in this paragraph are from Dickler, Jessica (2008). The incredible shrinking cereal box. CNN Money.

67. Ratneshwar, Srinivasan, Cornelia Pechmann, and Allan D. Shocker (1996). Goal-derived categories and the antecedents of across-category consideration. Journal of Consumer Research, 23(3), 240-250. In this paper, the authors argue that goal-derived categories make more sense for customers in their purchase decision process. One of the examples they use is "Get a birthday present for my sister" while another was "foods that help you to cool down when you are hot." These categories may not necessarily map onto product categories as marketers tend to think of them.

68. The original model can be found in Emery, F., (1969). Some psychological aspects of price. In B. Taylor, & G. Wills (Eds.), Pricing Strategy (pp. 98-111). Staples Press. An accessible description of this model is available in Johnson, Michael D. (1997), Customer Orientation and Market Action, New York: Prentice Hall.

69. Thomas, M. (2013). Commentary on behavioral price research: the role of subjective experiences in price cognition. AMS Review, 3(3), 141-145.

70. Barbaro, Michael (2007). Is Wal-Mart too cheap for its own good? New York Times, May 30.

71. Copeland, Nick, and Christine Labuski (2013), The World of Wal-Mart: Discounting the American Dream. Routledge.

72. Kaptchuk, T. J. (2001). The double-blind, randomized, placebo-controlled trial: gold standard or golden calf? Journal of Clinical Epidemiology, 54(6), 541-549.

73. Waber, R. L., Shiv, B., Carmon, Z., & Ariely, D. (2008). Commercial Features of Placebo and Therapeutic. JAMA, 299(9), 1016-1017.

74. This study is Study 1 in Shiv, B., Carmon, Z., & Ariely, D. (2005). Placebo effects of marketing actions: Consumers may get what they pay for. Journal of Marketing Research, 42(4), 383-393.

75. Plassmann, H., O'Doherty, J., Shiv, B., & Rangel, A. (2008). Marketing actions can modulate neural representations of experienced pleasantness. Proceedings of the National Academy of Sciences, 105(3), 1050-1054.

Chapter 4 Is it Worth the Price?

76. For an in-depth academic discussion of this topic, see Gigerenzer, Gerd and Wolfgang Gaissmaier (2011). Heuristic Decision Making. Annual Review of Psychology, 62, 451-482; Gilovich, Thomas, Dale Griffin, and Daniel Kahneman (2002), Heuristics and Biases: The Psychology of Intuitive Judgment. Cambridge, UK: Cambridge University Press.

77. This point has been highlighted extensively over the past decade, most notably in Barry Schwartz's book, The Paradox of Choice, which was published in 2003. Schwartz and his co-authors argued that beyond a handful of options, providing more choices reduces customer welfare instead of increasing it. Since then, however, newer research has cast some doubt on this relationship. Today, the general opinion is that instead of treating the "more choice is bad" association as a generalization, it is more reasonable to treat it as dependent on various

moderating factors. See Schwartz, Barry (2014). Is the famous 'paradox of choice' a myth?, PBS Newshour, January 29, 2014; Scheibehenne, B., Greifeneder, R., & Todd, P. M. (2010). Can there ever be too many options? A meta-analytic review of choice overload. Journal of Consumer Research, 37(3), 409-425.

78. Source: Food Marketing Institute, Supermarket Facts, which reported that the average number of items carried in a supermarket in 2016 was 38,900. Available at fmi.org.

79. Consumer Reports. What to do when there are too many product choices on the store shelves? March 2014.

80. Available at Statista, Number of existing and new car models offered in the US market from 2000 to 2017. See also Duff, Mike (2017). Mercedes and BMW Admit They Have Too Many Models, But the Solution Is a Bummer. Car and Driver, March 15.

81. See Shah, Anuj K., and Daniel M. Oppenheimer (2008). Heuristics made easy: An effort-reduction framework. Psychological Bulletin, 134(2), 207-222, for a detailed discussion of these factors.

82. See for example Chandon, Pierre, J. Hutchinson, Eric Bradlow, and Scott H. Young (2006). Does in-store marketing work? Effects of the number and position of shelf facings on brand attention and evaluation at the point of purchase. Journal of Marketing, 73(6), 1-17.

83. This view of a sequential decision making process where alternatives are pared down from a large initial set to a smaller set for in-depth consideration can be traced to consumer behavior research in the 1970s and 1980s. See Shocker, Allan D., Moshe Ben-Akiva, Bruno Boccara, and Prakash Nenungadi (1991). Consideration set influences on consumer decision-making and choice: Issues, models and suggestions. Marketing Letters, 2(3), 181-197. Note that in the discussion that follows here, my focus is on product options that are directly available to the consumer and I ignore the role played by options that the consumer may know about and have in their memory. This is because our focus is on the role of prices, and specifically, on factors that managers can influence directly during the consumer's decision making process.

84. This point is commonsensical, but retailers pay a great deal of attention to this form of rejection behavior by consumers. See for instance, Rigby, Darrell (2011). The future of shopping. Harvard Business Review.

85. This story is described in Escobar, Samantha (2015). Here's where the 2-Month's Salary Engagement Ring Thing Started. Good Housekeeping, May 20; Buhler, Konstantine (2016). A Diamond is For Never. Medium, October 10; Cawley, Laurence (2014). De Beers Myth: Do people spend a month's salary on a diamond engagement ring? BBC News Magazine, May 16.

86. Cooper, Mariah (2017). 'Real is Rare' diamond ad shows romantic lesbian love story. Washington Blade, October 13.

87. Flint, Noam (2014). George Clooney's $750,000 canary engagement ring to Amal Alamuddin. Naturally Colored, May 18.

88. See Prakash, Neha (2019). This Is How Much the Average Couple Spent on an Engagement Ring in 2018. Yahoo.

89. Schindler, Robert M. (1991). Symbolic Meanings of a Price Ending. in NA - Advances in Consumer Research Volume 18, eds. Rebecca H. Holman and Michael R. Solomon, Provo, UT : Association for Consumer Research, Pages: 794-801.

90. Muller, George (2014). Everything you wanted to know about raising prices, but were afraid to ask: A manager's guide, Monitor Deloitte White Paper.

91. Burlington Coat Factory site accessed on April 6, 2018. Of the 54 men's jacket choices available on the site priced between $100 and $250, 18 (or a third) were priced at either $149 or $199.

92. Nielsen FCMG and Research Insights (2018). Heard it through the grapevine: Wine trends to watch for in 2018. January 16.

93. Tuttle, Brad (2013). In Fast Food, Five—As in $5—Is Now the Magic Number. Time, June 10.

94. Boyle, Matthew (2009). The Accidental Hero. Bloomberg BusinessWeek, November 5.

95. Horovitz, Bruce (2013). Pizza Hut deal gets you a $5.55 pizza. USA Today, June 4.

96. The Alysa Milano video for UNICEF USA can be found at: https://bit.ly/2fpQWpP

97. Gourville, John T. (1998). Pennies-a-day: The effect of temporal reframing on transaction evaluation. Journal of Consumer Research, 24(4), 395-408.

98. Gourville, John T. (1999). The effect of implicit versus explicit comparisons on temporal pricing claims. Marketing Letters, 10(2), 113-124.

99. Bambauer-Sachse, S., & Grewal, D. (2011). Temporal reframing of prices: when is it beneficial? Journal of Retailing, 87(2), 156-165.

100. Elliott, Stuart (1994). Advertising; Cereal sticker shock is forcing makers of well-known brands to emphasize their value. New York Times.

101. Tiffany, Kaitlin (2018). The absurd quest to make the "best" razor, Vox, December.

102. Livsey, Alan (2017). Dollar Shave Club wins market share and customers with back-to-basics approach. Financial Times, March 16.

103. Terlep, Sharon (2017). Rather Than Add More Blades to Its Razors, Gillette Trims Prices. Wall Street Journal, November 29.

104. Harper, Elizabeth (2017). Is Dollar Shave Club worth the money? Deal News, April 26.

105. Trop, Jaclyn (2017). How Dollar Shave Club's founder built a $1 billion company that changed the industry. Entrepreneur, March 28. See also Solomon, Steven Davidoff (2016). $1 billion for Dollar Shave Club: Why every company should worry. New York Times, July 26.

106. Leighton, Mara (2018). Here's how Amazon's Subscribe & Save program works — and how you can use it to save money. Business Insider, March 26.

107. This study appears in Hsee, Christopher K. (1996). The evaluability hypothesis: An explanation for preference reversals between joint and separate evaluations of alternatives. Organizational Behavior and Human Decision Processes, 67(3), 247-257. The quote that follows later is also from this paper on page 255. See also Hsee, Chrisopher K., George F. Loewenstein, Sally Blount, and Max H. Bazerman (1999). Preference reversals between joint and separate evaluations

of options: a review and theoretical analysis. Psychological Bulletin, 125(5), 576-590.

108. This quote appears in the Hsee (1996) paper on page 255.

109. Zevnik, Neil (2017). Inca Treasure: The Delights of Quinoa. Huffington Post, November 11.

110. Bowler, Graham (2019). How Apple tricks our brains into accepting high prices. Cult of Mac, June 14.

111. See the section on Costs under the "Advice and Retirement" tab at Vanguard.com.

112. Khuri, Fuad (1968). The etiquette of bargaining in the Middle East. American Anthropologist, 70(4), 698-706.

113. Velthuis, O. (2003). Symbolic meanings of prices: Constructing the value of contemporary art in Amsterdam and New York galleries. Theory and Society, 32(2), 181-215.

114. Blackman, Brad (2016). How I price my paintings.

115. Chaperon, Rebecca (2018). Pricing artwork by the inch, Artist Run Website.

116. Brophy, Maria (2010). How to price your original artworks. MariaBrophy.com

117. Rahim, Amira (2014). 7 things I learned about pricing my artwork this year. AmiraRahim.com

Chapter 5 The Price in Context

118. Bekker, Henk (2019). 2018 (Full Year) USA: Toyota North America and Lexus Sales. Car Sales Statistics.

119. A key issue in pricing product lines is to account for both potential cannibalization as well as cost-interdependencies associated with offering a product line as best as possible. This is no mean feat, and outside the scope of this book. A detailed discussion of the pricing challenges resulting from demand and cost interdependencies and potential solutions is discussed in Chen, Yuxin (2009). Product line pricing, Handbook of Pricing Research in Marketing, Chapter 10, 216-231.

120. Harvey, Leslie (2018). Disney Park Hopper tickets: Worth it or a waste of money? TravelingMom.com

121. The Weber-Fechner law (also called as Weber's law) dates back to 1834 and has a checkered history in psychology. For a detailed description of how it can be used in designing product line prices, see Chapter 15 of Monroe, Kent (2003), Pricing: Making Profitable Decisions, Third Edition, McGraw-Hill.

122. Draganska, M., & Jain, D. C. (2006). Consumer preferences and product-line pricing strategies: An empirical analysis. Marketing Science, 25(2), 164-174.

123. Epstein, Adam (2016). It's not your imagination: US Netflix has a much smaller selection than it used to. Quartz, March 24.

124. Dudlicek, Jim (2015). Stack the meat case with value and simplicity, Progressive Grocer, November 25.

125. See Peck, J., & Childers, T. L. (2006). If I touch it I have to have it: Individual and environmental influences on impulse purchasing. Journal of Business Research, 59(6), 765-769.

126. Dhar, R., & Simonson, I. (1999). Making complementary choices in consumption episodes: Highlighting versus balancing. Journal of Marketing Research, 36(1), 29-44.

127. The description of the Business Select upgrade is available on Southwest.com

128. Mohammed, Rafi (2013). Why good-better-best prices are so effective, Harvard Business Review, February 8.

129. Farley, Amy (2014). Is premium economy worth it? Travel & Leisure Magazine, June 9.

130. Michaels, Daniel (2014). Why this plane seat is the most profitable. Wall Street Journal, March 4.

131. Sunstein, C. R. (2014). Nudging: A very short guide. Journal of Consumer Policy, 37(4), 583-588.

132. Frenkel, Lior (2014). Can designers steal the best pricing techniques from restaurants?

133. Miller, Aaron (2013). 10 stupidly expensive burgers you need to eat before you die. Thrillist, August 17. The $140 burger I mentioned is the DB Royale Double Truffle Burger at celebrity chef Daniel Bouloud's restaurant DB Bistro Moderne in New York City.

134. BusinessWeek's subscription offers are available here: https://www.bloomberg.com/subscriptions/ and the Economist's offers are here: https://econ.st/2PJyqpD. While terms may vary over time, the use of decoys has remained.

135. Nunes, J. C., & Boatwright, P. (2004). Incidental prices and their effect on willingness to pay. Journal of Marketing Research, 41(4), 457-466.

136. See Morwitz, Vicki G., Eric A. Greenleaf, and Eric J. Johnson (1998). Divide and prosper: consumers' reactions to partitioned prices. Journal of Marketing Research, 35(4), 453-463.

137. Zhang, Benjamin (2018). Mysterious airline fees are costing passengers hundreds of dollars and no one knows what they go to pay for. Business Insider, July 3.

138. Cox, Kate (2016). The Consumerist guide to understanding your Comcast Bill. February 1. The source of this Southwest Airlines' definition is Southwest.com.

140. Quirk, Mary Beth (2011). Zappos CSR's kindness warms our cold hearts. Consumerist, January 17.

141. Schindler, Robert M., Maureen Morrin, and Nada Nasr Bechwati (2005). Shipping charges and shipping-charge skepticism: Implications for direct marketers' pricing formats. Journal of Interactive Marketing 19(1), 41-53.

142. Greenleaf, Eric A., Eric J. Johnson, Vicki G. Morwitz, and Edith Shalev (2016). The price does not include additional taxes, fees, and surcharges: a review of research on partitioned pricing. Journal of Consumer Psychology, 26(1), 105-124. The quote appears on p. 107.

143. This study is reported as Experiment Two in the Morwitz, Greenleaf and Johnson (1998) paper.

144. Abraham, A. T., & Hamilton, R. W. (2018). When does partitioned pricing lead to more favorable consumer preferences? Meta-analytic evidence. Journal of Marketing Research, 55(5), 686-703.

145. Clark, John M., and Sidne G. Ward (2008). Consumer behavior in online auctions: An examination of partitioned prices on eBay. Journal of Marketing Theory and Practice, 16(1), 57-66.

146. Xia, Lan, and Kent B. Monroe (2004). Price partitioning on the internet. Journal of Interactive Marketing, 18(4), 63-73.

147. Voester, J., Ivens, B., & Leischnig, A. (2017). Partitioned pricing: review of the literature and directions for further research. Review of Managerial Science, 11(4), 879-931.

148. Bertini, Marco, and Luc Wathieu (2008). Research note—Attention arousal through price partitioning. Marketing Science, 27(2), 236-246.

149. Hamilton, R. W., Srivastava, J., & Abraham, A. T. (2010). When should you nickel-and-dime your customers. MIT Sloan Management Review, 52(1), 59-67.

150. McCartney, Scott (2018). The airline fee that exists for no apparent reason. Wall Street Journal, June 27.

151. Hamilton, R. W., & Srivastava, J. (2009). When 2+ 2 Is Not the Same as 1+ 3: Understanding Customer Reactions to Partitioned Prices. GfK Marketing Intelligence Review, 1(2), 24-31.

Chapter 6 Negotiating Price

152. Morris, James (1962). One-price policy among antebellum country stores. Business History Review, 36(4), 455-458.

153. Strasser, Susan (2004), Satisfaction guaranteed: The making of the American Mass Market, Smithsonian.

154. Goodman, Jillian (2006). The everything guide to haggling. New York Magazine Everything Guide.

155. Gelber, Steven (2005). Horseless horses: Car dealing and the survival of retail bargaining. In P. N. Stearns (Ed.), American Behavioral History (pp. 118–140). New York University Press

156. McGee, William (2016). How to Get the Lowest Airfares. Consumer Reports, October.

157. Jones, Michael (2016). The recession mentality: 3 ways frugality has shaped today's consumer. Forbes, May 31.

158. Scherer, Jenna (2019). Why everyone is so obsessed with Marie Kondo. Rolling Stone, February 7.

159. Rosenbloom, Stephanie (2009). High-end retailers offering more discounts. New York Times, July 31.

160. James, Kyle (2016). Negotiate better prices on these 6 grocery store buys. Wisebread.

161. Hathaway, Matthew (2010). Recession-weary consumers find haggling can cut costs. Chicago Tribune, March 14.

162. Spann, Martin, Robert Zeithammer, Marco Bertini, Ernan Haruvy, Sandy D. Jap, Oded Koenigsberg, Vincent Mak, Peter Popkowski Leszczyc, Bernd Skiera, and Manoj Thomas (2018). Beyond Posted Prices: The Past, Present, and Future of Participative Pricing Mechanisms. Customer Needs and Solutions, 5(1-2),121-136.

163. Planet Money Podcast (2019). The Pay-What-You-Want Experiment.

164. Blau, Peter (1986), Exchange and power in social life, Second Edition. Routledge.

165. DePillis, Lydia (2013). Panera's pay-as-you-go pricing experiment failed. Here's how they could fix it. Washington Post, July 14.

166. An example of an ad agency that uses PWYW pricing is 8k in Poland, see http://paywhatyouwant.eu/

167. Danovich, Tove (2015). How do pay-what-you-want restaurants work? Eater, May 6.

168. Swanson, Ana (2016). Americans are less trusting than ever before. That could also make us poor. Washington Post, Wonkblog.

169. Shanghaist (2018). Guiyang restaurant tries out 'pay what you want' policy, loses 100,000 RMB in a week. May 5.

170. Pomranz, Mike (2017). A Chinese restaurant's 'pay what you want' policy lost it $15,000 in a single week. Food & Wine, June 22.

171. Phillips, Tom (2013). Restaurant confronts China's moral crisis with free food. The Telegraph, November 28.

172. Caird, Jo (2011). Pay what you can: how low and how far can theatres go? The Guardian Theatre blog, August 17.

173. Shelle Santana and Vicki Morwitz (2015). Because We're Partners: How Social Values and Relationship Norms Influence Consumer Payments in Pay-What-You-Want Contexts. Working paper.

174. Gneezy, Ayelet, Uri Gneezy, Gerhard Riener, and Leif D. Nelson (2012). Pay-what-you-want, identity, and self-signaling in markets.

Proceedings of the National Academy of Sciences, 109(19), 7236-7240.

175. Lotus, Jean (2017). Pay-what-you-want cafes evolve in Colorado. Patch Denver, September 8. Available online at: http://bit.ly/31dj7vo

176. Gneezy, Ayelet, Uri Gneezy, Leif D. Nelson, and Amber Brown (2010). Shared social responsibility: A field experiment in pay-what-you-want pricing and charitable giving. Science, 329(5989), 325-327.

177. Saccardo, Silvia, Charis Li, Anya Samek, and Ayelet Gneezy (2015). Shifting mindset in consumer elective pricing. Working paper.

178. Jung, M. H., Nelson, L. D., Gneezy, U., & Gneezy, A. (2017). Signaling virtue: Charitable behavior under consumer elective pricing. Marketing Science, 36(2), 187-194.

179. Scott, Juliet (2015). In the cafe where you can pay what you want, what would you choose? The Guardian, April 18.

180. Jung, M. H., Perfecto, H., & Nelson, L. D. (2016). Anchoring in payment: Evaluating a judgmental heuristic in field experimental settings. Journal of Marketing Research, 53(3), 354-368.

181. An excellent, detailed description of Priceline's method is given in Anderson, Chris K., and John G. Wilson (2011). Name-your-own price auction mechanisms–Modeling and future implications. Journal of Revenue and Pricing Management, 10(1), 32-39.

182. See Chen, Rachel R., Esther Gal-Or, and Paolo Roma (2014). Opaque distribution channels for competing service providers: Posted price vs. name-your-own-price mechanisms. Operations Research, 62(4), 733-750.

183. See Hann, Il-Horn, and Christian Terwiesch (2003). Measuring the frictional costs of online transactions: The case of a name-your-own-price channel. Management Science, 49(11), 1563-1579.

184. Levina, Tatsiana, Yuri Levin, Jeff McGill, and Mikhail Nediak (2015). Strategic Consumer Cooperation in a Name-Your-Own-Price Channel. Production and Operations Management, 24 (12), 1883-1900.

185. Schaal, Dennis (2018). The death of Priceline's name your own price is likely drawing near. Skift, March 26.

186. Milnes, Hilary (2017). Startup Spotlight: Garmentory wants to bring independent boutiques online. Glossy, February 27.

187. Bergen, M. E., Kauffman, R. J., & Lee, D. (2005). Beyond the hype of frictionless markets: Evidence of heterogeneity in price rigidity on the Internet. Journal of Management Information Systems, 22(2), 57-89.

188. Ham, Tim, & Bertini, Marco (2013). The right price, at the right moment, to the right customer. Business Strategy Review, 24(1), 49-53; see also Wilson, Amy (2011). Price plan boosts AutoNation profits. Automotive News, 86(6483), 8.

189. Mohammed, Rafi (2013). Why baseball seats should be priced like airline tickets. HBR Blog, April 5. See also Broderick, Mark (2015). What's the price now? Communications of the ACM, 58(4), 21-23; and Lewis, Len (2015). How low should you go? Stores Magazine, 97(2), 40-42.

190. Levy, Daniel, Mark Bergen, Shantanu Dutta, and Robert Venable (1997). The magnitude of menu costs: direct evidence from large US supermarket chains. The Quarterly Journal of Economics, 112(3), 791-825.

191. Mohammed, Rafi (2015). Price-sensitive customers will tolerate uncertainty. HBR Blog, March 26.

192. Schechter, Dan and John Calkins (2016). Should movie theaters use flexible ticket prices like airlines do? The Wrap. Sampson, Hannah (2016). The future of theme park pricing is creative and dynamic. Skift, August 11. East, Andy (2015). Mobile app brings dynamic pricing to the dinner table. MIT Technology Review. Martin, Grant (2019), Lufthansa will adopt dynamic award pricing for its loyalty program. Skift, May 28.

193. Park, C. W., Mothersbaugh, D. L., & Feick, L. (1994). Consumer knowledge assessment. Journal of Consumer Research, 21(1), 71-82.

194. Jacobson, R., & Obermiller, C. (1990). The formation of expected future price: A reference price for forward-looking consumers. Journal of Consumer Research, 16(4), 420-432.

195. Greenleaf, E. A., & Lehmann, D. R. (1995). Reasons for substantial delay in consumer decision making. Journal of Consumer Research, 22(2), 186-199.

196. D'Innocenzio, Anne (2014). The online price of a sweater can change dozens of times a day, leaving shoppers confused. Associated Press.

197. Bertini, Marco and Wathieu, Luc (2010). How to Stop Customers from Fixating on Price, Harvard Business Review, 88(5).

198. Rotemberg, J. J. (2005). Customer anger at price increases, changes in the frequency of price adjustment and monetary policy. Journal of Monetary Economics, 52(4), 829-852.

199. Shoemaker, P. J. (1996). Hardwired for news: Using biological and cultural evolution to explain the surveillance function. Journal of Communication, 46(3), 32-47.

200. Fader, P. S., & Lodish, L. M. (1990). A cross-category analysis of category structure and promotional activity for grocery products. Journal of Marketing, 54(4), 52-65.

201. See Chapter 9 of Kapferer, J. N. (2012). The Luxury Strategy: Break the Rules of Marketing to Build Luxury Brands. Kogan Page Publishers.

202. Heil, O. P., & Helsen, K. (2001). Toward an understanding of price wars: Their nature and how they erupt. International Journal of Research in Marketing, 18(1), 83-98.

203. Economists call this point as the "equilibrium of demand and supply" and the price at this level as the equilibrium price. This Khan Academy video provides an easy-to-understand explanation of these concepts: http://bit.ly/2XyeERQ

204. Pinsker, Joe (2015). The risky business of reselling Super Bowl tickets. The Atlantic.

205. On its own website, Uber has a succinct and clear explanation of surge pricing. It is available here: https://ubr.to/2WPYhmr

206. Journalism professor Nick Diakopoulos has a nice discussion of potential effects of surge pricing in this Washington Post article: Diakopoulos, Nicholas (2015). How Uber surge pricing really works. Washington Post, April 17.

207. The study was done by two Uber employees and a University of Chicago economics professor. Hall, Jonathan, Cory Kendrick and Chris Nosko (2015). The effects of Uber's surge pricing: A case study. Working paper, University of Chicago.

208. Chen, M. K., Chevalier, J. A., Rossi, P. E., & Oehlsen, E. (2017). The value of flexible work: Evidence from uber drivers, Working paper No. w23296. National Bureau of Economic Research.

209. Cohen, Peter, Robert Hahn, Jonathan Hall, Steven Levitt, and Robert Metcalfe (2016). Using big data to estimate consumer surplus: The case of Uber. Working paper No. w22627. National Bureau of Economic Research.

210. Lam, C. T., & Liu, M. (2017). Demand and consumer surplus in the on-demand economy: the case of ride sharing. Social Science Electronic Publishing, 17(8), 376-388. See also, Hahn, Robert, and Robert Metcalfe (2017). The Ridesharing revolution: economic survey and synthesis. Working paper, Brookings Institution.

211. The test conducted in October 2014 compared prices for Uber and a taxicab for the same trip in 21 US cities and found that after factoring in tips for the cab driver, Uber was cheaper than a taxi in every single city. Even without the tips, Uber's price beat taxi fare everywhere except in New York city. Silverstein, Sal (2014). These animated charts tell you everything about Uber prices in 21 cities.

212. Lowrey, Annie (2014). Is Uber's surge pricing an example of high-tech gouging? The New York Times Magazine.

213. Economy, Peter (2017). Uber surge pricing snafu results in a shocking $14,400 charge for a 20-minute ride. Inc. Magazine.

214. Ismail, Levi (2019). Rodeo fans wait for hours while ride shares cash in on surge prices. KHOU 11.

215. Diakopoulos, Nicholas (2015). How Uber surge pricing really works. The Washington Post, April 17.

216. O'Reilly, Tim (2015). Improving Uber's surge pricing. Medium.

217. Diakopoulos, Nicholas (2013). Rage against the algorithms. The Atlantic.

218. Shontell, Alyson (2014). Is this the highest surge price ever recorded in Uber history? Business Insider.

219. Roberts, Jeff John (2016). Uber slammed for surge pricing after New York City bombing. Fortune.

220. Chen, L., Mislove, A., & Wilson, C. (2015). Peeking beneath the hood of Uber. In Proceedings of the 2015 Internet Measurement Conference, 495-508. ACM.

221. I have used Merriam-Webster dictionary's definition of surge.

Chapter 7 How Can I Get You to Buy?

222. Strassmann, Mark (2013). How a great sale affects your brain. CBS News.

223. Inman, J. J., & McAlister, L. (1993). A retailer promotion policy model considering promotion signal sensitivity. Marketing Science, 12(4), 339-356.

224. Anderson and Simester (2009) provide an excellent review of the academic literature on different pricing cues including sale signs. Anderson, E. T., & Simester, D. I. (2009). Price cues and customer price knowledge. Handbook of Pricing Research in Marketing. Northampton, MA: Edward Elgar, 150-66.

225. Anderson, E. T., & Simester, D. I. (1998). The role of sale signs. Marketing Science, 17(2), 139-155.

226. The quote appears on page 74 of Inman, J. J., McAlister, L., & Hoyer, W. D. (1990). Promotion signal: proxy for a price cut? Journal of Consumer Research, 17(1), 74-81.

227. Holmes, Elizabeth (2016). Beware signs that say 'Final Sale. Wall Street Journal, August 2.

228. This quote appears in Anderson and Simester (2009) on page 156.

229. Howland, Daphne (2018). Ross to settle $4.9 million lawsuit over 'deceptive' price tags. Retail Dive.

230. Rosenbloom, Stephanie (2009). High-end retailers offering more discounts. New York Times.

231. Feiereisen, Sharon (2019). 11 stores where you'll probably never buy anything on sale. Business Insider, May 23.

232. Dholakia, Utpal M. and Tsabar, Gur (2011). A Startup's Experience with Running a Groupon Promotion. SSRN Report.

233. Inman, J. J., & McAlister, L. (1994). Do coupon expiration dates affect consumer behavior? Journal of Marketing Research, 31(3), 423-428.

234. Krishna, A., & Zhang, Z. J. (1999). Short-or long-duration coupons: The effect of the expiration date on the profitability of coupon promotions. Management Science, 45(8), 1041-1056.

235. Scott D. Swain, Richard Hanna, and Lisa J. Abendroth (2006). How Time Restrictions Work: the Roles of Urgency, Anticipated Regret, and Deal Evaluations, in NA - Advances in Consumer Research Volume 33, eds. Connie Pechmann and Linda Price, Duluth, MN : Association for Consumer Research, Pages: 523-525.

236. Sahni, N., Zou, D., & Chintagunta, P. K. (2014). Effects of targeted promotions: Evidence from field experiments. Available at SSRN.

237. Danny the Deal Guru, 4/27 only, get a Lowe's coupon for $5-$500 off in-store.

238. Fitzpatrick, Jason (2010). The complete guide to capturing Woot! Off loot. Lifehacker.

239. Maynard, Micheline (2018). Starbucks' holiday cup offer gets off to a crashing start. Forbes.

240. Taylor, Kate (2019). Build-A-Bear declares 'Pay Your Age Day' deal that plunged stores into chaos a massive success 'bigger than anyone could have possibly imagined'. Business Insider.

241. Lacy, Lisa (2018). Price matching ain't what it used to be. July 18, Adweek.

242. Showrooming is the practice of visiting physical stores to examine and experience products, then buying it online from the seller with the lowest price. Showrooming is particularly detrimental to retailers with a substantial physical presence and higher operating costs, who found it difficult to offer prices as low as those offered by online retailers.

243. Roesler, Peter (2015). Use price matching to stand out from competitors. Business Journals.

244. Roose, Kevin (2017). Best Buy's secrets for thriving in the Amazon age. New York Times, September 18.

245. This is Best Buy's price match guarantee available on its website at: http://bit.ly/2ZesnOa

246. Target's price-matching guarantee is available on its corporate website. Available at: http://bit.ly/2XDW1vu

247. The list of the design factors is adapted from Hviid, Morten. (2010). Summary of the literature on price guarantees. ESRC Centre for Competition Policy and UEA Law School, Working paper.

248. Srivastava, J., & Lurie, N. (2001). A consumer perspective on price-matching refund policies: Effect on price perceptions and search behavior. Journal of Consumer Research, 28(2), 296-307.

249. Mohammed, Rafi (2012), Why price match guarantees can be bad for consumers. Harvard Business Review.

250. Lurie, N. H., & Srivastava, J. (2005). Price-matching guarantees and consumer evaluations of price information. Journal of Consumer Psychology, 15(2), 149-158.

251. Mago, S. D., & Pate, J. G. (2009). An experimental examination of competitor-based price matching guarantees. Journal of Economic Behavior & Organization, 70(1-2), 342-360.

252. Arbatskaya, M., Hviid, M., & Shaffer, G. (2006). On the use of low-price guarantees to discourage price cutting. International Journal of Industrial Organization, 24(6), 1139-1156.

253. Dudley, Renee and Rupp, Lindsey (2013). The perils of price-matching. Bloomberg Businessweek, May 13-19,

254. Lee, Timothy (2015). Mattress stores want to rip you off. Here's how to fight back. Vox, August 10.

255. Rachman, Gideon (1999). The price puzzle. The Economist,

256. See for example, NRG Editorial Services (2019). What Texas businesses need to know about scarcity pricing this summer. Available online at: http://bit.ly/2WgdYPn

257. Ricardo, David (1817/ 1925), Principles of political economy and taxation, London: G. Bell & Sons. The quote appears on page 6 of the 1925 edition.

258. Specia, Megan (2019). Japan's 'King of Tuna' pays record $3 million for bluefin at new Tokyo fish market. New York Times, January.

259. Associated Press (2012). Bluefin tuna sells for record $736,000 in Japan. January 12.

260. Zerbo, Julie (2019). Can the Birkin bag survive the resale market? New York Times, April 9.

261. In this review article, the authors provide a detailed analysis of the different ways that scarcity perceptions affect consumers in each of the stages of their decision journey. Hamilton, Rebecca, Debora Thompson, Sterling Bone, Lan Nguyen Chaplin, Vladas Griskevicius, Kelly Goldsmith, Ronald Hill et al. (2019). The effects of scarcity on consumer decision journeys. Journal of the Academy of Marketing Science, 47(3), 532-550.

262. Lynn, M. (1991). Scarcity effects on value: A quantitative review of the commodity theory literature. Psychology & Marketing, 8(1), 43-57.

263. Worchel, S., Lee, J., & Adewole, A. (1975). Effects of supply and demand on ratings of object value. Journal of Personality and Social Psychology, 32(5), 906-914.

264. Clifton, Jamie (2016). Why are so many people obsessed with Supreme? Vice UK.

266. Hilton, Boyd (2019). Why my love for Supreme will never die. GQ Style Magazine.

267. Inman, J. J., Peter, A. C., & Raghubir, P. (1997). Framing the deal: The role of restrictions in accentuating deal value. Journal of Consumer Research, 24(1), 68-79.

268. Tan, S. J., & Hwang Chua, S. (2004). While stocks last! Impact of framing on consumers' perception of sales promotions. Journal of Consumer Marketing, 21(5), 343-355.

269. Bloom, Jonathan (2019). Toronto restaurant fights waste by chopping menu prices till food is gone. The Salt, National Public Radio.

270. For a detailed but understandable discussion of the idea, see Heilizer, Fred (1977). A review of theory and research on the assumptions of Miller's response competition (conflict) models: Response gradients. The Journal of General Psychology, 97(1), 17-71.

271. Hull, Clark L. (1934). The rat's speed-of-locomotion gradient in the approach to food. Journal of Comparative Psychology, 17(3), 393-422. For an early review of Clark Hull's research on the goal gradient hypothesis, see Hull, Clark L. (1932). The goal gradient hypothesis and maze learning. Psychological Review, 39(1), 25-43.

272. Kivetz, Ran, Oleg Urminsky, and Yuhuang Zheng (2006). The goal gradient hypothesis resurrected: Purchase acceleration, illusionary goal progress, and customer retention. Journal of Marketing Research, 43(1), 39-58.

273. See Barron, Kenneth E., and Judith M. Harackiewicz (2001). Achievement goals and optimal motivation: Testing multiple goal models. Journal of Personality and Social Psychology, 80(5), 706-722.

274. Mutter, Tobias and Dennis Kundisch (2014). Behavioral mechanisms prompted by badges: The goal gradient hypothesis. Paper presented at Thirty Fifth International Conference on Information Systems, Auckland.

275. Cheema, Amar, & Rajesh Bagchi (2011). The effect of goal visualization on goal pursuit: Implications for consumers and managers. Journal of Marketing, 75(2), 109-123.

276. Cryder, Cynthia E., George Loewenstein, and Howard Seltman (2013). Goal gradient in helping behavior. Journal of Experimental Social Psychology, 49(6), 1078-1083.

ABOUT THE AUTHOR

Utpal Dholakia is a professor of marketing and holds the George R. Brown Chair of Marketing at Rice University in Houston, Texas. He teaches pricing strategies and customer experience management to MBA students, and conducts research on consumer welfare, digital marketing, and marketing strategy. He provides consulting and expert witness services to law firms, and financial services, technology, healthcare, and energy companies.

Utpal's popular blog on Psychology Today is called *The Science Behind Behavior*. You can learn more about him and his work and connect with him at **utpaldholakia.com**.

Made in the USA
Middletown, DE
15 June 2023

32626728R00139